MAKING AN IMPACT

MAKING AN IMPACT

A Handbook on Counselor Advocacy

Karen Eriksen, M.S., LPC

ACCELERATED DEVELOPMENT
A member of the Taylor & Francis Group

USA	Publishing Office:	ACCELERATED DEVELOPMENT
		A member of the Taylor & Francis Group
		1101 Vermont Ave., N.W., Ste. 200
		Washington, DC 20005-3521
		Tel: (202) 289-2174
		Fax: (202) 289-3665
	Distribution Center:	ACCELERATED DEVELOPMENT
		A member of the Taylor & Francis Group
		1900 Frost Road
		Suite 101
		Bristol, PA 19007-1598
		Tel: (215) 785-5800
		Fax: (215) 785-5515
UK		Taylor & Francis, Ltd.
		1 Gunpowder Square
		London EC4A 3DE
		Tel: 071 405 2237
		Fax: 071 831 2035

MAKING AN IMPACT: A Handbook on Counselor Advocacy

1 2 3 4 5 6 7 8 9 0 BRBR 9 8 7 6

This book was set in Times Roman by Princeton Editorial Associates.
Editing and technical development by Alice S. M. Rowan. Additional technical development by Cynthia Long.
Cover design by Michelle Fleitz.

Printing and binding by Braun-Brumfield, Inc.

A CIP catalog record for this book is available from the British Library.
∞ The paper in this publication meets the requirements of the ANSI Standard Z39.48-1984 (Permanence of Paper)

Library of Congress Cataloging-in-Publication Data
Eriksen, Karen
    Making an impact : a handbook on counselor advocacy / Karen
Eriksen.
        p. cm.
    Includes bibliographical references and index.

    1. Counselors. 2. Counselors—Government policy. 3. Counselors—Legal
status, laws, etc. I. Title.
BF637.C6E75 1997
361.3'23—DC20   96-31393
                                                  CIP

ISBN 1-56032-544-5

TABLE OF CONTENTS

PART I
THE STAGES OF ADVOCACY

PART II
ADVANCED ADVOCACY

ACKNOWLEDGEMENTS

In conceiving this book and bringing it to fruition, I owe gratitude to many people. In particular, I thank my husband, my first and foremost critic, supporter, and editor. I would also like to thank Harriet Glosoff, under whose guidance I did an internship at the American Counseling Association, who introduced me to some of the most exciting people in the counseling profession, and who reviewed the book. Priscilla Regan served as my mentor in public policy at George Mason University, checking not only the facts of my writing but introducing me to the best authors in the public policy field and reviewing many drafts. Stuart Eriksen was kind enough to provide graphic design assistance. And last, but certainly not least, all of the people I interviewed for the book, who made time available to talk with me about their experiences in advocacy, deserve my utmost gratitude. They are Sandra Barker, James Benshoff, Joyce Breasure, Theron M. Covin, Cheryl Davis, Peter Emerson, Diana Emory, Harriet Glosoff, Thomas Hosie, Budd Kendrick, Dennis Maki, Sally Mallery, Robert Mattox, James Messina, Beverly O'Bryant, Larry Parker, Randa Piccard, MaryLyn Pike, Walter Roberts, Gail Robinson, Nancy Schlossburg, James Schmidt, Jeri Stevens, Helen Stidham, Thomas Sweeney, Warren Throckmorton, Marion Turowsky, and Richard Yep.

LIST OF FIGURES

LIST OF TABLES

Chapter 1

INTRODUCTION

Advocacy efforts on behalf of the counseling profession are designed to promote the profession and are critical to its future. It is only through many long years of effort on the part of advocates that counselors in most states have reached their current status as respected professionals, able to practice without too many constraints what they are trained to do. Counselors owe a great debt of gratitude to the many people who have written letters and made phone calls to insurance companies, legislators, and employers; who have served on professional association, credentialing, and licensing boards; who have instituted counseling programs in schools, acquired counselor licensure, and successfully included counselors in state and federal insurance and health care legislation. All of these achievements have been accomplished by energetic advocacy efforts.

Counselors still have a long way to go, however. As President Clinton developed the 1993 Health Security Act, and as other legislators proposed other health care reform bills, counselors struggled to be included as mental health providers, because most of the proposed bills excluded counselors. If those bills—which intended to unify public and private health care—had become law, financing for counselors' work would have ended and, thus, their professional livelihoods would have been threatened. As the Elementary and Secondary School Education Act came up for reauthorization in 1994, counselors in schools actively and successfully advocated to retain school counseling programs. They had worked *for eight or nine years* to get the Elementary School Counseling Demonstration Act passed so that school districts would have enough elementary school counselors. When it became clear that this act would not pass on its own, it was amended to the Elementary and Secondary School Education Act, which became law as the Improving America's Schools Act.

If they do not stay on top of policy changes, counselors cannot be assured that their interests will be protected by laws, regulations, and policies. The pressure to reduce costs is tremendous, and mental health agencies and other institutions where counselors are employed are feeling the financial stress. The financial challenges include the growing number of service providers, increasingly limited government money, and increasing demands for efficiency and accountability (Gilchrist & Stringer, 1992).

As the counselor advocates whose interviews formed the basis for this book said, among mental health providers, counselors are "the new kid on the block" and thus need to advocate a great deal more than related professions to develop a strong sense of professional identity, develop ethical standards, guarantee quality services, and gain recognition of all of these elements by the purchasers of the services. "You have to advocate on behalf of your profession if you want that profession to change in a positive direction. . . . You must advocate on behalf of your profession in order to safeguard it, if nothing else," said one advocate. Another advocate suggested a further motivation when she stated, "I don't think that it's that if we don't change the way we've done business, we're not going to have clients, 'cause we're not going to be around."

The field of public relations concurs, claiming that counselors can be great at what they do, but if no one knows about it, or knows what they do, clients will not be able to access their services, legislators and insurance companies will not see the benefit of their services, employers will not hire counselors, and referral sources will not refer to counselors. Counselors not only need to communicate to these publics what they do but they also need to accurately assess client, employer, referral source, and legislator needs, and to demonstrate through research both the needs and counselors' effectiveness in meeting these needs (Newsom, Scott, & Turk, 1993). Otherwise, the profession is in danger. Only a true commitment to advocacy guarantees progress for the profession, parity with other mental health providers, funding for essential mental health programs, and critical, competent services for clients.

PURPOSE OF THE BOOK

This book was developed because counselor advocacy is important. Professional associations have advocated, but no one has researched advocacy in the counseling field. The only literature in existence is newsletter articles written by advocacy and government relations staff or by board members of counseling professional associations. Further, when political scientists focus on advocacy and interest groups (counselors are an interest group), they address changing only public policy. While this focus has been very helpful—and a great deal of that literature is included in this book—it informs only one aspect of promoting the counseling profession. It neglects many of the other advocacy activities that are necessary to building a viable profession. The public relations and conflict resolution fields have approached advocacy more broadly. The author's research results have therefore been compared with the public policy, public relations, and conflict resolution literature, and the attempt has been made to consolidate these materials into a model that is relevant and practical for counselors.

Overall, when the advocacy practices of organizations like the American Counseling Association (ACA) and the activities of its division and state branch leaders were compared with the practices suggested by experts in public policy and public relations, it was pleasant to discover that these organizations have been "doing the right thing." They have been educating counselors to do exactly what big-name lobbyists do. However, many counselors lack confidence that these organizations have been doing the right thing. They surmise that their advocacy and government relations staffs or committees are doing the best they can given a lack of funding and limited know-how. They believe that counseling is "small potatoes" and cannot compete with major corporations and other interests when trying to influence legislators, the courts, the public health system, or insurance companies.

In fact, however, highly paid, full-time, professional lobbyists are jealous of what counselors have. These lobbyists continually work to create the grassroots organizations and substantive expertise that counselors have. Furthermore, the staff of trade and professional associations (like ACA) are actually the people with the most political influence in Washington, despite the hype about lobbyists influencing decisionmakers through a good ol' boys network and backroom deals. Trade and professional organizations have even more clout at the state level, where access is easier. This discovery was reassuring, and the author hopes that this information will increase readers' confidence in their advocacy efforts.

CONTENTS OF THE BOOK

This book combines three types of information for counselors to draw on to facilitate their advocacy efforts: (a) the results of the author's qualitative research; (b) the literature of three related fields—public policy, public relations, and conflict resolution; and (c) the illustrative stories of two counselors that demonstrate the application of advocacy principles.

The qualitative research was done at the ACA Headquarters and the ACA's 1994 convention. (The research procedures, preconceptions, and limitations are described in detail in Appendix One). For the purposes of the research, advocacy was defined as promotion of the profession, although advocacy principles can also be applied to the promotion of individual counselors or to the promotion of solutions to social or client problems. Counselor advocacy includes such activities as demonstrating through research that counseling is effective, persuading insurance companies to reimburse counselors, educating various audiences about what counselors do, or lobbying for legislation that includes counselors as mental health providers or recognizes and funds counseling programs.

Chapters Three through Seven begin with the stories of two counselors. Each story was developed to elucidate the principles in the chapter. One counselor, Kaylan Sanders, is a mental health counselor who works within the context of a state counseling association. The other, Daniel Wong, is a school counselor who works independently, outside the context of an interest group. The point of using both an independent and a group-affiliated counselor is to demonstrate how counselors can advocate for themselves and the profession both individually and collectively.

Comparisons are made throughout the book between the results of the research done for this book (those who participated in the research are referred to as "participant advocates") and what authors in the public policy, public relations, and conflict resolution literature have concluded.

Part One presents a model of the stages in the advocacy process generated from the author's research. It begins with "Counselors Should Be Counselors," a chapter designed to identify specifically some of the struggles counselors have with the advocacy process and to address these struggles by clarifying the similarities between counselors' personalities and skills and those of effective advocates. Each of the remaining chapters in Part One addresses a particular stage of the advocacy process by (a) telling an illustrative story, (b) discussing the research done for this book as well as other findings in the literature, and (c) providing exercises for individuals and groups to assist them in organizing and conducting each stage of the advocacy process.

The model, illustrated in Figure 1.1 and discussed throughout Part One, presents an approach to organizing and managing an advocacy campaign. Advocacy can be thought of as a *seven-stage process* beginning with the development of a sense of professional identity (Stage One). Advocates next identify the problem to which they would like to direct their attention (Stage Two) and assess the resources they possess to solve that problem (Stage Three). Individuals can then take action, while groups need to invest some time and energy in planning their strategies (Stage Four) and training their membership (Stage Five). Most counselors, either individually or as part of a group, have been involved in the next step: taking action (Stage Six). Many, however, have not been included in Stage Seven: celebrating, evaluating, and regrouping.

The public relations literature suggests very similar stages for advocacy (McElreath & Miller, 1991; Newsom et al., 1993; Richards, 1990), while the public policy literature suggests primarily stages correlating with the strategic-planning and taking-action stages in the model (Advocacy Institute, 1990; Wittenberg & Wittenberg, 1989).

Part Two provides a comprehensive discussion designed for advanced advocates. The chapters offer a more sophisticated explanation than Part One of the judicial, executive, and legislative processes and of how counselors might impact them. Part Two also presents more comprehensive chapters on coalition building and conflict management, two processes that counselors often fail to consider or to use as effectively as they could in their advocacy activities.

Although this book is written by one who enjoys the process of advocacy, many counselors obviously do not share this enthusiasm. It is hoped that after reading this book counselors will understand the advocacy process better, realize that many of their current activities already are part of the advocacy process, and have greater confidence that their current skills provide a solid foundation for successful advocacy efforts. Almond and Verba (1963) have indicated that those who have a greater sense of civic competence—that is, the belief that they are able to be politically influential—will be more active. It is hoped that this book will increase counselors' civic competence so that they will participate more fully and willingly in advocating for their profession.

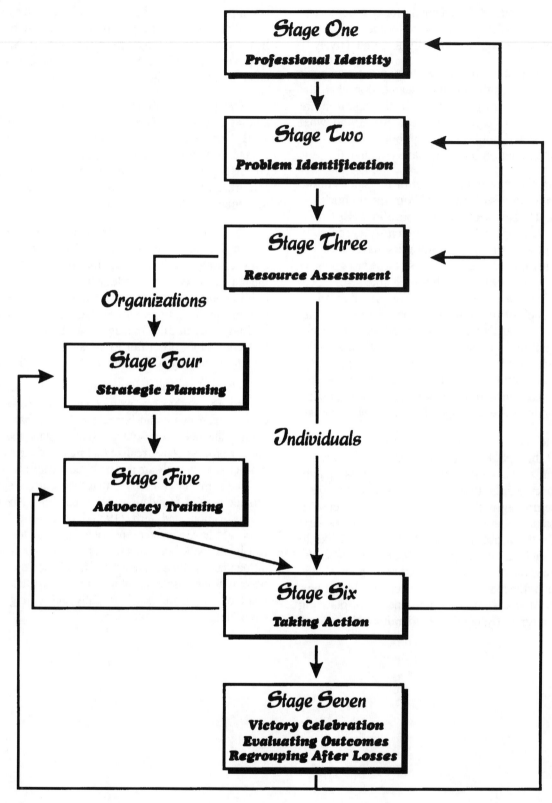

Figure 1.1. Stages of Counselor Advocacy.

Part I
THE STAGES OF ADVOCACY

Chapter 2

COUNSELORS SHOULD BE COUNSELORS!

Counselors are often reluctant to involve themselves in advocacy. This reluctance generates from the mistaken notion that counselors' values, personalities, and skills differ dramatically from those of advocates. Counselors see public relations (PR) and public policy people as possessing intricate knowledge of political and business systems, and as being manipulative, "hard sell" people. They view this style as conflicting with their desire for integrity and intimacy, and as detracting from the energy available for the provision of quality services. However, counselors, in fact, typically have the kinds of values, skills, and personalities needed for successful advocacy.

VALUES

Participant advocates (those advocates who participated in the research done for this book) indicated that four values promulgated by the counseling profession—inclusiveness, an educational approach, good communication, and relationship building— were essential elements in their advocacy.

When speaking of *inclusiveness,* participant advocates pointed frequently to the many specialties included by ACA, and the necessity of valuing what each specialty has to offer. They also urged counselors to adopt an inclusive rather than exclusive attitude toward other mental health providers.

Counselors of all persuasions often point to *education* as their heritage, and they consider educating people as valuable in much of what they do. Participant advocates indicated that approaching advocacy as education—rather than taking an angry, threatening approach—contributed most to desired changes.

Good communication is something counselors work at each day, and participant advocates con-

sidered it essential to advocacy as well. The various types of communication necessary to advocacy will be discussed throughout this book.

Finally, the three previous values contribute to *relationship building.* Cigler and Loomis (1995) and Birnbaum (1992) concurred on the importance of relationship building, indicating that the best way to get a target to respond to requests is for a counselor to establish a relationship with the target prior to the request—a relationship that demonstrates the counselor's value to the target.

Relationship building includes earning the right to be heard. If you were approached on the street by someone who asked you to do something for him or her, the first thing you would ask is "Who are you?" In fact, most people would not even approach someone who did not already know the answer to that question. Within a school, a counselor who has done his or her job well or served as a resource to a principal by helping that principal solve a problem is better positioned to make requests of that principal. A counselor who has worked on a legislator's campaign or honored the legislator for outstanding efforts in mental health legislation is better positioned to make requests of that legislator. A professional association that has researched an issue for a congressional committee will have easier access to that committee in the future. A counselor who has performed well for a managed care company and has been easy to work with can make requests of that company that others cannot. The value of relationship building cannot be overstated.

SKILLS

Just as counseling values are advocacy values, counseling skills are also advocacy skills. Participant advocates claimed that counselors should approach advocacy targets the same way they approach clients.

They should listen, ask questions until they understand their target's needs; gather information from a one-down, not-knowing position; and clarify what they are hearing to make sure they understand. Further, effective counselors know how to use language that clients can hear or understand, to clearly communicate how the changes clients need to make are related to the *clients'* perceived needs. This is no less necessary with advocacy targets.

Participant advocates also urged counselors to use their counseling skills in relating to other counselors. "If we are a profession that believes in empowering others, then why don't we do it with ourselves?" questioned one participant advocate. He and others further urged counselor advocates to support their colleagues who advocate, to focus on and build on their strengths, and to be very appreciative of their efforts. "If we want anyone to do anything, we call them, we answer their questions, we explain the necessary steps. People who followed through in advocating were people we talked with personally."

The public relations literature has identified other skills necessary to advocacy, skills that counselors also recognize as necessary to their work. These are problem sensing and problem solving, planning, educating, communicating, cheerleading, working as a team, building consensus, negotiating conflicts, changing systems, and gathering different views and hammering them together into a solution. Public relations experts devote whole chapters in their books to theories of communication, persuasion, and change—theories that are right out of counseling textbooks (Bernays, 1982, as cited in Newsom et al., 1993; Newsom et al., 1993).

PERSONALITIES

Of the three elements discussed here—values, skills, and personalities—counselors' personalities are most often thought to be contrary to those necessary for advocacy. Some counselors believe that only outgoing, forceful, articulate presenters— people with personalities similar to salespeople or politicians—succeed at advocacy. Bernays (1982, as cited in Newsom et al., 1993), however, cited the following characteristics as necessary for good PR people: character and integrity, a sense of judgment and logic, the ability to think creatively and imaginatively, truthfulness and discretion, objectivity,

a deep interest in the solution of problems, a broad cultural background, intellectual curiosity, effective powers of analysis and synthesis, intuition, and training in the social sciences. Seitel (1994) further emphasized the following characteristics for people in public relations positions:

1. A communications orientation—a bias toward disclosing rather than withholding information; they should want to communicate with the public and should practice the belief that the public has a right to know.

2. An advocacy orientation—a desire to be advocates for their group.

3. A counseling orientation—a compelling desire to advise decisionmakers; they must be willing to disagree at times with decisionmakers.

4. Personal confidence—a strong sense of honesty and ethics, a willingness to take risks, a sense of humor, and the courage of their convictions.

Most counselors would also consider these personality traits important for service providers in the mental health field.

Some of the participant advocates were indeed energetic, forceful, enthusiastic, upbeat, very intelligent, and had a "can do" attitude. However, just as many respondents were shy, soft-spoken, introverted, and understated. This group effected change by going through the "back door" rather than the "front door."

For example, one participant advocate unintentionally created massive changes by doing research on insurance companies. As he asked them questions—from a one-down, not-knowing position—about their policies and the reasons behind those policies, he discovered that the companies were often misinformed. When he supplied them with documentation to correct the misinformation, they changed their policies to include counselors.

Another introverted, soft-spoken counselor employed other interesting techniques. She started meetings on time whether or not the psychiatrists had arrived, to communicate that everyone's time was important, not just the doctors'. If the doctors addressed her by her first name, she did so in return, to emphasize parity. She decided how things ought to be and then acted on those decisions, without any up-front discussion. It seems that counselors like her accomplish a great deal by being non-threatening.

Most advocates observed during the research for this book, whether introverted or extroverted, seemed to be "overfunctioners" with hundreds of activities on their plates. They seemed crisis oriented, scattered, and a bit frenetic. It was intriguing how they managed to keep enough organization in their advocacy to finish tasks. In fact, some of the advocates reported that they regularly worked 10- to 16-hour days, and stayed up until all hours of the night working on advocacy projects.

Again and again, the research pointed to different personalities being necessary for different advocacy efforts. Assessing personality resources and matching those resources to particular advocacy activities may be a more helpful, albeit less used,

advocacy strategy. But regardless of personality, participant advocates indicated that a sense of humor and a passionate belief in what they are advocating for are necessary characteristics.

Whatever the reputation public relations people and lobbyists have acquired, it is clear that professionals and researchers in these fields concur with counselor advocates in encouraging the values, personalities, and skills taught in counseling programs and necessary to success as a counselor. Inclusiveness, good relationships, effective communication, integrity, creativity, diversity, curiosity, intuition, assessment skills, personal confidence, a sense of humor, empowerment, educative persuasion, and problem solving are all valued as much in public relations and lobbying as they are in counseling. Counselors do not have to "play a game" that contradicts who they are in order to be successful advocates. Their advocacy can benefit from who they are and who they desire to be.

Chapter 3

STAGE ONE: WHO ARE WE?

Kaylan Sanders and Daniel Wong were two counselors living in an average state in middle America. Kaylan was the president of the state's Association of Clinical Counselors (ACC). She had become very worried about counselors being excluded from health care reform bills and about the presentation of managed care as the only solution to the need for health care cost containment. Kaylan knew that mental health counselors are as qualified as other mental health professionals, and she knew that exclusion from major federal legislation such as health care reform would mean that she and other mental health counselors would be prohibited from practicing their profession as fully as they had been trained to do. She had also been hearing complaints from counselors about the inefficiency of managed care, and about the lesser quality client care that generates from applying the short-term therapy model to all mental health problems.

Daniel was a school counselor who had run into some difficulties with parents who were trying to eliminate some school programs, including some school counseling programs. These parents wanted to make sure that no relaxation training, self-esteem enhancement training, or other humanistic tools would be used on their children. They claimed that such practices were against their religious principles. School counselors had defined this problem as "censorship."

A precondition for Kaylan's and Daniel's disturbance about their respective situations and for their motivation to take action was their clear sense of professional identity. After all, why would counselors be upset about others not valuing or respecting who they are if they do not know and value who they are and what they do? Kaylan and Daniel reviewed this identity in preparation for their advocacy efforts. They knew their own credentials: what types of graduate study they had completed, what

kinds of supervised experiences they had had, and what types of licenses and certifications they had earned. They talked with other counselors to find out whether they had comparable experiences and perceptions. They talked with mental health professionals from different disciplines to find out how the other disciplines differed from or were similar to the counseling profession. Kaylan reviewed the state's licensing requirements and wrote to the psychiatry, psychology, nursing, social work, and marriage and family licensing boards to find out how the different licenses compared. She wrote to the American Counseling Association (ACA) and to the American Mental Health Counselors' Association (AMHCA) to find out how counselors were licensed or certified in other states, and she asked ACA and AMHCA for information on how counselor qualifications compared with those of the other mental health professions.

Daniel looked at his credentials and reviewed the state requirements for those credentials. He talked with the school social worker and the school psychologist in his school to clarify how their professional preparation differed from his own. He wrote to the American School Counselors Association (ASCA) to get their materials on what school counselors do and what their qualifications are.

Both Kaylan and Daniel began a process of introspection, asking themselves what they had to offer that was valuable enough that others ought to listen to their assessment of problems and suggestions of solutions. They assumed that others would not be as disturbed as they were and thus would not be automatically willing to fix the perceived problems. Kaylan also asked the board of directors of ACC to assess the counseling profession. She and Daniel developed the following list of counselor qualifications:

1. *Counselors are well-educated in the theories, research, and practice of counseling.* The education that counselors receive is comparable to and sometimes exceeds that of other mental health professionals. In Kaylan and Daniel's state, licensure as a mental health counselor requires 48 semester credits of graduate course work. Kaylan and Daniel discovered that ACA/AMHCA and the Council on Accreditation for Counseling and Related Educational Programs (CACREP) established a national standard of 60 semester credits for clinical mental health counselor preparation. For community counseling, the CACREP standards are 48 semester credits. In comparison, social workers in their state need 60 semester credits for clinical licensure, marriage and family therapists are required to have 48, and psychiatric nurses are only required to have a master's degree, with no credit hours specified. For school counselors, the state requires 48 graduate credits for credentialing, and CACREP accreditation requires 48 graduate credits. In comparison, school social workers generally need 45 to 60 graduate credits for their master's degree, while school psychologists need 45 credits for theirs.

2. *Counselors are well-supervised prior to receiving their credentials or licenses.* In Kaylan and Daniel's state, school counseling credentials require one year of supervised practicum experience in a school during the master's program. This requirement equals or exceeds requirements for school social workers and school psychologists. Mental health counseling requires two years or 3,000 hours of supervised experience beyond a master's degree. This equals or exceeds the postgraduate requirements for clinical social workers, psychologists (postdoctorate), and marriage and family therapists.

3. *School counselors are the only mental health professionals some children will ever see.* School counselors' developmental counseling objectives include working with students on (a) understanding self and others, (b) decision making and problem solving, (c) interpersonal and communication skills, (d) school success skills, and (e) career awareness skills (Myrick, 1993). School counselors' support groups contribute to many students improving their self-esteem and assertiveness, overcoming substance abuse, and learn-

ing to get along with others (Brigman & Moore, 1994). School counseling decreases school failure and dropouts, and reduces disciplinary problems (American School Counselor Association, 1979, 1981; Baker, Swisher, Nadenicheck, & Popowicz, 1984; Borders & Drury, 1992; Braun, 1976; Carledge & Milburn, 1978; Cobb & Richards, 1983; Deffenbacker & Kemper, 1974; Gerler, 1980, 1985; Gerler & Anderson, 1986; Glosoff & Koprovicz, 1990; Hoge & Luce, 1979; Wehlage & Rutter, 1986; Wirth, 1977). What school counselors offer in support and guidance when children are going through difficult times with peers, dealing with divorcing parents or the death of a family member, or having trouble getting along with a parent is invaluable to these children. School counseling increases positive attitudes toward school and learning and improves academic achievement.

School counselors are often the only people assisting teenagers in deciding what they want to do and are capable of doing for a career. Counseling eases the school-to-work transition by teaching employment skills and knowledge. School counselors may be a teenager's only resource for finding out about colleges or vocational training schools, and the financial aid available to attend these institutions.

4. *Mental health counselors provide top-quality mental health care to clients with a variety of problems.* The quality of this care is comparable to the quality of care provided by psychiatrists, psychologists, social workers, nurses, and marriage and family counselors in treating mental health and emotional problems. However, the care provided by counselors is also unique. Because counselors' heritage is education and vocational counseling, their treatment is not limited to remediation of problems but includes helping clients achieve optimum mental health. Counselors thus focus more on the whole client, considering satisfaction at work and in interpersonal relationships as essential elements in being mentally healthy. Counselors also offer prevention and early intervention in the form of psychoeducational classes given in the community. Many times these classes prevent mental health problems from developing. Counselors offer career guidance to people whose job difficulties are contributing to their mental health problems. Further, mental health treatment is

important to overall health care because it reduces the incidence and costs of medical problems.

As a result of their introspection and conversations with others, Kaylan and Daniel concluded that while other mental health professionals offer very valuable services, counselors are unique in what they have to offer consumers. This realization gave them a greater sense of pride in what they do and made them more willing to work at persuading others about the value of their work.

RESEARCH RESULTS AND THE LITERATURE ON PROFESSIONAL IDENTITY

The advocates who participated in the research for this book said that a clear sense of professional identity is fundamental to any advocacy effort. Before people can promote themselves as groups or individuals, they must know well what they are promoting. According to Schrader (1989, p. 230),

> If counselors do not determine what they should be doing, offer good reasons for doing it, and communicate their programs to other staff members, someone else will be certain to step in and tell them what they should be doing. And the chances are excellent that it won't be what the counselors want to do or think they should be doing.

This sense of professional identity can be explored across increasingly broader contexts. Counselors can examine who they are as individual counselors or as members of organizations. They can determine who counselors are as mental health professionals. They can explore where counselors fit in the broader health care or educational environment. They can also decide who counselors are as an interest group in the political universe.

Counselors as Individuals or Organizations

"It must be emphasized in the beginning that people's own sense of self is what will determine success in their marketing efforts. . . . Therapists should look to themselves first, making sure they feel good about themselves and are prepared to start marketing" (Richards, 1990, pp. 129–130). Advocacy must be based on confidence, assuredness, and stability in personal beliefs. Counselors should ask themselves what they do and what they are qualified to do. What makes them qualified to do these things? What makes their approach different from others? If they are mental health counselors, why

should clients come to them or why should referral sources refer clients to them rather than to someone else? Included in this assessment should be questions about the counselors' specific certifications, their specialties, the populations with whom they work well, their hours, the type of therapy they do, and the insurances that reimburse them.

School counselors can ask what role they play in their schools. Are they respected by the principal, their colleagues, the teachers, the students, and the parents? Are their recommendations heard and acted on by the other professionals in the school? Is counseling considered essential to the school's functioning? Are the students they counsel succeeding in school, improving their attitudes toward school, getting into colleges or vocational training?

Counselors serving in other organizations need to assess what their organization does, what it says, and how other people see it (Newsom et al., 1993). What role does the organization play in the community? Who does it serve? What does it do that other organizations do not? What can it be proud of? What should people know about it? Finally, counselors can do assessments to discover whether their own perceptions of who they are and what they do match the assessments of those around them.

In discovering the answers to these questions, counselors will need to determine with whom they have relationships because relationships determine, to a large extent, who a person becomes. The public relations field concurs, and refers to those with whom individuals, groups, or organizations have relationships as "publics" (Newsom et al., 1993). In the field of public policy, publics are groups that intervene between a perceived problem and governmental intervention, "a group of affected parties, aroused, engaged in conjoint activity, growing conscious of itself, organizing and seeking to influence officials" (Smith, 1964, p. 16). The publics that school counselors relate to may include

students,

teachers,

school social workers,

school psychologists,

the principal,

parents,

the school board,

legislators,

the state's department of education,

and parent-teacher organizations.

Mental health counselors' publics may include

clients,

legislators,

insurance companies,

licensing boards,

hospitals,

members of their professional association,

potential clients,

referral sources,

counseling services administrators,

and consumer advocate groups.

Of course, each of these publics may be divided further as counselors research particular views on specific issues. Jerry Hendrix's (1992) categories, presented in Table 3.1, give a more comprehensive look at the publics counselors might potentially engage.

Establishing a clear sense of professional identity means not only knowing one's position vis-à-vis these publics and how these publics impact the counseling profession but knowing where there is a disconnection between who counselors are and how they are treated by these publics (Newsom et al., 1993).

Counselors as Mental Health Professionals

Counselors can understand themselves in the context of mental health professionals if they know their "substance"—that is, their standards, credentials, and roles—and how it compares with that of other mental health professionals. Kaylan and Daniel identified important information as they asked questions about this substance. Table 3.2 is a chart

developed by the Virginia Association of Clinical Counselors to help their many publics understand more fully where mental health counselors fit in Virginia's credentialing world.

Participant advocates strongly emphasized the need for counselors to believe in their profession and to refuse to operate from an underdog mentality. As one advocate trainer said, "I think a real key in this for me has been helping counselors behave in a way that says they believe that they're peers, that they have parity, that they are not second class, that they are there because they belong, that they are part of the scene. It's expected that we would be participants."

In some cases, expecting recognition from their publics for the substance of who they are is more difficult for counselors because ethical and practice standards, credentials, educational and training programs, and licensure and certifications have yet to be developed. Further, because of the diversity of counselors, group cohesion and unity are sometimes difficult, making it hard to develop a unified set of credentials. However, because a highly unified group is more influential and provides greater security for its members (Truman, 1951; Zisk, 1969), decisions about professional identity should not be undertaken lightly. Wittenberg and Wittenberg (1989) urge groups interested in political ends to speak with one voice: "Any dissension about approaches, goals, or allowable compromises should be kept as far away from the capital as possible. Dissension sends confusing messages to Washington" (p. 103).

Counselors in Health Care and Education

The value of counselors within the health care and educational environments was not mentioned by participant advocates. However, the continuing struggles over issues such as health care reform and censorship make it clear that establishing a widespread understanding of the value of counseling in these environments is critical, not only to the future of the counseling profession but to the physical health of clients and the educational success of students.

Counseling's role in the health care environment was brought into focus during the 1993-94 national debate on health care reform. Tipper Gore, whose degree is in marriage and family counseling, led the way in insisting that mental health care be

Table 3.1 Categories of Publics

Media Publics

Mass media
  Local
    Print publications
      Newspapers
      Magazines
    TV stations
    Radio stations
  National
    Print publications
    Broadcast or cable networks
    Wire services

Specialized media
  Local
    Trade, industry and association publications
    Organizational house and membership publications
    Ethnic publications
    Publications of special groups
    Specialized broadcast or cable programs and stations
  National
    General business publications
    National trade, industry, and association publications
    National organizational house and membership
      publications
    National ethnic publications
    Publications of national special groups
    National specialized broadcast or cable programs and net-
      works

Member Publics

Organizational employees
  Headquarters management
  Headquarters nonmanagement (staff)
  Other headquarters personnel

Organization officers
  Elected officers
  Appointed officers
  Legislative groups
  Boards, committees

Organization members
  Regular members
  Members in special categories
  Honorary members or groups

Prospective organization members

State or local chapters
  Organization employees
  Organization officers
  Organization members
  Prospective organization members
  Related or other allied organizations

Co-Worker Publics

Management
  Upper-level administrators
  Midlevel administrators
  Lower-level administrators

Nonmanagement (staff)
  Specialists
  Clerical personnel

Secretarial personnel
Uniformed personnel
Equipment operators
Drivers
Security personnel
Other uniformed personnel
Union representatives

Other nonmanagement personnel

Funding Publics

Government funding agencies
Insurance companies
Foundations
Private payers

Government Publics

Federal
  Legislative branch
    Representatives, staff, committee personnel
    Senators, staff, committee personnel
  Executive branch
    President
    White House staff, advisers, committees
    Cabinet officers, departments, agencies, commissions

State
  Legislative branch
    Representatives, delegates, staff, committee personnel
    Senators, staff, committee personnel
  Executive branch
    Governor
    Governor's staff, advisers, committees
    Cabinet officers, departments, agencies, commissions

County
  County executive
  Other county officials, commissions, departments

City
  Mayor or city manager
  City council
  Other city officials, commissions, departments

Community Publics

Community media
  Mass
  Specialized

Community leaders
  Public officials
  Educators
  Religious leaders
  Professionals
  Executives
  Bankers
  Union leaders
  Ethnic leaders
  Neighborhood leaders

Community organizations
  Civic
  Service
  Social
  Business
  Cultural

(Table continues on next page)

Table 3.1 Categories of Publics (*Continued*)

Community organizations (*Continued*)	**Special Publics**
Religious	Media consumed by this public
Youth	Mass
Political	Specialized
Special interest	Leaders of this public
Other	Public officials
Consumer Publics	Professional leaders
Company employees	Ethnic leaders
Customers	Neighborhood leaders
Professionals	Organizations composing this public
Middle-class	Civil
Working-class	Political
Minorities	Service
Other	Businesses
Activist consumer groups	Cultural
Consumer publications	Religious
	Youth

Source: From *Public Relations Cases* (2nd ed.) (pp. 13–16), by J. A. Hendrix, 1992, Belmont, CA: Wadsworth. Copyright © 1992 by Wadsworth Publishing Company. Adapted with permission.

included on a par with medical care. The reasons that she and the Mental Health Liaison Group (1993) cited were (a) the high degree of success in treating mental illness in comparison with the success of already-covered and commonly used medical procedures; (b) research demonstrating "medical offsets"—that is, that mental health treatment reduces the incidence and thus the costs of medical problems; and (c) research demonstrating that the availability of unlimited outpatient benefits did not generate spiraling usage or costs. As a result of the health care reform debates, the linkage between mental and physical health is now somewhat better understood, and the importance of counseling to physical health has begun to be acknowledged.

Table 3.2. Commonwealth of Virginia Licensure Requirements for Mental Health Professionals

	Clinical Psychologist	Professional Counselor	Clinical Social Worker	Psychiatrist	Clinical Nurse Specialist
Minimum Education	Ph.D. / Psy.D.	MA / MS / Ms.Ed.	MSW	M.D.	M.S.N. or B.S.N. with master's in mental health field
Mental Health Courses Required	90+ graduate semester hours in 13 areas	60 graduate semester hours in 9 areas	60 graduate semester hours, content unspecified	None	Minimum of 24 graduate academic hours in mental health theory
Supervised Psychotherapy Experience Required	1-year internship 1-year postdoctoral residency (Total = 4,000 hours)	2 years of post-master's supervised experience in clinical setting (Total = 4,000 hours)	2 years of post-master's supervised experience in clinical setting (Total = 3,000 hours)	1-year residency (Minimum of 2,000 hours)	2 years of post-master's supervised experience (Total = 832 hours)
Face-to-face Supervision in Psychotherapy Required	200 hours	200 hours	100 hours	Unspecified	100 hours
Written Exam	Yes	Yes	Yes	Yes	Yes

Source: Developed by M. Nahl and K. Eriksen, Virginia Association of Clinical Counselors (VACC) members.

Counseling's role in the educational environment receives continuing attention through court cases and publicity surrounding the censorship of various public school activities, including school counseling activities. School counselors, principals, and teachers defend counseling programming on the basis of the value of school counseling to the total school environment. Research clearly shows that school counseling programs reduce dropout rates, decrease school failure, and improve attendance. They also increase students' self-esteem, assertiveness, and social skills, and decrease delinquency, which in turn increases students' abilities to learn (American School Counselor Association, 1979, 1981; Baker, Swisher, Nadenicheck, & Popowicz, 1984; Borders & Drury, 1992; Braun, 1976; Brookover, 1969, as cited in Brigman & Moore, 1994; Caine & Caine, 1991; Carledge & Milburn, 1978; Cobb & Richards, 1983; Coopersmith, 1981; Deffenbacker & Kemper, 1974; Gerler, 1980, 1985; Gerler & Anderson, 1986; Glaser, 1969; Glosoff & Koprovicz, 1990; Gurney, 1987; Hoge & Luce, 1979; Marsh, 1984; Nagel-Harmon, 1989, as cited in Brigman & Moore, 1994; Purkey, 1970; Wehlage & Rutter, 1986; Wirth, 1977).

Counselors as an Interest Group

Finally, counselors are an interest group among other interest groups in the political arena. "Once the political community grows beyond the manageable boundaries of the town meeting, some kind of private associational life becomes essential to democracy; in fact, it is difficult to imagine large-scale democracy without it" (Schlozman & Tierney, 1986, p. 4). Interest groups serve as a major link between the citizen and the government (Berry, 1989a; Zisk, 1969), providing a means for citizens to be educated about issues and to participate in the political process, and a means for government to respond to constituent needs and desires (Berry, 1977, 1989a). Interest groups form "a channel of access through which [group] members voice their opinions to those who govern them" (Berry, 1989a, p. 6). Interest groups also serve as bargaining agents in the allocation of material and human resources (Zisk, 1969).

Historically, the political process has been characterized in terms of the dynamic relations among many contending groups. Growth in the size and reach of government over the years has led to the greater need for interest groups to promote their interests, particularly as budget deficits have made competition between interests more intense (Loomis & Cigler, 1986; Petracca, 1992b; Schlozman & Tierney, 1986). Schlozman and Tierney (1986, p. x) claimed that this process

> enhances the mechanisms of representation, guaranteeing to ordinary citizens an effective voice in the halls of government; protects them from the coercive exercise of governmental power; precludes majority tyranny by accommodating the preferences of the most intensely concerned; ensures moderate policies and therefore political stability; and promotes political outcomes that approximate the public interest.

Wilson (1992, p. 95) further claimed, "No interest group system exceeds the capacity of the American one to represent effectively a wide diversity of views." It is hoped that as groups struggle on an issue, the adversarial process will give rise to a degree of rationality that would otherwise be unattainable (Hayes, 1986). In this process, interest groups

- *educate* the public and their members about the issues,

- *persuade* decisionmakers to attend to their concerns,

- *monitor* existing programs to draw attention to shortcomings in these programs,

- *provide a place* for individuals to belong and to join with others to more effectively impact systems (Berry, 1989b; Petracca, 1992a),

- *gather information* increasingly needed by overworked government officials,

- *link* group members with broader community values, and

- *transform* the values of members or government officials (Petracca, 1992a).

Many types of interest groups involve themselves in the political process. Counselors are generally part of member organizations called "professional associations." Other types of member organizations are

- *peak business associations,* or organizations of organizations like the chamber of commerce;

- *trade associations,* which unite companies in a single industry and are the most numerous of the interest groups;

- *labor unions,* which have the largest membership and act not only on issues affecting their members, but on social justice issues;

- *farm groups,* which advocate for the farming community;

- *citizens' groups,* which try to advance government policies that will benefit the public at large;

- *advocacy groups,* which seek selective benefits on behalf of groups that are in some way incapacitated or unable to represent their own interests;

- *cause groups,* which care intensely about a single issue (such as abortion); and

- *civil rights and social welfare organizations,* which combat discrimination on the basis of race, ethnicity, or gender.

Nonmember organizations such as corporations and public interest law firms also pursue political interests. Finally, foreign governments, the intergovernmental lobby, and the executive branch of government also lobby for their interests (Schlozman & Tierney, 1986). Interest groups thus serve a valuable function in a democracy, helping to keep the people informed, to keep the government informed, and to increase the representativeness of government.

PROFESSIONAL IDENTITY EXERCISE

The following exercise will help you conduct your own process of introspection and thereby enrich your awareness of your own professional identity. Ask yourself the following questions, and spend a little time really considering their importance to your work. Write down your answers so that you can share them with others, and add to those answers as your sense of professional identity grows and matures.

1. What is counseling to me, and what is my role as a counselor? What do I do with clients? What is my role in my employing organization and my value to it?

2. What qualifications do I have that prepare me to be a counselor? (If you do not remember your state licensure or credentialing requirements, you may want to pull them out to refresh your memory.)

3. What do I plan to do in the next few years to add to these qualifications and keep my current skills and knowledge up-to-date? Do I, for instance, hold a value, or is there a requirement in my profession, that insists on more training, supervision, or continuing education?

4. How do my qualifications and roles differ from those of social workers, psychologists, nurses, marriage and family therapists, psychiatrists, and other mental health professionals? (You may need to question these other professionals or write to your state licensing or credentialing board to find the answers to this question.)

5. How are my qualifications similar to those of the above professionals?

6. How do my qualifications compare with other counselors around the country? (ACA keeps an up-to-date list of the requirements for licensure, certification, and credentialing in all of the states. They also keep the state licensure laws on file. You may want to contact them for some documentation at 703-823-9800.)

7. What preparation standards and what certifications exist for counselors? (To find out more about the National Board for Certified Counselors [NBCC] certification and Certified Clinical Mental Health Counselor [CCMHC] certification, write or call NBCC, 3-D Terrace Way, Greensboro, NC 27403, 910/547-0607. To find out more about CACREP, contact their office at ACA, 5999 Stevenson Avenue, Alexandria, VA 22304, 703-823-9800.)

8. What has the counseling profession done that it can brag about? (Professional associations often publish in their newsletters a "brag list" of what they have accomplished during the past year or since the inception of the association. This is important information for you to know about your profession.)

9. What have I done that I can brag about? (Remember, anyone you talk to is going to be asking themselves, "Who is this person, and why should I listen to [hire, refer to, reimburse, change legislation, fund programs for] them?")

10. What role does my organization play in the community?

11. Who benefits from counseling services and how?

12. To ascertain your publics, divide the inner circle in Figure 3.1 into pie wedges representing the different roles you play and according to the percentages of time you spend in these roles. In the outer circle, write the names of people and organizations with which you interact as a regular part of your role. Also write down those publics that impact you in your role. (Figure 3.2 contains a completed example.)

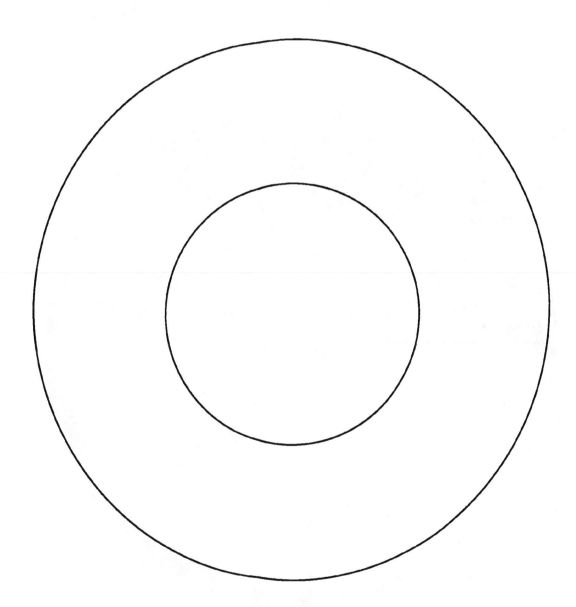

Figure 3.1. Template for Roles and Publics Exercise. Permission is given to enlarge and photocopy for individual use.

SUMMARY

Only when counselors fully understand who they are as individual and organizational providers, as mental health professionals, as players in the educational and health care delivery systems, and as an interest group in a political system can they believe enough in their value to persuade others of their importance. Participant advocates indicated that the lack of professional identity is a real obstacle to advocacy efforts. Continual conflicts among counselors about who they are and what they do results in a lack of uniformity and translates into difficulties telling their publics who counselors are. The publics then receive conflicting and confusing messages. While counselors value diversity, it seems that there are currently so many competing voices that counselors may become distracted from their goals, coalitions may fall apart, and decisionmakers may become confused. "We do more damage to ourselves and the way we define ourselves than anyone else," said one advocate. Advocacy efforts must thus be grounded in a firm sense of professional identity, and if this identity is lacking, counselors must first seek to generate it.

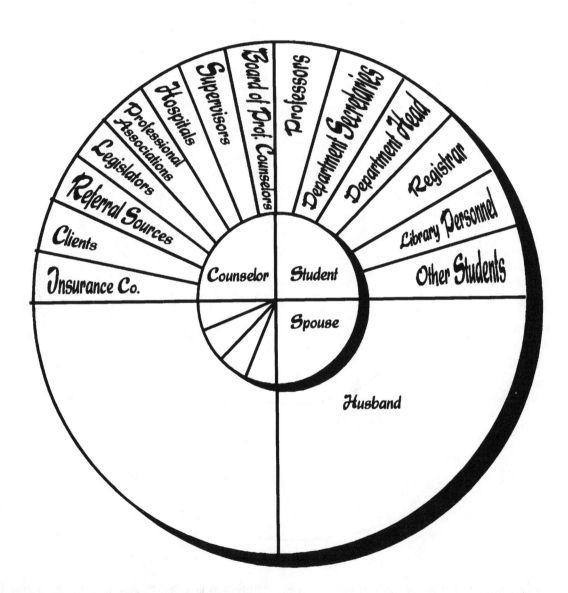

Figure 3.2. Example for Roles and Publics Exercise.

Chapter 4

STAGE TWO: WHY START?

Kaylan Sanders and Daniel Wong would not have begun the advocacy process if they had not noticed some problem, inequity, or need. If, in fact, they had not had confidence in themselves as counselors, if they had not believed that what they do is valuable, and if they had not felt that someone was treating them or their clients unfairly, they probably would not have been disturbed enough to take action.

Kaylan had been in private practice for 10 years and was known as one of the finest therapists in her region. She had contributed to the reconciliation of more marriages, the remission of more depression, the well-being of more people than she could count. Her clients valued her services enough to refer their friends and family to her, and she had a thriving and profitable practice. Most people, however, could not afford to pay $60 per hour out of their own pockets for counseling. They relied on the health insurance provided by their employers to pay for at least half of it.

Health care reform was designed to make America's health care system more efficient. It proposed to use such tools as managed care to contain the rising costs of health care. While Kaylan agreed with the aim of health care reform, she was alarmed that most of the health care reform bills submitted to Congress only recognized psychiatrists, psychologists, social workers, and nurses as mental health providers. Since some health care reform proposals hoped to consolidate private and public health care under one system, counselors would be out of work if they were not included as providers.

Since Kaylan knew that 50 percent of all mental health care was provided by master's level counselors, she was not only concerned for herself and her fellow counselors, she was also concerned for all of the clients who would have difficulty accessing mental health care if counselors were removed as providers. Further, she knew that in rural and inner city areas in her state there were already shortages of mental health providers. Removing financing for qualified mental health providers could only make these shortages worse. Those most hurt by this lack of accessible providers would be the disadvantaged and seriously mentally ill clients.

Kaylan was further alarmed at the ease with which the idea of managed care was being "sold" while many providers she knew were complaining about managed care. Clients in crisis were calling their managed care companies and being put on hold, or reaching answering machines and sometimes not having their calls returned for a week. Those with long-standing and serious mental health problems were having difficulty acquiring authorization for more than six to eight sessions. Clients also found that highly recommended therapists were not on managed care panels because of the difficulties these therapists encountered in dealing with managed care. Finally, the reluctance of some therapists to see managed care clients resulted in clients having to call multiple therapists before finding one with a reasonable appointment time.

Counselors were concerned not only for their clients' welfare but for their own welfare. They were being told that if they averaged more than six to eight sessions they would be dropped from the provider panels. So, they struggled with the conflict between their clients' clinical needs and their own livelihood needs, an interesting ethical problem involving dual relationships. Further, while they agreed to see clients at rates only half of what they usually charged, in return for the promise of increased client referrals, they rarely received increased referrals from the managed care companies. Most of the referrals came from their own marketing efforts. Finally, because the managed care companies handled claims processing so poorly, it often took providers months and many phone calls and re-submissions before they received any money for the services they performed. These developments alarmed Kaylan enough to take action.

Daniel faced a different problem. He had been an elementary school counselor for 12 years. His latest promotion had made him the director of guidance with responsibility for supervision of the school counseling programs in a "pyramid" of schools—one high school, three intermediate schools, and eight elementary schools. He had received many commendations for his work with students, particularly for a "Just Say No" program he had instituted in several schools. The students with whom he worked wrote to him for years after they graduated to thank him and to let him know what they were doing with their lives. Daniel watched many other school counselors achieve just as much as he had with students in need.

While Daniel could understand and accept that different people have different beliefs, he could not understand why some parents were condemning all the good work he and other school counselors were doing as against their religion, antifamily, and harmful to children. These accusations were provocative, at the very least.

Further, what these parents were demanding was new "opt-in" state legislation instead of the current "opt-out" requirements. This change would require school counselors to get written permission from parents for each meeting they had with a student, rather than requiring parents to indicate that they did not want their children participating in counseling programs. The delays involved in the process could be disastrous, because the permission process would make it difficult for school counselors to be available to students and teachers in an emergency; would make it impossible for students to initiate counseling that they might want but that their parents might not want for them; would encourage students to believe that adults were not available to them when they wanted help with issues difficult to talk about with parents, like sex or drug abuse; and would make it harder for students to access needed support when parents were abusive or unavailable to them. Further, he knew that research indicated that many children would fail or drop out of school if it were not for school counseling programs.

Daniel felt that the opt-in legislation was unfair both to counselors and to students. He was concerned that the actions of a small group of parents might eliminate some school counseling programs, cause top-quality counselors to lose their jobs, and cause children to lose needed services. He was very worried that the time and finances needed to combat the litigation by these parents would further deplete the already low funds for counseling programs and the already drained energies of overworked school counselors. He also felt personally angry about the vehemence with which some of these parents were denouncing his own profession. He knew that this anger was increasing his stress level. He became upset enough to take action.

As Kaylan and Daniel began speaking with their colleagues, they found that other counselors had similar concerns. The belief that joint action could generate greater results inspired them further.

RESEARCH RESULTS AND THE LITERATURE ON PROBLEM IDENTIFICATION

The most important decision in the advocacy process is not what strategies or tactics to use but whether to become active on an issue in the first place (Berry, 1977). According to the advocates who participated in the research done for this book, motivation for action depends on identifying a problem or need that is of significant magnitude to motivate action or be defined as a problem (see also Foreman, 1995). Almond and Verba (1963) and Loomis and Cigler (1986) concurred that direct action is more likely to generate from stressful situations in which citizens believe that government activity will injure them, or from "substantial cleavages among society's citizens" (Loomis & Cigler, 1986, p. 5). Stage Two of counselor advocacy (see Figure 1.1) is the identification of a problem and the framing of that problem in language that mandates action.

Counselors who are content with their jobs, status, and salaries will rarely feel any compunction to advocate for themselves. Any discrepancy, however, between a counselor's own image of his or her abilities and the ability to fully use those abilities generates a sense of need or injustice. In other words, anger at such things as being excluded from a client's insurance policy, losing those clients whose insurance policies do not cover counselors and who cannot afford to pay out of pocket, being unable to find work because the schools and mental health agencies do not hire counselors, losing a promotion because counselors cannot supervise, being unable to find funding for a program employing counselors, or having one's counseling students excluded from federal training subsidies generally arouses a sense of need or injustice, thus defining the problem as one needing action. Concern for clients who, because of a shortage of mental health providers, cannot receive mental health services, combined with anger at the failure of legislation to legitimize a qualified solution to these shortages, may also generate this sense of injustice. Thus, advocacy is often motivated by the unjust exclusion of one's profession, frustration with abuses in systems, the pain of those unable to fight for themselves, and panic about losing one's livelihood. As one participant advocate said, however, "I think that may be the most challenging part of advocacy . . . coming to some agreement among ourselves" as to what problems should receive priority attention.

Another challenge is that the public, the media, employers, and other targets have limited amounts of time and energy and therefore can focus on only a limited number of issues. Thus, although society has many problems, not all of them get enough attention to be rectified. As Salmon (1990) said, "It is an enduring characteristic of society that certain behaviors, products or ideas periodically become 'defined' as social problems through the efforts of advocacy groups" (p. 23). Efforts to address issues will fail if those efforts are not promoted by capable organizations. Only with backing will social conditions even be viewed as needing attention, much less get the attention they need. A person or organization may also choose to advocate on problems that give them the opportunity to promote their favorite solution, to block initiatives that will hurt them, or to promote a solution that precedent indicates policy makers will act upon. Sometimes action is determined externally by other political actors, such as someone suing a counselor or the government making policy changes (Schlozman & Tierney, 1986). In other words, defining a social condition as a problem that warrants attention is a subjective process.

While it may be easy for counselors to identify a problem, they may neglect the politicking that is necessary to get it the attention it warrants. Problem definition involves using language to frame the problem so that decisionmakers and the wider public will be motivated to take action. Problem definition is thus of such importance that public policy experts address it in depth, and in this book it is considered more fully in chapter 6. Here, however, it can be acknowledged that individuals will define a situation as a problem and be motivated to action when the threat is perceived as great enough and when the probable solution seems within their power to achieve. When problems are perceived as having enough magnitude to require more than individual action, groups of people must come to some consensus on which problems are most significant. As with individuals, groups choose to elevate a problem to their agendas if group members can agree that it is indeed a problem, and if they can perceive an attainable solution. Other "bad" situations are still problems but do not become actionable. They float around until the political atmosphere changes, solutions become attainable, actionable language can be found, or powerful, monied people adopt the issue.

MOTIVATION EXERCISE

The following exercise will help you identify needs or injustices on which you might be motivated to take action.

1. List some professional needs of yours that are not being met and that cause you frustration (or identify areas of frustration and work backward to identify the need). Use the concentric circles from the exercise in chapter 3 (Figure 3.1) to trigger your thoughts.

2. List some unmet needs and frustrations of your clients or of your employing organization. (Groups may want to make one list combining the unmet needs and frustrations of counselors, clients, and the organization.)

3. Prioritize these lists by placing a number from 1 to 10 next to each item, with 1 being the most stressful or urgent.

4. Decide whether any of these items could be grouped together because action on one would help resolve another.

5. Beginning with the most stressful or urgent, identify who is being hurt or may be hurt by the situation and how they are being or might be hurt.

6. What are you afraid will happen if action is not taken to correct this problem?

7. What do you envision happening if action is taken to correct this problem?

SUMMARY

Counselors identify problems based on the stress they experience in interfacing with one of their publics. If this stress threatens something they value, they will probably talk about it with other counselors. If enough counselors feel similarly, they may define the problem in terms that will motivate other counselors, decisionmakers, and the wider public to take action. Framing problems in order to generate consensus and coalitions is addressed in greater depth in chapter 8.

Chapter 5

STAGE THREE: WHO AND WHAT IS ON OUR SIDE?

As president of the Association of Clinical Counselors (ACC), Kaylan realized that before ACC began advocating on behalf of counselors, they had better have a clear idea of what resources they could bring to bear on their priority issues. At ACC's board retreat, she led the leadership through part of the strategic planning process used by the American Mental Health Counselor's Association (AMHCA). First she asked the board to consider what ACC's strengths and weaknesses were, and then what external assets and liabilities existed for them. They came up with the following list of strengths and assets:

- strong, willing, active core group of 10 people;

- one successful legislative season that gave ACC visibility;

- a liaison person with close connections to the advocacy department of the American Counseling Association (ACA);

- an ACA grant and willingness on the part of ACA to help ACC become a strong group;

- licensure in the state for licensed professional counselors (LPCs);

- a newsletter to keep members informed;

- a cause about which many people are concerned;

- an issue with the potential for involving other mental health provider groups;

- a board member who had served on Tipper Gore's mental health working group;

- a board member working on a dissertation related to managed care; and

- a great deal of passion over the loss of income being experienced by counselors and organizations in the state.

The board also identified the following weaknesses and liabilities:

- inexperienced leadership;

- lack of a history of working together for a cause;

- no grassroots organization;

- the death of the initial drive-toward-licensure passion, without reorganizing for group maintenance;

- a budget of only $2,000;

- licensure at a lower level than the national standard;

- the seeming failure of health care reform to get off the ground; and

- the risk of counselors losing their provider status if they are vocal about problems with managed care.

Daniel, too, assessed his resources, in order to be intentional about selecting actions to take. Like most school guidance personnel, he was somewhat overworked, so his time was at a premium. However, because of his recent promotion to director of guidance for a pyramid of schools, he had not yet fully prioritized his list of projects.

He decided he would set aside two hours per week to think about and work on the censorship problem.

Daniel was not thinking about finances at this point, because as an individual he could decide whether to spend money as situations arose, based on his financial resources at the time. Besides, he was fairly sure he could use some school resources since the issue related to his pyramid's programs.

What Daniel was particularly proud of was his substantive knowledge and network of contacts built up over the years. In preparation for taking on the new position, he had collected statistics on the counseling programs in his pyramid. These data included

- the numbers of students and parents served;

- postservice satisfaction ratings;

- postservice academic and behavioral improvements; and

- community and parent public relations contacts.

In addition, Daniel wrote down the names and positions of people with whom he had good relationships and who might be interested in the issue:

- Jan Mason, school board member;

- Jerry Tomlinson, principal;

- Sandy Wu, internship supervisor at the local college;

- Franklin Benjamin, director of guidance at the high school;

- the counselors in his pyramid;

- Jennifer Tallfeather, PTA president;

- Joseph Perry, county supervisor; and

- a number of special education teachers.

Finally, Daniel felt very strongly about finding some solutions, and he felt he could effectively communicate his ideas and passion both orally and in writing.

RESEARCH RESULTS AND THE LITERATURE ON ASSESSING RESOURCES

"Without sufficient resources interest groups cannot expect even to survive as organizations, much less to have an effect on political outcomes" (Schlozman & Tierney, 1986, p. 88). Thus, key questions in advocacy efforts are the following: What resources can an individual or organization bring to bear on a problem? Which resources are most necessary to effective problem resolution? And how can advocacy plans be designed to match available resources? Stage Three of the counselor advocacy model (see Figure 1.1) involves identifying these resources.

Public policy researchers and writers have been much more explicit about the resources necessary to an advocacy campaign than were the advocates who participated in the research for this book, even though counselors are often concerned that they lack sufficient resources to make an impact. "Money remains the mother's milk of politics," said Loomis and Cigler (1986; see also Cigler, 1986; and Schlozman & Tierney, 1986). Birnbaum (1992, p. 161) further claimed that

> few lobbyists entered the fray of Washington without first making sure they had a ready hoard of dollars to spread around. PAC and personal political contributions were expected of anyone who wanted to get his point across. Though money rarely bought votes outright, it did buy a lobbyist the chance to make his views known, a chance not everyone had. Access to the powers that be was rationed, and the size of one's political pocketbook was important to making the cut. The importance of money in politics was openly acknowledged by both the lawmakers who took it and the lobbyists who doled it out. "Money is power," said Democratic Representative Bill Alexander of Arkansas. And the lobbyists who were able to provide money were able to wield more than their share of power. "Access to Congress can't be bought, but it can be acquired with the help of campaign contributions," said Democratic Senator Brock Adams of Washington State, in a marvelous example of doublespeak.

Birnbaum quoted one lobbyist as saying, "'Chances are you are not going to get your phone calls returned' if you don't help a lawmaker raise money" (p. 165). He also noted that "often political money [works] for lobbyists in subtle ways. It [is] not just a way to buy access and win friends; it also [is] the ticket to some of the biggest lobbying fests in Washington: political fundraisers" (p. 167). In addition, media skill and access are a helpful resource to public relations or public policy efforts, and large sums of money are often necessary to make full use of the media (Foreman, 1995).

Both individual counselors and groups of counselors have worried about lacking the large sums of money that they feel would enable them to compete with corporations. These companies have major departments and staff specifically designated to advocate on their behalf. Counselors also have worried about a powerful elite of lobbyists who make backroom deals, precluding access by the average person. Finally, counselors have worried that, relative to highly paid lobbyists, they have lacked the time to contact targets.

However, the mechanisms of influence have changed over the years (Birnbaum, 1992). Money is still a primary influence, but it is far from the only one. Less money can be compensated for with other resources (Schlozman & Tierney, 1986). Also, sources of money other than membership dues have become available for activities that do require money. For example, the government and other foundations fund organizations that are engaged in worthwhile causes (Berry, 1977). Further, lobbying has become more open and competitive, requiring greater ingenuity, more use of the grass roots, and greater substantive knowledge (Berry, 1989a; Wittenberg & Wittenberg, 1989).

Research by Heinz and his colleagues (Heinz, Laumann, Nelson, & Salisbury, 1993) explored who the policy influencers were in Washington and how they wielded their influences. The research disproved the notion that only an elite group that has special connections to other elites or to government officials with whom they worked in the past has sufficient power and connections to influence public policy. Their research found that even though the list of notables they interviewed included

> Washington representatives of great prominence, accomplishment, and reputed influence, [they found] no identifiable set of core actors. This suggests that autonomous brokers who have the capacity to bridge the four policy areas either do not exist or [they] were not able to find them. (p. 301)

Even when looking at only one domain, they found no notables holding the field together or mediating between different groups on different issues.

Heinz and his colleagues also disproved the revolving door hypothesis: that most lobbyists previously held jobs in government and that that is where they acquired their contacts, their access, and thus their effectiveness. Heinz and his colleagues also disproved the importance of the good ol' boy network—that who you know is more important than what you know. Only 5 percent of those questioned had previously worked in a government organization with which they needed contact as lobbyists. Knowledge of the subject matter and knowledge of the legal process were considered more important than good ol' boy contacts. The only exception to this was that contacts were considered more important to the work of lobbyists who had congressional experience, probably because of the lesser formality and greater accessibility of Congress.

Washington representatives (currently a more popular term for lobbyist) are usually recruited from within the organizations for whom they work—like the normal staff people we know in organizations like ACA, AMHCA, and the American School Counselors Association (ASCA)—not some world-impacting political gurus. In fact, 76 percent of all lobbying is done by full-time employees of this type of organization, only sometimes in collaboration with outside representatives. (Outside representatives play a comparatively small role.)

Heinz and his colleagues also found that Washington representatives are constrained by their client organizations, and scholars suggest that that means relative stability as positions and patterns of alliance and opposition shift only within narrow limits. The influence of representatives derives primarily from substantive expertise or professional status. Lawyers do not dominate the field. Instead, lawyers are found where the primary institutional actors are courts or regulatory agencies. Lawyers specialize more narrowly than other representatives. What they specialize in—the formalities of procedural due process—are much less the rule "than are telephone calls, personal visits to members of Congress, and other public officials, give-and-take negotiations with allies and adversaries, and close monitoring of the trade press" (Heinz et al., 1993, p. 104).

Finally, Heinz and his colleagues explored how much contact government officials had with Washington representatives. According to the government officials they questioned, "only ten of the large, visible interest groups received as many as ten nominations from the three hundred officials" (p. 240). According to Heinz and his colleagues, this meant that the interest group universe is very diverse. Also, on 29 percent of the issues, no official was contacted by a representative. In 53 percent of the issues, at least three groups contacted the officials; more than 75 percent of the time these contacts were on the same side of the issue. Also, groups were more likely to contact officials when the groups and official were on the same side of the issue (73 percent of contacts). Further, typical representatives see only 16 to 20 targets per year. It does appear, according to Heinz and his colleagues, that these contacts enhance the groups' success in achieving their policy objectives.

What does this research mean for counselors? Because money is not the only resource; because the staff of organizations like ACA are the primary lobbyists; because full-time, professional, highly paid lobbyists make so few government contacts; and because there are no elite lobbyists who make it happen for everyone, counselors are clearly better situated than they generally consider themselves to be. Counselors are not "small fry" in the political arena, and they clearly should not consider themselves to be without influence.

Readers should note, however, that participant advocates and the public relations literature said little about assessing resources. This means that the following discussion of resources properly applies only to advocacy with government. A discussion at the end of the chapter explores which of the principles can be applied to other types of advocacy activities.

TYPES OF RESOURCES

So, what form can counselors' influence take? What resources can counselors bring to bear on target publics? Resources in the public policy domain can be roughly divided into the following categories: political expertise, substantive knowledge, access, merits of the cause, media skill, allies, fervor, and organizational resources.

Political Expertise

Much of this book is about developing political expertise. It helps to understand the structure and function of government organizations and the policy making or public relations process before launching advocacy efforts. Advocates need to have political information, to be on top of the political situation, to have the "ability to frame issues in such a way as to attract allies and divide opponents, [to have] a sense of timing, a facility in marshaling facts and presenting arguments, and a nose for assessing the strengths and vulnerabilities of one's antagonists" (Schlozman & Tierney, 1986, p. 97). It also helps to be flexible and to be able to compromise (Wittenberg & Wittenberg, 1989).

Groups can hire people who have these skills or otherwise retain them from outside. Lawyers are one type of outside expert. They monitor government activity for any developments that might affect the group's interests. They also draft bills and regulations, compose testimony and statements, assemble research and technical information, gain access to decisionmakers, talk with government officials, plan political strategy, and set up and run political action committees.

Public relations agencies are another type of outside expert. They provide a much wider array of services, including mobilizing grassroots efforts, conducting opinion surveys, building press relations, holding social events and receptions, and developing advertising campaigns (Schlozman & Tierney, 1986). The AMHCA, for example, hired a managed care expert to assist individual members and the organization as a whole to interact more effectively with managed care organizations.

Outside experts generally do the same things as organizations' salaried staff members. Outsiders are hired primarily because they have access to Congress or executive branch officials, access the organization staff might not have (Schlozman & Tierney, 1986). Counselors may also seek the advice of lobbyists and public relations firms if they do not have the political or other substantive expertise within their ranks on a full-time basis. However, at the national level of policy making, outside experts usually have no more political expertise than the staff of such organizations as ACA, AMHCA, or ASCA.

Substantive Knowledge

Substantive knowledge is knowledge about the particular policy domain. For counselors, substantive knowledge is information about the process and effectiveness of counseling and counseling programs, the impact of legislation or organizational policies on counselors and consumers, or possible alternatives to solving problem situations. Clearly, counselors themselves have the greatest access to this type of information. The value of this information has increased as the public policy environment has changed (Birnbaum, 1992; Foreman, 1995; Schlozman & Tierney, 1986; Wittenberg & Wittenberg, 1989).

Browne (1986) indicated that "single issue organizations," such as ACA and its state branches or divisions, have the "political advantages of specialized expertise, the need for routine access to only a few policy makers, and the group's ability to focus on one item of interest" (p. 194). They maintain an image of expertise and experience. Their "political relationships best replicate the subsystems model, in which a few lobbyists work with highly specialized legislative subcommittees and relatively small federal agencies" (p. 194). These lobbyists "see policy makers regularly, engage them in ongoing policy dialogues, establish relationships of trust, and advance their own proposals early in the deliberative process" (p. 194–195). They and the legislators they contact have an ongoing and comprehensive concern about regulations that affect a commodity or product—such as counseling.

Access

Any of the resources discussed in this chapter can gain counselors access to decisionmakers, but sometimes access is simpler. Counselors may know targets—such as legislators, their staff, administrators of insurance companies, government officials, school board members—personally, as friends or as co-workers in other capacities. This type of access is not to be undervalued. After all, counselors would make time available for giving vocational advice to the child of a friend. They would not mind being approached for advice on a psychoeducational program to be held in their church. They frequently advise friends or friends of friends who are considering a counseling career. Why should counselors expect less from their friends and colleagues?

Merits of the Cause

Counselors may consider many issues to have merit, but of critical importance is whether their publics or targets also consider the issues to have merit. Are the problems that counselors would like

to solve considered problems widely? Are decisionmakers already aware of these problems and motivated to seek solutions? Will they value the solutions counselors prefer? Are there precedents for choosing the solutions counselors prefer? What are the arguments for and against what counselors would like to see happen (Schlozman & Tierney, 1986; Wittenberg & Wittenberg, 1989)?

Related to the merits of the cause is the number of other groups or people who are likely to be in favor of or in opposition to the proposed solution. Clearly, counselors must consider early on who they can count on to support their cause. (Coalition and consensus building are covered extensively in chapter 8.)

Fervor

Certainly not the least of the potential resources to be considered are fervor and determination, which clearly reflect the importance of the issue to those attached to the profession. These sentiments have often attained results despite the lack of other resources (Advocacy Institute, 1990; Berry, 1977; Schlozman & Tierney, 1986; Wittenberg & Wittenberg, 1989). For example, as noted in chapter 4, threats to counselors or their clients' well-being can certainly motivate counselors to overcome many other obstacles.

Organizational Resources

Latham (1952) indicated that organized groups are structures of power because they concentrate "human wit, energy, and muscle for the achievement of received purposes" (p. 382). Groups organize for the security and self-expression of their members. If these goals are not fulfilled, the group loses energy, morale, and dedication. The goals are achieved "through control of the physical and social environment which surrounds each group and in the midst of which it dwells" (p. 386). This control is established in three ways: by putting restraints on the environment or destroying the opposition; by neutralizing the environment with counterpropaganda; and by conciliation to make the environment more friendly. Gaining control is a ceaseless struggle because the environment is constantly changing. Organized groups have advantages, therefore, over unorganized groups, and the better-run, more efficient organizations have the greatest advantages.

Any discussion of organizational resources must address organizational development, leadership, membership, and group cohesion.

Why Groups Develop. Although theories abound on why groups develop, the discussion that follows will show that to induce people to join a group, organizational leaders ultimately must have some sort of available resources.

Group theory grew out of theories in sociology and psychology that posited that people are naturally affiliative. Proliferation theory followed, claiming that as the population achieves more and more specialization of function, people within each function have disparate interests and values from those in other functions, and the natural social response is to form associations with those who have the same interests and values. A homeostatic element was then added, which posited that a fluctuation in group membership occurs as some socially disruptive force (such as a war) disturbs the equilibrium among social groups. This disequilibrium generates a response from the disadvantaged sectors as they attempt to restore a viable balance. Other organizations arise in opposition, until a different level of equilibrium is achieved (Truman, 1971).

Mancur Olson (1965, p. 2), however, articulated the "free-rider" problem and thus challenged the notion that people will join together for their collective benefit—that is, for the purpose of achieving benefits for everyone in that group (such as for all counselors or teachers or mothers). Olson said that it is more rational *not* to join groups if as a result of someone else's effort a person will gain the benefits without joining. In fact, Olson's research showed that unless a group is quite small, or unless there is some coercion or other incentive to make individuals act in their common interest, "rational, self-interested individuals will not act to achieve their common or group interests" (p. 2).

Olson's (1965) research demonstrated instead that "the large and powerful economic lobbies are in fact the by-products of organizations that obtain their strength and support because they perform some function in addition to lobbying for collective goods" (p. 132). He thus distinguished between collective benefits and selective benefits. He defined *selective benefits* as those benefits that are available only through group membership. These

benefits manifest as some form of coercion or positive incentives. For instance, to get liability insurance and to get the journals or information affecting their schools and practices, counselors must usually belong to a professional association. This is a form of subtle coercion. "An organization that did nothing except lobby to obtain a collective good for some large group would not have a source of rewards or positive selective incentives it could offer potential members" (Olson, 1965, p. 133), and the group would not survive.

In their "incentive theory," Clark and Wilson (1961) described both selective and collective benefits, calling them material, solidary, or purposive (sometimes referred to as expressive) incentives. *Material incentives* are tangible rewards of goods or services, or the means by which these may be obtained. They have monetary value and are extrinsic to individuals. For instance, counselors might join the ACA for liability insurance, for journals, or for a credential that makes it possible for them to get a job. They might also join to acquire information or to contribute to public policy objectives that will benefit them materially. *Solidary benefits* are intrinsic, experienced directly and within the self, and include rewards such as camaraderie, fun, a sense of group membership and identification, and status and prestige. *Purposive* or *expressive incentives* involve the realization of suprapersonal, ideological group goals that are more general, like "quality mental health for all." These benefits cannot be cost analyzed and they accrue to many people who take no part in efforts to secure them.

In his entrepreneurial theory, Salisbury (1969) claimed that entrepreneurs manipulate these benefits in such a way as to lure members into groups. Thus, leaders must have the resources available to provide these benefits if they are to motivate new members or other supporters to join them in accomplishing their goals.

Membership Size. At this point the question arises as to how important a large membership is. In fact, many small groups have had a great deal of impact because they have relied on resources other than member dues. "Group theory traditionally has assumed that entrepreneurs will rely heavily, if not exclusively, on member dues for funds sufficient to sustain their operations. The free-rider problem was seen as posing a serious obstacle to organizations" (Hayes, 1986, p. 136). Recent empirical research indicates that groups have circumvented the free-rider problem by securing alternative sources of funding. In one study, 89 percent of the groups required outside funding to get started, and relied heavily on it even after becoming established (Berry, 1977; Walker, 1983; see also Schlozman & Tierney, 1986). So, small size does not have to mean failure; in fact, small size can mean lower maintenance, easier cohesion, and less need for selective benefits (Foreman, 1995).

Further, research by Heinz and his colleagues (1993) demonstrated that the number of organizations or representatives supporting a proposal did not affect success; however, the number opposing the proposal did affect success. Only a small number of people supporting a proposal are necessary to gain success if there is no opposition. So, although a large membership can provide legitimacy and clout (Schlozman & Tierney, 1986)—and this needs to be considered when assessing resources—more important is the relationship between membership and finances, and between membership and opposition. If a group finds external financing, a large membership may not be necessary. If a group's issues are unlikely to engender opposition, then a large membership may not be necessary.

Stages of Development. Groups need different resources during their different stages of development. The initial stage, mobilization, involves the identification of a problem and agreement on the need for collective action. "Group leaders develop a package of incentives for group involvement and offer them to potential participants with distinct wants, needs, and preferences" (Cigler, 1986, p. 47). In the beginning, the attempt is to rouse members' passion over a single issue. Most of the appeal is expressive and is conveyed by skillful, inspiring speakers who emphasize the ideological attraction of standing against the "enemy." Mobilization often involves a loose organizational structure and very personal involvement of the grass roots (Cigler, 1986).

After the initial issue is taken care of the passion usually dies and the group may lose members if sides are taken on other issues. Some members will try to keep the group going, but they will have to regroup, strategize, and redefine issues in order to be successful (Cigler, 1986). At this stage the group needs to find an ongoing source of money. Private

sector groups draw about two-thirds of their money from membership dues. Some groups also draw funds from foundations, some draw from various fees and publications, others draw from government grants, and still others draw from "sugar daddies"—individuals willing to make large donations (Berry, 1989a, p. 63).

Achieving the next stage—group maintenance—usually involves changing and formalizing the group's structure, developing a permanent presence in the capital, and building slowly. During this stage, leaders have to be creative to keep up with changing events and needs. "While skillful group entrepreneurs often are able to mobilize people in the short run by collective material and expressive appeals (through the use of symbolism, emotionalism, and rhetoric), the 'free-rider' problem is still significant" (Cigler, 1986, p. 48). So, to maintain the group, leaders generally have to shift from collective benefits to selective benefits. The incentive package has to be continually modified to stay relevant. Decisions about the incentive package often cause internal conflict, however, posing a threat to what originally motivated people to join.

For a group to maintain itself as an interest group it must move toward mainstream political activity and demonstrate political effectiveness, which occur after a group has developed an identity as a political collectivity in the eyes of relevant political actors (Cigler, 1986). Continued group existence can be threatened by goal attainment, unstable leadership, erosion of financial resources, fragmentation or exhaustion over the long run (which happens more in groups with "in your face" tactics), and the inability to contain conflict and sustain a sense of shared purpose (Foreman, 1995).

Thus, when assessing organizational resources, groups need to consider from what developmental stage they are operating. While an early developmental stage implies greater resources of passion, energy, and determination, a later stage may yield greater political and public relations skill, a more significant reputation, more money and membership, and relationships with key decisionmakers.

Leadership. Skilled leadership is required for effective advocacy (Cigler, 1986). One might assume that effective leadership is representative, democratic leadership. In fact, research has demonstrated that although many groups observe the external forms of democracy, very few have any means other than elections to assess their members' views (Berry, 1977, 1989b; Hayes, 1986; Luttberg & Zeigler, 1966). Michels (1958) asserted that "organization implies the tendency toward oligarchy" (p. 37). While initially most members select leaders to represent their interests, eventually it is the leaders who determine the direction of the organization:

> The more extended and the more ramified the official apparatus of the organization, the greater the number of its members, the fuller its treasury, and the more widely circulated its press, the less efficient becomes the direct control exercised by the rank and file, and the more is this control replaced by the increasing power of committees. (Michels, 1958, p. 38)

As the organization develops, tasks become more difficult and complicated, so the group members have to hand them over to salaried people with specialized skills and content themselves with summary reports. This is a technical and practical necessity, according to Michels. Considering groups to be representative is therefore a mistake. Yet, Michels considered the membership-at-large to be incapable of self-government, which explains, he said, why oligarchies exist in all organizations.

Does this lack of democracy matter? Michels claimed that it matters in some situations and not in others. It does not matter when there is little controversy on an issue. Then, democracy wastes valuable time and resources. Michels claimed that democracy also does not matter when the organization's members are limited in their commitment to the organization and its activities and are free to leave if they are dissatisfied, or when subunits are in place to deal with differences in interest. Democracy matters, he said, when there are differences of interest or when greater legitimacy is needed for the organization's decisions. If democratic procedures are not built-in, and if there is no freedom to leave the organization for another organization, the disadvantaged will be continually without representation.

Leaders' responsiveness to membership is complicated by the need to consider both the intragroup and extragroup impacts of the leaders' decisions and actions. Leaders cannot act without considering the responses of other political actors and the effects of these responses on the organization's long-term goals. Leaders must, however, have a sense of their members' desires because they may not have jobs if they fail to satisfy the members.

Leaders' passions, then, generally dictate the directions and activities of the group (Schlozman & Tierney, 1986). Leaders generally are more committed to collective benefits than the membership-at-large, and they generally commit greater amounts of their own resources to the cause (Foreman, 1995; Sabatier, 1992; Schlozman & Tierney, 1986). They succeed to the degree that they can generate cohesion and cohesive action among the membership (Foreman, 1995; Schlozman & Tierney, 1986).

In a voluntary organization, cohesion primarily generates from member satisfaction with leaders. Luttberg and Zeigler's (1966) research found that if leaders operated on the basis of their own personal values they would not be representative of the membership. If they were purely representative, they would actually end up being more conservative and restrained than the membership would actually desire. If they simply followed their understanding of the members' desires, then they were actually closer to what the members desired, and thus satisfied the members to a greater degree.

Cohesion through member satisfaction, however, is difficult to accomplish because of the members' diverse interests and reasons for joining the organization. No assurance exists that the members will agree on objectives. Organizations are torn between membership needs and those actions necessary to achieve success with advocacy targets. Leaders in organizations, who are more aware of what it takes to be successful with advocacy targets, feel that they need to organize and make use of grassroots involvement. The grassroots organizations feel that the leadership is tainted and does not know the organizations' members and their talents (Advocacy Institute, 1990). Yet, it is necessary for organizations to build a history of cohesive action because such a history establishes an organization's reputation for credibility, trustworthiness, and power.

Because leadership plays such a central and critical role in the success of interest groups, any assessment of resources must assess the strength, vision, talent, and effectiveness of the leadership. Effective leadership requires that leaders be able to accurately discriminate when democracy is needed and when it is not, to offer desirable selective benefits, to balance member needs with target or environmental needs, and to satisfy members enough to develop group cohesion. Leadership resources may be even more critical than membership resources.

EXERCISE FOR ASSESSING RESOURCES

The following exercise will enable you and/or your group to assess available resources.

For Individuals

Write as many ideas as you can think of in each of the following categories. Make sure to attend specifically to those resources that distinguish you from other people. Decide whether it is worth it to you to expend these resources.

1. Training

2. Expertise

3. Personality characteristics

4. Interests

5. Key contacts and relationships (You may want to refer back to the concentric circles exercise in chapter 3 to refresh your memory.)

6. Time (How much are you willing to set aside?)

7. Money (How much is it worth to you?)

8. Commitment and passion (How strongly do you feel?)

For Groups

Write as many ideas as you can think of in response to the following list. Then discuss these ideas as a group and develop a group composite analysis. Make sure to attend particularly to those resources that are unique to your group. Also, make sure to compare your resources to those of other interest groups in order to reach an accurate comparative analysis.

1. Financial resources

2. Media skill and contacts

3. Access to substantive knowledge (that is, information about counseling and counseling programs, and statistics about effectiveness)

4. Political expertise and experience

5. Access to decisionmakers

6. Attractiveness of your cause

7. Potential allies and opponents

8. Passion of membership and leaders

9. Membership size

10. Leadership skills

11. Ability to provide selective resources

SUMMARY

Counselor advocates need to assess their financial resources, their media skill and contacts, their substantive knowledge, their political expertise, their access to decisionmakers, the merits of their cause, their allies and opponents, their passion, their membership size, the skills of their leaders, their ability to provide selective benefits, and their developmental stage and its corresponding resources. They need to have an accurate idea of how their resources compare with those of other groups. They need to write a credit-and-debit ledger and see if they can increase the credit-to-debit ratio (Wittenberg & Wittenberg, 1989).

Counselors need to keep in mind, however, that the types of resources necessary to success are situation specific and that all groups seem to view themselves as having fewer resources than the next guy (Heinz et al., 1993; Schlozman & Tierney, 1986). Counselors therefore need to find ways to maximize the resources they have, and they should try not to worry if it seems that other organizations have more resources. Those others are probably worrying about the same thing.

Chapter 6

STAGES FOUR AND FIVE: WHERE ARE WE GOING AND HOW CAN WE GET THERE?

Two months before the annual board retreat, Kaylan scheduled a meeting with ACC's board of directors. Also, because the board was composed primarily of private practitioners and counselor educators, she asked the director of a community mental health center, Janice, and the clinical director of a large private psychiatric hospital, Suzanne, to serve as members-at-large on the board to make it more representative of counselors in her state.

At the meeting, the directors first identified their goals. They wanted to achieve

1. health care delivery systems that provide everyone with access to quality mental health care;

2. parity with other mental health providers for the profession of counseling; and

3. parity with medical care for mental health care.

The more specific goals they wanted to achieve that particular year, related to the problem situation identified in Chapter Three (that counselors were being excluded from health care reform bills and that managed care was being presented as the only solution to the need for health care cost containment), were

1. inclusion of counselors in any new health care reform legislation, and

2. advancement of a broader, more comprehensive health care delivery system than that currently available through managed care.

The board next decided that the following publics would be concerned about or affected by this issue: (a) consumers of mental health services, (b) the other four mental health provider groups in the state, (c) insurance and managed care companies, (d) state and national legislators, (e) government agencies that administer health benefits plans, (f) employers, specifically benefits administrators, and (g) counselors.

The board members then embarked on background research.

1. *Stan,* the board member with close connections to ACA's advocacy department, was appointed as liaison to ACA to find out what ACA was doing on the issue, what ACA thought ought to be done, and what resource materials ACA could provide to support ACC's effort. Stan was also expected to check with ACA's lobbyist on the current political climate.

2. Another board member, *Richard,* was assigned to contact the professional associations of psychiatrists and social workers, and another, *Jamie,* was assigned to contact the professional associations of marriage and family counselors, nurses, and psychologists. These two board members would try to serve as liaisons with the other groups' boards of directors. They would also try to set up a meeting with representatives from each organization to assess their willingness to work together, to discover what they thought ought to be done on these issues, and to find out what they were already doing.

3. *Sarah,* who was working on her dissertation on managed care, was asked to provide a literature review on the need for a reformed health care delivery system, and an assessment of what the possible

options were, what the causes were for escalating health care costs, how the managed health care system was working thus far in addressing mental health needs, and what the impact would be of expanding the provider pool to add another provider group. Sarah committed to researching questions that would be helpful to ACC's pursuits. Janice and Suzanne, the hospital and community mental health center directors, agreed to provide her with information from their facilities on the impact of managed care.

4. *Avis,* the board member who had worked on Tipper Gore's working committee, had some contacts in the administration and legislature, so she volunteered to find out which state and national legislators and committees were interested in or working on this issue. She would also find out which local, state, and federal agencies administered mental health-related programs and ask them for their documentation or publications on this issue.

5. *George,* another board member, decided to research and contact any groups that might represent consumers of mental health services.

6. Because she had worked in several big corporations, *Nicole* volunteered to research and contact groups representing corporate benefits administrators.

7. *Dan* said he would come up with a plan for contacting counselors around the state and maintaining communication with them. He would also give some thought to a committee structure for ACC that would facilitate any action plan the board developed.

At their retreat two months later, the board members brought all this information together to formulate a strategic plan. They decided on the following problem definitions:

- *For government officials:* discrimination by the current health care delivery systems against the poor and those with chronic mental health problems; shortages of mental health providers in inner city and rural areas

- *For insurance companies and employers:* rising health care costs due to failure to use inno-

vative and preventive care overall, and mental health care specifically

- *For consumers:* inability to get timely, quality mental health care at a reasonable cost

- *For counselors and other mental health care providers:* inability to provide the services they were trained to provide, and the increasing trend toward non-mental health providers making clinical decisions

On the basis of these problem definitions and the board members' research, the ACC board developed one-page flyers—a different one for each target public—that stated

- the problem cited for that group, with research backing up the existence of the problem;

- the solutions, with research supporting them;

- the anticipated opposition and answers to this opposition; and

- specific requests for action.

Then, because of their limited financial resources, the board decided on a two-pronged approach for the upcoming year: a grassroots approach and a more centralized approach.

The grassroots approach: ACC knew that to accomplish any broad plan they needed to involve the 1,200 counselors in their state and request that each take on a task. The first step would be asking each board member to form a local group in their area and to structure communication to include bimonthly meetings and a telephone strike force. The second step would be to assess the strengths and contacts of each local group member and to create a database with the information. Third, the central group would then assign each local member to an advocacy target, ask them to build a relationship and communicate certain information to that target, and request that they report back to the local group leadership. Fourth, at the statewide ACC conference the core group would train these local members and give them supporting documentation.

The centralized approach: The board members committed themselves to developing a model mental health care delivery system based on conferencing with all the publics involved and on research. They would prepare a series of position papers, present symposia, and publish articles on the model. They would publish in the journals that their targeted decisionmakers read. The position papers would be distributed to ACA and other counseling organizations. The symposia would be presented for both state and local decisionmakers. While the grassroots approach would be simple, concise, and very targeted, the centralized plan would be scientific, academic, and broad.

Once the plans were laid, Kaylan assisted the board in developing a budget and setting time lines for the advocacy activities.

RESEARCH RESULTS AND THE LITERATURE ON STRATEGIC PLANNING

While individuals can move easily from assessing resources into taking action, according to both the advocates who participated in the research for this book and the public policy literature (Berry, 1989b; Schlozman & Tierney, 1986), groups need to plan their strategies first. This is Stage Four of counselor advocacy (see Figure 1.1). Participant advocates further indicated that planning is usually done by a small core of the larger group. They emphasized that the core group must be committed to solving the identified problem and determined to "hang in" for the long haul. The core group needs to include diverse perspectives and should be composed of representatives of those groups that have vested interests in the particular problem. The core group needs to establish a "structure for advocacy." According to one participant advocate: "There must be a line of authority for making pinch hit decisions in a bind, in a crunch." There must be a structure for disseminating information quickly. Participant advocates also suggested that out-of-town retreats facilitate core group processing by focusing, building momentum and a sense of mission, and creating a sense of unity. Retreats may also be useful later for evaluating progress and, according to one participant advocate, for "reexamin[ing] policies that we currently have, looking at why we even have the policies, why are we buying into this, and coming up with stronger statements on policies."

The core group needs to convert what it perceives to be the desires of its constituents into easily articulated policies and goals (Birnbaum, 1992; Wittenberg & Wittenberg, 1989). These goals should reflect long-term vision but they should be achievable in reasonable increments. Strategies and tactics should be organic—they must adjust to changing circumstances—and positions and progress should be reassessed constantly in light of these changing conditions and opinions. Further, flexibility should be built into the initial decisions to assist in the compromises necessary for achieving the group's goals. Advocates need to be prepared to recognize the best deal when it comes along (Wittenberg & Wittenberg, 1989).

Participant advocates concurred that the core group must consider a variety of factors when establishing short- and long-term goals. Goals must be based on a realistic assessment of resources. During goal setting, the core-group members "need to lay out any possible contingency and plan for each eventuality." In developing a strategic plan, they need to take the long view and the broad view, and they must decide which battles are worth fighting. They need to set priorities and develop proposals. The participant advocates also agreed with the need to be flexible. As one advocate cautioned, developing a strategic plan "doesn't mean that you don't take advantage of opportunities that are sometimes staring at [you]."

Many models for planning and strategizing exist in the public policy and public relations literature. Berry's (1977) model is a decision-making framework that uses goals, resources, and environmental factors to decide on the overall strategies of influence. These then determine the specific actions (tactics) to be taken.

Zisk's (1969) evaluation of interest groups in the policy-making process indicates less about strategies than Berry's approach but shows the importance of the interactive process among the interest group's resources or characteristics; other groups and unaffiliated individuals; the economic, legal, and social environment; and decisionmakers. This model suggests that groups must consider various systems when trying to influence policy.

Newsom, Scott, and Turk (1993), public relations experts, proposed a checklist that is useful to planners in walking through the advocacy process. Their checklist suggests that an organization should be structured so that different people stay cognizant

different arenas (such as finance, mar-
law). This broad look at issues seems
nt to counselors than other approaches,
since counselors are not involved solely in the public policy arena.

Newsom and his colleagues have suggested that
groups should first research the issue and the climate thoroughly. They should then identify and
research their publics and prepare suitable documentation. Next they should decide on specific advocacy activities. Preparation of inside people
proceeds advocacy with the external targets. Once
the action plan has been decided upon, timetables,
budgets, and methods of review and evaluation are
decided. The only missing link in Newsom's model
is matching the plan to the available resources and
prioritizing actions based on the usual limitations in
resources. Perhaps this is because public relations
professionals work within large companies that usually have more extensive resources than do counselors and counseling organizations.

Other public policy literature (Berry, 1989b;
Schlozman & Tierney, 1986) concurs that groups
designing any strategy must consider resources and
the political environment in deciding which tactics
to use. Figure 6.1 summarizes the most useful components of the approaches presented here. The
model presented in the figure will guide the following discussion from goal setting to questions about
which strategies are most effective, from problem
definition and other strategies to political action
committees and lobbyists, and finally to preparing
the group to take action.

GOAL SETTING

Groups must have both an inside strategy and
an outside strategy, according to Wittenberg and
Wittenberg (1989). An inside strategy is the overall
game plan, known to those in the group, including
preparing the group for action. The outside plan
posits how to convince the legislator or other target
to take action. Green (1988, p. 186) suggested the
broad inside goals of "elevating the self-esteem of
individual counselors and the status of the profession" by increasing public awareness and appreciation of the essentialness, exclusivity, and
complexity of professional counselors' skills.
Achieving these goals would serve to increase
counselors' autonomy, which is dependent upon

demonstrating one's superior and specialized knowledge base, and it would establish credibility, so that
others would listen to counselors' recommendations.

Participant advocates suggested setting specific
internal and external objectives for reaching these
overarching goals. *Internal objectives* focus on
counselors themselves. When advocating internally, counselor advocates assist other counselors in
establishing a sense of professional identity, and
they promulgate shared beliefs that are fundamental
and helpful to the counseling profession and to
advocacy. For instance, advocates might focus on
developing a philosophy of inclusion among a
group's membership. They might develop certain
stances that they feel will help the advocacy process,
like persuading counselors to separate the issue of
licensure from that of reimbursement so as to clearly
separate the pursuit of a consumer benefit from the
pursuit of a counselor benefit. A slightly different
twist on internal objectives are efforts to improve
the profession of counseling. Improving the profession requires developing and upgrading ethical and
practice standards, credentials, and training programs. Promulgating information supporting these
objectives to membership and self-policing complete the cycle of this advocacy focus.

External objectives address two types of issues: consumer issues and counselor issues. The
distinction between the two is often unclear because counselors may portray a change as being
"for the consumer" in order to draw attention to
the issue when in fact the change also upgrades
the counselors' own status, recognition, or salaries. The issues that are more clearly related to
consumers are:

- seeking privileged communication rights for
  clients of counselors;

- seeking increased access to mental health care
  for those in need, who may not be able to
  advocate for themselves;

- attempting to improve health care delivery systems that currently provide poor quality care or
  that discriminate unfairly against those with
  chronic mental health problems;

- working for the parity of mental health treat-
  ment/coverage with medical treatment/cover-

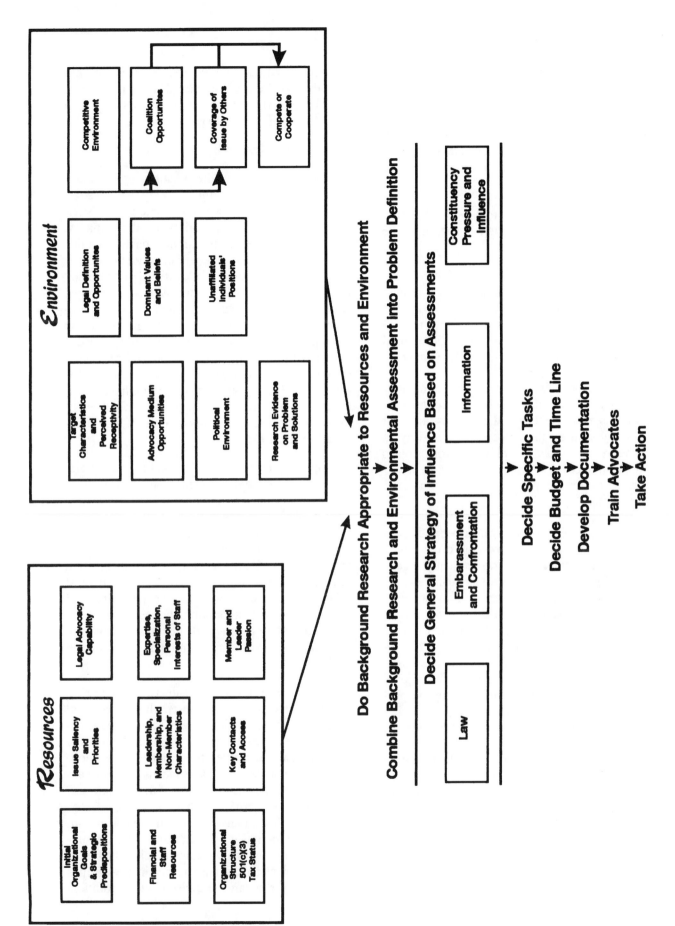

Figure 6.1. Strategies and Tactics: A Model for Influencing Key Decisions.

age, because of the belief that the two are equally worthy and that mental health care reduces the need for medical care;

- working for funding of a continuum of care so that major problems and their attendant high costs can be forestalled by early preventive care; and

- preventing the sunset of professional licensure legislation so that the public will continue to be protected.

The counselor-related issues involve counselors advocating for themselves or for their profession, seeking the right to do what they were trained to do and recognition that the value of what they do is comparable to the value of what other mental health professionals do. They might, for instance,

- seek insurance reimbursement. Such reimbursement in fact would recognize that counselors' services meet critical medical needs, and that counselors meet these needs as effectively as other reimbursable mental health professionals do. Insurance reimbursement would also broaden counselors' opportunities to practice their profession.

- advocate with employers, trying to persuade them to hire counselors or rewrite job classification systems to include counselors explicitly. Again, this effort seeks recognition that counselors are qualified mental health service providers and should be recognized as such, as other mental health providers are. Changing job classification systems may also increase the number of jobs available to counselors. Broadening job classification systems to include the full range of counselors' skills might mean adding hospital admissions, hospital commitments, or psychological testing to counselors' responsibilities.

- seek further recognition from other professionals—from those who refer clients for counseling services, from those who seek counseling services (the public-at-large, parents, and even students themselves), and from sources of funding for counseling-related programs.

- invest great energy toward legislative changes that license counselors to practice indepen-

dently and that include counselors along with other professionals in mental health legislation. This is perhaps the function of advocacy with which counselors are most familiar.

Effectiveness Research

Before a group decides what strategies to use, it would be good for members to know what strategies are most effective at influencing decision-makers. Despite many claims to the contrary, however, public policy researchers have had a difficult time determining what actually is effective. Interest groups certainly work very hard at influencing their targets. "Private interests have developed elaborate organizational structures in order to provide control over the processes through which they are represented" (Heinz et al., 1993, p. 5; see also Browne, 1986). Further, the "choice of behavioral style of any group seems to vary little over time" (Browne, 1986, p. 189). Perhaps groups have developed clear structures of strategy and influence because of the increasing uncertainty of outcomes (Heinz et al., 1993).

Opinions on the effectiveness of group strategies have varied widely: interest groups have been seen as determining policy, then as having very little impact, then as a powerful part of the political system, although far weaker in influencing the legislative system than previously supposed (Petracca, 1992c). Members of Congress themselves have provided some of the evidence of interest group effectiveness; some have even retired because of the relentless pressure they feel from interest groups. Many complain that interest groups have become too powerful and intimidating (Schlozman & Tierney, 1986).

How does a researcher or interest group prove that the group's activity caused the government officials to change their behavior? So many factors influence the course of a policy: the "preferences of policymakers themselves, the residues of past policies, the limitations on what is technically or financially feasible, and the decisions of foreign powers" (Schlozman & Tierney, 1986, p. 8; see also Berry, 1989b). Further, in any research using self-report, administrators and government officials are unlikely to admit that they changed their behavior as a result of interest group activity, and interest groups are likely to overestimate their effect. In addition, success is defined differently by different actors at different times on different issues. Many times, "in making inferences from cases about organized interest influence, what matters is not simply who won or lost, but whether the score would have been different had interest organizations not been active" (Schlozman & Tierney, 1986, p. 392; see also Tierney, 1992). "Policy defeats are usually seen as being beyond the control of the lobbyist's group. . . . If they lose, it is because they were overwhelmed by superior resources on the 'other side'" (Berry, 1977, p. 278). So, clearly there are operational difficulties in measuring interest group influence, and little consensus on how to rectify these difficulties. As a result, "academic studies of interest groups have demonstrated few conclusive links between campaign or lobbying efforts and actual patterns of influence. This does not mean . . . that such patterns or individual instances do not exist. Rather . . . the question of determining impact [is] exceedingly difficult to answer" (Loomis & Cigler, 1986, p. 21).

The public policy literature and research *suggest* the following, however, about the effectiveness of advocacy efforts. When choosing their strategies, counselors need to keep in mind that greater effectiveness occurs:

- in efforts targeting the House rather than the Senate;

- in blocking issues than in promulgating new issues;

- with less visible, less conflictual issues (Petracca, 1992c);

- when an issue is linked to an identifiable constituency that is pressuring a legislator (Petracca, 1992c; Tierney, 1992);

- in raising money and mobilizing campaign volunteers;

- in intensifying the support of legislators who are already leaning in that direction (Petracca, 1992c);

- in using more tactics on big issues over which conflict is great and that affect many people, and fewer tactics when fewer people are affected and conflict is minimal (Heinz et al., 1993);

- in the details, which ensures that policy outcome is substantially more congenial than it would have been had the organization not acted;

- in helping political discourse to be carried on in a more moderate voice (Kornhauser, 1959);

- if jointly interested individuals are represented by an organization acting in concert with others (Schlozman & Tierney, 1986).

- for those who seek narrow, technical ends;

- for those whose contacts within Congress are also concerned about the issue;

- for those who have more resources, although money is not the determining resource;

- for those who have greater ability to locate the controversy in an arena that is more likely to yield favorable outcome (Schlozman & Tierney, 1986); and

- if the merits of the case are strong (Heinz et al., 1993).

Heinz and his colleagues (1993) indicated that in the health domain, Washington representatives employed by professional associations report a higher degree of success than representatives from other domains, although those representing not-for-profit groups are the least successful. Notables (i.e., those people in positions of power) and representatives who have government experience have greater success in advocacy efforts. The amount of time devoted to a particular domain does not affect success. Doing more of anything results in greater success, with the exception of litigation. Economic conservatism has more success than efforts to spend money. Heinz and his colleagues also indicated that "newcomers would do well to take the advice of regulars. Insiders who know their way around in the agencies will usually obtain better results" (p. 4). Finally, lobbying is not, for the most part, a last-minute vocation; rather, it relies on an accumulation of actions over time (Birnbaum, 1992). Overall, however, "it is dangerous to assume that conventional notions of influence will accurately predict policy outcomes. Policy results are uncertain; hence the success or failure of particular groups on specific issues is also uncertain" (Heinz, 1993, p. 4).

The Background of a Strategy

Conducting background research is a critical first step in developing an advocacy strategy, and it is the advocacy activity most overlooked by counselors. Core group members need to collect and compare information from others who have advocated on similar issues. They need to explore extensively—through review of the literature and by conducting original research—the problem, the law, the alternative solutions, the publics, the opposition, and the political environment (McElreath & Miller, 1991; Newsom et al., 1993). Researchers provide outcomes and effectiveness data, client satisfaction information, and service utilization data (Gilchrist & Stringer, 1992). This information can be used in other advocacy efforts, such as testifying before legislative committees. It is crucial in convincing others of the importance of counseling. One participant advocate said:

> If you want to convince me that we must have counselors in the schools, rather than social workers, that counselors bring something very unique because of their training into a school system, and that it should be a K through twelve comprehensive program, you've got to show me some dollar signs on why it is cost effective and how that's linked with such things as students finishing school or lower truancy rates.

Birnbaum (1992) urged advocates to do the research, calculate the figures, then meet to negotiate. Wittenberg and Wittenberg (1989) urged advocates to take their time in this process, to check and recheck the facts, to find precedents, to order opinion polls and surveys to back up their position, to prepare a presentation based on the belief that the opposition will show up next and that the advocate needs to prevent the member or staffer from being embarrassed.

One of the results of counselors' research needs to be a statement of the perceived impact of their proposed solution, demonstrating scrupulous attention to detail. Sometimes it is necessary to find notable people to do serious academic research to develop this impact statement. Because legitimizing problems and solutions through research is so critical to lobbying, Washington representatives even have set up think tanks (Birnbaum, 1992; Wilson, 1986) and foundations to add academic and scientific legitimacy to their causes and to store essential information in databases (Cigler, 1986). Already-established think tanks are also useful if counselors' ideas are compatible with those of the think tank. "The books [that think tanks] produce are reviewed by major media, and their ideas are accorded serious treatment" (Wittenberg & Wittenberg, 1989, p. 139). Think-tank representatives are invited to hearings and television debates; their expertise is sought. University researchers, by contrast, are usually not as fresh and experienced in government as think-tank representatives. Think tanks need success and recognition for their ideas so that funds will keep coming in, so they tend to stay up-to-date on issues. "We are in the business of making ideas ready for legislation," says Stuart Butler of the Heritage Foundation. "So is every so-called think tank" (Wittenberg & Wittenberg, 1989, p. 141).

Both academia and think tanks hold conferences, seminars, and lectures as part of their research and to disseminate their research (Birnbaum, 1992). These events can be very helpful in educating a broader group about counseling issues and solutions.

Counselors also need to research the political environment for likely receptivity. Kingdon (1984) asserted that for the target to take action the political climate must be right. For instance, an administrator looking for a success in order to clinch a promotion might be particularly open to a counselor's solution to a problem. A national mood of concern about the mentally ill homeless freezing in the streets of Washington, D.C., might motivate a legislator to take action to expand the mental health provider pool. Counselor advocates report the necessity of staying aware of their target's needs, jobs, and interests in order to time their efforts to match the current political climate. Hiring a lobbyist or consultant can assist this process, but the relationships already formed with targets are perhaps just as effective at keeping counselors informed.

Counselors need to research the law related to their issue. One participant advocate indicated that a careful reading of his state's licensure law revealed a loophole that precluded an extensive effort in pursuit of freedom-of-choice legislation. The state mental health association discovered that counselors could be covered by insurance policies as long as a physician reviewed their treatment plan. While physician review might not be the ideal situation, the discovery resulted in many counselors receiving insurance reimbursement without having to pass new legislation.

Counselors also need to research their publics. Chapter Three noted how to identify publics. Newsom and his colleagues (1993, p. 139) indicated that "publics are any group of people tied together, however loosely, by some common bond of interest or concern." Any public may become the target for an advocacy effort. Counselors need to be fully aware of each public that is affected by or involved in a project. Research is the key to finding out who publics really are and what they think. Counselors can categorize a public by describe it demographically or psychographically—that is, by looking at its emotional and behavioral characteristics.

Knowing the target publics "implies knowing what to say to them and how to say it, how various messages are likely to affect the various publics you depend on for goodwill" (Newsom et al., 1993, p. 163), and how to prioritize these publics. Anticipating responses from all publics is part of issues evaluation and management. Counselors need to know about relationships between the target public and their publics. Proactively pursuing this information can prevent counselors from being caught off guard.

One of counselors' publics is clearly the government. Wolpe (1990, p. 19) said that it is important to know this public's key players, "who they are, where they are from, what motivates them, and where they stand and why." What is the tone of their political dialogue, the effectiveness of their interaction, their ideology, their worldview? What are their interests? Advocates also need to be conscious of the atmosphere of Congress, of what the big issues and problems are; they need appropriate knowledge of these issues and the ability to appropriately react to them. Acquiring this kind of information requires participation in and observation of the political process and review of legislators' voting records.

This knowledge is necessary when it comes time to select a "horse"—a sponsor for a piece of legislation—to "carry your water" (Birnbaum, 1992, p. 193). A committee or subcommittee chair is the best choice for a horse, so counselors need to know who the chairs are. A good alternative horse is a member who is well-placed and respected on his or her committee. It is critical to select someone who

is well-known on the issue (Birnbaum, 1992; Wittenberg & Wittenberg, 1989; Wolpe, 1990). If the desired powerful person is unwilling to play this role, counselors can put together a coalition of legislators. Counselors need to keep even the "uninvolved" informed because people in these positions change frequently. Also important in selecting a horse is considering their personal strengths and deficiencies, political position, effectiveness, and relations with other important members of Congress (Wolpe, 1990).

Wolpe also urged counselors to know the committees and their staff, who do most of the important work and make most of the important decisions. Different committees have different ways of operating and different leadership. Wolpe stressed that advocates need to know this when planning strategy. They must also know what is happening in other committees or in parallel arenas in order to know the potential impact on their issue, and to know what strategies are currently working. Participant advocates further recommend reading the *Federal Register* and *Bills in Print,* and using the Internet, to keep abreast of current legislative and executive branch proposals and other developments.

It is no insignificant task to gather this information. As one lobbyist said,

> We're talking to everybody we can about what the general mood of the Congress is. What issues are they going to deem important? How are the members lining up? How strongly do they feel, for example, about new taxes to deal with the deficit problem? That is what we do, it's a network, it's a game. All the people that we know, and we've done favors for, gotten jobs for, sent them business, are part of it. What you know and your ability to interpret it—your ability to understand what's important and what's not—is what it's all about. (Birnbaum, 1992, p. 31)

Counselors also need to know which publics oppose them. Who doesn't like counselors, who will get hurt by policy? When counselors find this out, they then can develop strategies designed to defuse this opposition (Birnbaum, 1992; Wolpe, 1990).

Developing the Strategy

Once the research has been completed, counselor advocates can begin the strategy development process by joining their research on the problem and their research on publics or targets into a problem definition. This was touched on in Chapter Four in the discussion of problem identification; it deserves a more in-depth discussion, however, because it is of such critical importance.

Problem Definition. Problem definition differs from identifying a counselor or client need. Kingdon (1984) asserted that many academics, interest groups, and legislators have favorite programs or solutions they would like to see enacted, but the likelihood of action depends on finding a problem to which the solution can be attached. Advocates must thus identify language that expresses the problem in such a way that the advocacy target will be highly motivated to apply the counselor's solution. Counselors must know what issues and problems are critical to legislators, insurers, employers, and other targets, and must then demonstrate that their solution—counselor inclusion or licensure or program funding—can help that person or organization solve the problem.

However, saying that language must be identified is an overly simplified way of saying that counselors need to try to come up with ideas that "change the terms of the debate" (Birnbaum, 1992, p. 44), that promote entirely new ways of thinking into which the smaller changes they want might fit naturally. Thus, the language and slogans used are very important, according to both participant advocates and Birnbaum. No one can successfully approach a target saying we want more money and more power. No legislator will buy that. Advocates must have other, more saleable reasons for a legislator to act on their behalf—not just so the legislator will buy the idea, but so the legislator can sell it to other legislators, to voters, and to other interest groups. For instance, as a legislator cited by Birnbaum (1992, p. 193) said, "We need to get across that this is not a fat cat issue but a jobs issue." Further, counselors need to choose problem definitions and solutions that do not draw battle lines, that will motivate action on the part of the entire membership.

The language of the problem definition should convey unity and values of importance to the public—"justice," "fairness," "equity," and "truth" all retain untold political clout—and the issue should be framed to appeal to prevailing public opinions and beliefs. The appeal should be addressed to the widest possible group of potential constituents, not just to the narrow body of existing supporters (Wittenberg & Wittenberg, 1989; Wolpe, 1990). The

Advocacy Institute (1990, pp. 11–12) pointed out that

> though we are a notoriously heterogeneous nation, Americans resonate with surprising unanimity to a set of core public values: freedom, security, family, health, fairness, opportunity, caring. The more an issue initiative positively evokes one or more of these values, the more likely it is that public attitudes toward that initiative will be favorable.
>
> Mirroring these affirmative public values are a set of negative values which evoke negative responses: unfairness, government or corporate oppression, harm, deceit, greed, favoritism, dependency. When an issue campaign succeeds in associating one or more affirmative values with its initiative, and associating its opposition with one or more negative values, its chances of generating broad public support are greatly enhanced.

"Before advocates can successfully frame an issue, they must understand the public's reaction to it" (Advocacy Institute, 1990, p. 14). This means polling the public, or carrying out other forms of research. Counselors can then use focus groups to test out themes for selling issues. Public service announcements can educate the public, increasing their awareness of an issue and calling attention to its relative importance. The overall objective in defining a problem is simplicity, clarity, and focus on a small number of basic themes.

An example of counselors effectively defining a problem to fit their solution has been attempts to get counselors included in the Public Health Service Act (the solution). Participant advocates indicated that first they identified a problem that Congress and the National Institutes of Mental Health were already struggling with: shortages of mental health providers in rural and inner city areas and shortages of providers to treat certain "priority populations." They then went to these decisionmakers, gave evidence of counselors' numbers and credentials, and said, "We can help you solve this problem if you will legitimize us by identifying us as providers in this legislation." When the decisionmakers have named counselors as providers in the referenced legislation, counselors will have accomplished an incremental step in the policy process. The next step would be to say, "You have seen how well we have provided services for the people in these inner city and rural areas. Are you now saying that these people deserve second class services?" Because decisionmakers could not politically afford to answer this question affirmatively, counselors should be better positioned for further inclusion.

Participant advocates identified many other examples of defining problems and solutions that do not draw battle lines. The conflict over whether to call themselves "professional" or "mental health" counselors has been a response to defining the problem as such: "Decision makers are confused by our lack of unity, and we need numbers to demonstrate our legitimacy." Endorsing counseling specialties in licensure laws is a solution that responds to the following problem: "Because there are many different types of counselors, licensure without specializations might exclude qualified providers." Endorsing specializations also increases the scope support for a new law. Urging national legislators to use "any qualified mental health provider" rather than a laundry list of specific providers answers the problem that "a laundry list might eventually exclude highly qualified and competent providers."

Participant advocates indicated that it is critical to define a problem and solution in a manner that generates the greatest support. Decisionmakers tend to be most interested in solving consumer problems and in reducing costs (see also Heinz et al., 1993). Thus, counselors are more likely to be effective if they define problems in terms of consumer needs and cost reductions rather than in terms of counselor needs. Schlozman and Tierney (1986) concurred that finding a problem or stance representing a public interest is more effective than one representing a private interest. A focus on consumer needs and cost controls can also often serve as a rallying point for many different mental health organizations.

Counselors have used a consumer and cost focus in their efforts to get counselors included in health insurance benefits. They have emphasized "improved and fairer consumer access to quality mental health care" (as per participant advocates) and the problems inherent in not providing this. Counselors have emphasized the cost benefits of expanding the provider pool: it increases competition and provides consumers access to a lower cost provider.

Developing Strategies. After defining the problem, counselors need to develop strategies specific to each target public, because each public will have different needs and priorities. Groups first need to prioritize these publics by determining the importance of each particular public to the group (Newsom et al., 1993). Newsom and his colleagues outlined a rating method that evaluates each public in terms of its potential for being influenced and the vulnerability of the group to that public. "The choice of tactics is the process by which resources and policy objectives are converted into specific acts of interest articulation and representation" (Berry, 1977, p. 5).

Next, the core planning group develops target-specific documentation that reflects their research and the problem definition, and that anticipates both the target's questions and needs and the opposition's position. Wolpe (1990) urged advocates to develop documentation that is clear, concise (one page), persuasive on the merits, and framed in terms that can be readily comprehended, and then to field-test the documentation. Because legislators are generalists rather than specialists, Wolpe's suggestion translates into having a noncounselor read the brief to make sure that generalists will understand the arguments. Participant advocates also urged that documentation be top quality and professional looking, and that it include such items as sample letters, fact sheets, how-to manuals, brochures, or directories.

Other principles operating in political systems that strategic planners need to remember are precedent, incrementalism, the need for the grass roots, and the scope of conflict.

When there is a **precedent**, decisionmakers tend to be more willing to do something, because it has been done before. For instance, counselor inclusion in the Public Health Service Act will serve as a valuable precedent in persuading decisionmakers to include counselors in other federal legislation. Another example comes from a hospital chain that considered counselors qualified enough to hire but whose insurance plan did not recognize counselors as qualified to counsel their employees. Letters pointing out the inconsistency resulted in the hospital changing their insurance coverage to include counselors. The decision to hire served as precedent for changing the insurance benefits. Wolpe (1990) went so far as to say that precedent controls process, claiming that it is very difficult to do something completely new. The legitimacy of a group's goals depends on what has been done before. Advocates should therefore use precedent in their arguments. Even failure may be useful, because a process that has been attempted once, even though it failed, may facilitate a second attempt.

A dispute exists in the public policy literature over whether big changes can ever be made or whether change only occurs incrementally (Lindblom, 1959). **Incremental change** often is called "muddling through." Muddling through is often criticized for its failure to consider the big picture or the long view, and its seeming failure in correcting major societal problems. Be that as it may, incrementalism still appears to rule the day. Heinz and his colleagues (1993) claimed it is clear that in the health domain (and others) dramatic initiatives draw formidable resistance. More often, small policy objectives are sought and gained, and this is where interest groups have the most effect. So, counselors should not discount small changes but should view them as one step in a long process (Lindblom, 1959).

The **grass roots** are the larger group of counselors who are impacted by the goals and actions of the smaller planning group and who must be mobilized if advocacy is to be successful. One participant advocate pointed out the importance of mobilizing grassroots support:

> Anything global begins locally. The strength of true leaders begins at the grassroots level. The stuff that comes from the top down is not nearly as successful as stuff that comes from the bottom up. True advocacy, therefore, must emerge from the bottom up. . . . You reach out to people at the grassroots level, and you ask them to participate, you find their strengths, you make them feel as if they are a part of the total and overall process, because then when some type of request comes top down . . . then it is going to be far more successful than if that work has never been done before.

Indeed, all of the public policy literature indicates that one of the major changes in lobbying in the 1990s has been the need for and use of the grass roots. How to mobilize them will be discussed more in chapter 7.

The **scope of conflict** refers to how many people will be interested in the issue at hand, and whether they will have different views on whether the issue is a problem and on what a reasonable solution ought to be. (See chapter 9 for a comprehensive examination of conflict in advocacy efforts). Heclo (1978) indicated that most policy is made by an "issue network"—a network of legislative, administrative, interest group, and academic actors invested in a particular issue. Levine and Thurber (1986) indicated further that if the actors in a

subsystem cannot quickly and successfully resolve conflict among themselves, outsiders from other committees, agencies, bureaus, groups, and the media or the general public will take the issue away from them. The influence of these outsiders and the probability of a policy change increase as internal subsystem conflict intensifies and becomes uncontrolled. A primary goal, therefore, of the actors in a policy subsystem is to control the scope and level of conflict associated with the programs and issues within its jurisdiction (Levine & Thurber, 1986, p. 206).

Those who find themselves outside the decision-making subsystem can learn from Levine and Thurber, who indicated that

> subsystems are naturally closed, low level operations in government, but they can be "opened" in several ways. Changing the scope of conflict, increasing the level of conflict, changing key personnel, reorganizing the jurisdiction over an issue, and using the regulatory process of administrative agencies and the courts are several important methods of changing the power of policy subsystems. . . . The relationship between the scope and level of policy conflict and the influence of policy subsystems can be expressed in the following hypotheses:
>
> • The wider the scope of policy conflict, the less influence policy subsystems have over policy outcomes.
>
> • The wider the scope of conflict, the higher the level of conflict.
>
> • The higher the level of conflict, the less influence policy subsystems have over policy outcomes. (p. 206)

Closed subsystems do not broaden their discussions to include the media, political parties, or the public. They decide issues, debate, research, and present finished legislation that has been negotiated by the subsystem. If counselors believe this to be unfair, or if they want to challenge a subsystem's power because they dislike the subsystem's decisions, they can broaden the scope and raise the level of conflict.

Thus, strategic planners need to consider whether to broaden the scope of a conflict or contain it. In situations in which there is likely to be little controversy, it is better not to involve too many people. In situations in which counselors are likely to be left out, planners may effectively achieve their ends if they involve a broader audience (Levine & Thurber, 1986).

Because the policy process is both inherently conflictual and inherently continuous, Wolpe (1990) urged advocates not to burn votes in the midst of a conflict. If counselors do not win today, they must start again tomorrow and they may need their opponents in the next round. Also, there are many issues that counselors will work on over the years, and opponents on one issue may be allies on another. So, Wolpe urged advocates not to alienate anyone. An opponent on one issue may want to make up or compensate by being helpful on another issue. Differences must remain professional, not become personal.

In conclusion, both the research done for this book and the public policy literature point to the need for a coordinated effort. When people go off on their own to try to change something, they often miss out on knowing how the problems are being defined by others concerned with the same issue, or they countermand the strategies that have been developed for a reason by the central organization and by people who are more expert and more experienced at the process. Further, an essential task of an advocate is to make it as easy as possible for a legislator to support an issue or request. Currently, the advocacy process is less of a behind-the-scenes, mysterious effort than it is the implementation of political strategy. It requires attention to detail and the big picture, knowledge, the touching of all political bases involved in the outcome of issues, and following through on commitments (Wolpe, 1990).

TO HIRE A LOBBYIST OR NOT

Participant advocates enthusiastically endorsed hiring a lobbyist for legislative efforts, yet all had tales of woe related to finding and keeping a good lobbyist. Many had difficulty discerning whether their lobbyist was actually working for them or not. Many told stories of lobbyists missing key legislation, resulting in counselors not being included along with other mental health providers in that legislation. Some indicated that at critical points their lobbyists indicated they could not act on an issue because they had a conflict of interest—usually with the insurance companies for whom they also worked. But despite these difficulties, participant advocates felt that the complexity of the legislative process and the political environment made a lobbyist necessary.

Lobbyists come in different shapes and sizes. Heinz and his colleagues (1993) identified three types:

- *Knowledge based:* The lobbyist has substantive expertise in the issue area, gained through working in an organization or government position that frequently confronts that issue, or political expertise, generated from training and experiences as a lobbyist, government official, or lawyer.

- *Institution based:* The lobbyist is hired on the basis of the access he or she has to particular offices or agencies in the government, perhaps as a result of previous employment.

- *Organization or client based:* The lobbyist is chosen from the within organization. Big companies have many needs, and may choose one lobbyist for each need. The lobbyist's work reflects the range of interests of the client organization. Specialization is based on the position the lobbyist has in the organization and the issues to which he or she is assigned.

The three types of lobbyists are not mutually exclusive. Expertise on a particular type of issue tends to be associated with contacts in the relevant government agency and with employment in an industry organization.

Thomas and Hrebenar (1992) categorized lobbyists somewhat differently, dividing them into contract lobbyists, in-house lobbyists, government legislative liaisons, citizen lobbyists, or private individuals. Counselors usually make use of contract, in-house, knowledge-based, or institution-based lobbyists.

Because many lobbyists work for several different industries, they often serve as arbiters between the different positions, working on drafting legislation that allows people of opposing views to come to some agreement with the legislators' input or prior to presenting their ideas to legislators. Sometimes lobbyists build coalitions in this manner (Birnbaum, 1992).

Counselors may need different types of lobbyists for different types of situations, so it is wise to be aware of the type of lobbyist being hired. In one state, the mental health counselors association hired an institution-based lobbyist who was very powerful and knew everyone. He also charged a great deal of money. The association became quite distressed, however, when he repeatedly allowed legislation that had an impact on counselors to slip through the cracks because his knowledge of what was relevant to counselors was limited. As a result, the association also selected a knowledge-based lobbyist to monitor issues relevant to counselors. They still used the expensive, institution-based lobbyist to get things done legislatively, connect them with the right sponsors, and give them advice on the political climate and the necessary legislative actions to take.

Both participant advocates and the public policy literature advised hiring a lobbyist through recommendations from people whose judgment is trusted, such as groups working on issues similar to the type of issues counselors are pursuing (for example, benefits in insurance plans, school programming, and professional licensure). Wittenberg and Wittenberg (1989) urged advocates to interview candidates until they feel confident that they have selected the one best suited to their needs. They also urged advocates to make sure they know who will actually be doing the work for their organization. In the state association referred to earlier, the expensive institution-based lobbyist did the handshaking and whispering in someone's ear—critical functions—but his staff did the rest. Knowing this up front is important, as is getting the staff's credentials.

What can counselors actually expect from a lobbyist? Will the lobbyist do everything? Can counselors place their legislative agenda in the lobbyist's hands and expect him or her to accomplish it? Perhaps big corporations with a team of lobbyists can, but because of the limited budgets counselors typically have, their expectations need to be scaled back. Lobbyists rarely know the counseling profession or its history like counselors do, so counselors need to be prepared to continually educate the lobbyist, to be prepared to be the experts on issues and on legal wording. In fact, counselors may be the appropriate party to draft their legislation, merely expecting lobbyists—if they are lawyers—to put it in its final form. Most participant advocates suggested that counselors should expect to do most of the legwork, advising and monitoring the lobbyist and expecting him or her to be the expert on the legislators, the legislative process, the political climate, and on what counselors need to do to be successful. Information gathering is one type of legwork crucial to lobbying, and counselors can

play a significant role in it, while lobbyists may be "the best informed about everything from the timing of legislative action to the inclinations of individual policymakers" (Birnbaum, 1992, p. 6).

In summary, the more informed counselors are, the more significant will be the dialogue they can have with their lobbyists, which will be more likely to lead to successful advocacy strategies and greater accountability on the part of the lobbyist. Counselors should also trust their own instincts, questioning anything a lobbyist may do that does not seem right.

POLITICAL ACTION COMMITTEES AND TAX EXEMPT STATUS

No discussion of strategy would be complete without discussing political action committees (PACs). PACs are fund-raising organizations, sometimes organized around certain ideological beliefs or issues, and designed to contribute money to political campaigns. PAC activity increased "by stunning proportions" during the mid-1980s (Schlozman & Tierney, 1986, p. 222).

> Maintaining the integrity of government means that we must somehow balance the need to fund campaigns, the desire to have people actively involved in elections, and the obligation to keep government from being unduly influenced by those with the most money to contribute (Berry, 1989b, p. 117).

In practical terms, this means regulating how much individuals or groups can contribute to candidates who are running for office.

The Federal Election Campaign Act of 1971 and its amendments enacted in 1974, 1976, and 1979, as well as the Revenue Act of 1971 and the regulations and advisory opinions of the Federal Election Commission govern PACs. As of 1995, contributions by individuals and organizations to a candidate for federal office are limited to $1,000 per election, contributions to the national political party committees are limited to $20,000 per year, and contributions to a campaign committee are limited to $5,000 per election. No individual may contribute more than $25,000 to PACs, national-level party organizations, and candidates for federal office in any one year. Multicandidate PACs—those that contribute to five or more candidates for federal office—have advantages over individuals and organizations. They can contribute as much as they can raise, as long as they do not give more than $5,000 to a candidate in one election. In addition, there are no limits on how much PACs can spend on behalf of a candidate (for instance, on making up and distributing promotional materials), as long as they do not coordinate with the candidate or his or her representatives (Conway & Green, 1995).

Counselors need to be cautious, however, that their tax exempt status is not threatened by their lobbying and PAC activities. Counseling organizations that have 501 (c) (3) tax exempt status are not allowed to form PACs or lobby legislators (although they can accomplish other policy objectives through attempting to influence the executive or judicial branches). They may only act in an "educational" capacity, providing Congress with technical assistance. Their members can fully deduct their dues for tax purposes. Private foundation money, which counseling organizations might have access to through grants, also cannot be used for lobbying because then the foundations' tax exempt status could be threatened. Sometimes organizations accommodate by developing affiliated foundations, one for lobbying and one to receive tax-deductible contributions to be used for nonlobbying advocacy campaigns, litigation, educational campaigns, and approaching the administrative branch. While the Internal Revenue Service exercises considerable discretion when removing an organization's tax exempt status, and while research shows that, despite the regulations, 44 percent of 501 (c) (3) groups are actively lobbying Congress, the importance of the 501 (c) (3) status as a constraint on the lobbying activities of interest groups should not be underestimated (Berry, 1977).

Counseling organizations that wish to form PACs or to lobby extensively must choose to give up their tax exempt status. If electoral and lobbying activities are not its primary activity, an organization can become a 501 (c) (6) corporation, which allows them to form a PAC and use up to 20 percent of their income for lobbying activities. In this case, members can only deduct that portion of their dues not used for lobbying activities.

So, why would counselors, or anyone else, need to contribute money to campaigns? Wittenberg and Wittenberg (1989) indicated that democracy is not a spectator sport, that advocates need to do more

than vote if they want to shape policy. Making contributions gets an advocate's name on the list, with the rest of the contributors. Green (1982) cited Justin Dart of Dart Industries as saying, "Talking to politicians is fine, but with a little money they hear you better" (p. 20). In *The Lobbyists,* Birnbaum (1992, p. 161) reported that a senator

> asked a lobbyist if he knew what the three most important things are to a member of Congress. The senator answered his own question: "Number one is getting reelected. Number two is getting reelected. And number three is getting reelected." Whatever a lobbyist could do to help the lawmaker stay in office, the lesson went, was certainly worth the effort.

Contributing money to campaigns puts counselors on equal footing with others who contribute. There is a growing attitude that says, "Without campaign contributions, my interests will not be heard as well in Congress" (Berry, 1989b, p. 139; see also Green, 1982). Interests groups therefore contribute plenty, to make sure that their access is as great as their opponents'. According to Berry (1989a, p. 138), "Money is the lifeblood of campaigns; candidates cannot be blamed for seeking out available funding. PACs provide such a large proportion of total campaign financing that candidates can place themselves at a serious disadvantage by refusing to take PAC donations."

If counselors form a PAC, how should they make decisions about contributions? The following principles from public policy research and literature may help guide those decisions. PACs usually contribute where their money buys the most—to incumbents, particularly early in the race to intimidate the opposition into not running; to challengers early in the race if trends are favorable to the challenger's party (Conway, 1986), because challengers need more money to win (Berry, 1989b); to those who have voting records and ideologies favorable to the group (Berry, 1989b; Conway, 1986; Conway & Green, 1995; Schlozman & Tierney, 1986); to those to whom the group already has access (Schlozman & Tierney, 1986); to marginal races (Conway & Green, 1995; Schlozman & Tierney, 1986); to issues that are noncontroversial and have low visibility (Evans, 1986; Schlozman & Tierney, 1986); to those likely to win, in order to buy access later; and to those on committees crucial to the issue (Schlozman & Tierney, 1986).

PACs have created a few innovations. The biggest innovation is *bundling,* in which the organization serves as a conduit for contributions. The PAC solicits checks made out to the candidate, then bundles them all together and sends them to the candidate under the organization's name. This method provides far more than individuals or PACs can otherwise contribute (Berry, 1989b; Sorauf, 1995). *In-kind contributions* are another innovation, in which PACs offer a noncash contribution, such as services, technology, or mailing lists.

PACs have certainly been criticized by those who consider them a method for buying votes (Berry, 1989b; Schlozman & Tierney, 1986). Some supporters have responded that PACs are buying access, not influence. Access is a kind of influence, however, because those who do not have access do not have influence (Schlozman & Tierney, 1986; and many others). Despite all the focus on PACs and the ethics related to them, they really dole out small amounts of money, usually from a few hundred to five thousand dollars. Many PACs remain inactive (in the 1991 and 1992 elections, 23 percent did not contribute anything to anyone) (Conway & Green, 1995). Further, Wolpe (1990) claimed that expertise can gain access as easily as contributions, and Birnbaum (1992) emphasized constituent power when he indicated that PACs increase the level of lobbyists' access to that of constituents. Again, counselors have a powerful means to influence public policy without the finances popularly considered necessary.

EXPANDING FROM THE CORE GROUP

As indicated earlier, most issue campaigns begin with a core group of supporters who quickly resonate to the themes evoked by the initiative. The critical framing task for the campaign, then, is to broaden that core base of supporters by finding and using themes that engage the intellect and emotions of those who are not yet supporters of the initiative (Advocacy Institute, 1990). Broadening support and training advocates are Stage Five of counselor advocacy (see Figure 1.1). Although these activities could be considered actions in themselves, they are properly considered preparation for taking action—which will be discussed in chapter 7.

During Stage Five, in order to broaden support, leaders speak out on the issues and stimulate discussion and analysis. They test ideas in conferences and workshops, examining the problem and possible solutions. For more serious debate, experts publish in journals and articles and give speeches. National organizations consult with their members, both listening to and educating them. The intensity and audience grows. Networks broaden. Coalitions are begun (Advocacy Institute, 1990).

Participant advocates indicated that training is necessary during this stage: "You have to educate your own people a lot before they can do a lot of direct advocacy." At workshops, at conferences, and on legislative days, the "expert advocates" assist members in assessing their own resources and contacts. The experts present documentation and the "talking points" (i.e., what counselors are to say to advocacy targets) on particular issues, overviewing the "problem" and pertinent facts. Training clearly articulates the target's specific needs, presents solutions, and backs them up with research and precedent. Advocacy trainers run through simulations and role-plays of actual advocating, and make suggestions of what actions are possible and necessary (see also Schlozman & Tierney, 1986). Group members might be trained in specific skills, such as how to deal with the media or how to testify before a legislative committee.

Training also ensures that everyone is "singing off the same sheet of music," as nothing is more detrimental to advocacy efforts than different counselors communicating opposing messages to the same decisionmakers. As already shown, cohesive groups have more impact. Consensus building is assisted when trainers encourage dialogue about the issues, present reasons for choosing particular solutions, and keep talking points simple.

Finally, training serves an essential role in motivating counselors and letting them "blow off steam." Getting trainees excited about advocacy brings new blood into the profession's leadership. Further, one advocate who addressed self-care urged counselors to scream, get out their frustrations, and work out their differences at home, with each other, *before* they approach their targets. She related this approach to one of her training goals: "A big part of what I try to do in training is get people to understand their triggers, what pushes their buttons, why they get defensive, and that they need to deal with that in a way that is not in front of who they are trying to influence."

STRATEGIC PLANNING EXERCISE

The following exercise should help you and your group in strategic planning.

1. What is your group's overarching mission?

2. What specific goals related to the current problem area would you like to see accomplished?

3. Who are the publics concerned about or affected by this problem area?

4. What background research needs to be done on the problem, solutions, publics? Who will do it?

5. Decide on problem definitions targeted to each public.

6. Develop documentation for each public, citing the following: the problem (as defined in #5), with research supporting your claims; the proposed solution, with research justifying it; possible opposition to your claims about the problem or solutions; answers to this opposition; and specific actions you want the target to take.

7. How much money needs to be budgeted for each activity planned?

8. Set up a time line for the action plan.

SUMMARY

Before taking action, a small core group of counselors needs to invest considerable time in planning strategies. First, the group needs to establish goals and decide what publics should be targeted in order to meet these goals. Next, the small group needs to research the problem, the possible solutions, the political environment, and the publics. The research results should be used to help the small group decide on a problem definition and language that will best promote their issue and draw allies toward their work. They also need to use the information gained through research to decide what activities would be the best use of their resources. Finally, they need to develop target-specific documentation and train the larger-group membership to carry out the proposed actions. Part of this process may involve hiring a lobbyist or starting a PAC.

According to participant advocates, naivete about advocacy and the political process is a major obstacle to counselors' achievement of their goals, resulting in the neglect of advocacy as an organizational goal and in a view of advocacy as only self-serving. "We haven't really fully mobilized ourselves to have a clear definition of advocacy, as I see it, of the client populations or the target populations we want to influence, and developed the kind of tools that we need to approach them and to follow through," said one participant advocate. Naivete has resulted in angry discussions with or documentation to legislators. One advocate, in response to some documentation counselors were using, said, "'God!' I literally said, 'If I were a legislator and I read this, knowing no more than the average person knows about the issues, I'd pat you all on your pointed little heads and tell you to stand around with the social workers and work it out.'" Naivete has also resulted in ineffective individual efforts: "To go out and think you can do it on your own when it has nothing to do with what we do. We aren't trained. We don't know how to do that stuff." Strategic planning by a small core group of counselors is the only way to overcome these obstacles.

Chapter 7

STAGES SIX AND SEVEN: ON THE MOVE AND VICTORY CELEBRATION

Kaylan Sanders Takes Action

Kaylan and her board members were ready for action. First, the board divided into committees responsible for overseeing the advocacy activities. The *Grassroots Task Force* was responsible for developing the grassroots network, advising the local leaders, and disseminating information for those leaders to give to their members. This committee also served government-relations functions, monitoring legislation and the political climate for those events relevant to counselors. The *Conference Committee* planned the state conference and the advocacy training to take place at that conference. This committee also planned the conferences designed to disseminate information to government officials and benefits administrators. The *Coalition Committee* was designed to facilitate coalition building with other mental health professions and with consumer groups. The *Research Committee* collected and performed research and prepared briefs and documents for dissemination. Because ACC felt they could accomplish more with more funds, they established a *Membership and Funding Committee.* This committee continually discussed and acted on ways to build membership. They also applied for a foundation grant to cover the research and publication costs involved in developing and disseminating their model comprehensive mental health care delivery system.

Next, the Grassroots Task Force began mobilizing the grass roots. They divided the organization's membership list by zip code for each local group leader. They did the same with the membership list of the American Mental Health Counselors' Association. Each local group leader sent out a letter outlining the board's plans and asking the counselors in their area to attend a meeting. They used the meeting to go over

the plans in depth, to dialogue about the problem and potential solutions, and to answer questions. They then asked each attendee to commit to one advocacy activity, and asked them to list their skills and contacts for entry into a database. Finally, they asked attendees to be part of a telephone strike force. ACC had purchased a computer program that enabled "Bob" the computer to call each member and deliver a message. The group leaders requested that members do as "Bob" requested.

When the database was fairly complete, ACC had 400 counselors willing to take some action. They were assigned as follows:

1. A constituent counselor was assigned to each legislator in an "adopt-a-legislator" program.

2. Counselors were assigned to each of 20 insurance and managed care companies.

3. Counselors were assigned to serve as liaisons to groups of mental health care consumers (such as the Alliance for the Mentally Ill and the Mental Health Association), schools, the school board, and other community groups (such as the Rotary club, the Elks, and the Chamber of Commerce).

4. Counselors were assigned to develop media contacts in each area, and to send press releases whenever counselors did something notable.

Next, the Coalition Committee began implementing the more centralized part of the plan by identifying the organizations that represented ACC's target publics:

1. The state branch of the American Mental Health Association and the state branch of the Alliance for the Mentally Ill represented mental health

consumers, and were known to be very concerned about funding for the treatment of those with mental and emotional disorders.

2. Groups representing referral sources—such as ministers, doctors, chiropractors, pediatricians, school counselors, and lawyers—included the State Medical Association, the Association of Pediatrics, the State Chiropractics Association, the local Ministerium (an ecumenical group of local ministers), the School Counselors Association, and the Bar Association.

3. Groups representing other health and mental health care providers included the Association of Social Workers, the State Psychologists Association, the Association of Psychiatrists, the Marriage and Family Therapy Association, and the State Nursing Association. Although the ACC's board of directors did not know what association represented the psychiatric hospitals, they decided to contact the local hospital to find out.

Each board member tried to identify contacts that they and other ACC members had with these organizations. Those who had contacts called them and asked if perhaps the contacts could serve as liaisons between their organizations and ACC. The board members also asked to be invited to the other groups' board meetings. For the next two months, the ACC members attended the other groups' board meetings and began building relationships with the board members. They listened closely to the agendas of these other groups. When members of the other groups asked them about ACC concerns, they shared their issues, goals, and plans. When it became clear which other groups were also concerned about ACC's main issue, the liaisons asked the other groups if they would be willing to meet to discuss the issue further and perhaps contribute time and/or money to the effort.

Kaylan and the ACC board were excited about the responses they received. They decided the time was right to gather these groups together, so they planned a symposium entitled "Ensuring Quality and Access for Mental Health Care in a Changing Health Care Environment." They sent out invitations to the boards of all the groups they had visited. They asked for a $500 contribution from each group to cover the costs of the symposium.

During the morning of the symposium, Kaylan divided the participants into small groups to discuss

their primary concerns. ACC board members facilitated the small-group discussions. Just before lunch, all the participants met together. They consolidated their concerns into a prioritized list. During the afternoon, they met again in small groups to determine what actions were needed, then joined together again to share proposed initiatives and to prioritize the next steps. They decided to collect information first, so their initial goals were to

1. have consumer groups collect documentation on difficulties their members were having accessing quality mental health care;

2. have each profession get its members to collect documentation on difficulties they were having with managed care;

3. have professional groups contact their national associations for assistance in getting information on the issue, financial support, and further action suggestions; and

4. identify potential opponents and their needs and positions, and through contacts with them, try to identify what compromises might neutralize this opposition.

After the conference, Kaylan wrote a report of the recommendations made, sent it to the attendees, and asked them to take the results to their boards of directors. She requested that each board discuss the initiatives and make suggestions. She also asked them to decide what their organization could contribute in time and money, and asked them to choose a representative to speak on behalf of their organization.

The coalition that emerged from this process began to meet regularly. First they decided what actions they could accomplish on the basis of their financial and human resources, then they prioritized these actions. Next, they divided the responsibilities and began to take action.

Initially they struggled because each of the group representatives knew more about their own group's priorities than they knew about the priorities of the other groups. Each representative spoke a different language related to mental health care, and many had been competitors in the marketplace. Consumers and providers often battled over priorities, with consumers claiming that providers were only interested in their pocketbooks and did not care for people who were truly hurting. Further, it seemed that some of the groups were willing to work hard while others were just along for the ride. Early enthusiasm waned.

Kaylan, however, learned how to facilitate communication about these differences, and eventually the coalition was able to arrive at plans, position statements, and documentation that everyone could support. Each group had to make compromises, and the final decisions often seemed watered down. The representatives faced difficulties explaining these compromises to their respective boards of directors, who had not been involved in the dialogue and conflict negotiations. Yet, with fits and starts the coalition moved ahead. In addition, a hoped-for side effect of Kaylan's excellent leadership was that coalition members came to regard counseling very favorably, and Kaylan had no difficulty getting counselors included in the coalition's health care proposals and documentation.

After eight months of doing research and developing position papers, the coalition was ready to prepare and publish their comprehensive plan. As they began to do so they alerted ACC's Conference Committee, asking them to expedite plans for two conferences: one for state and local government officials involved in mental health care and another for corporate benefits administrators. The Conference Committee hired big-name speakers for these events to help persuade the target audiences to attend. They used a half day for the speaker and for presenting their plan, and a half day for dialoguing and developing a strategy for instituting the plan. The Conference Committee called press conferences at the end of each of the conferences, submitting press releases about the conferences and the plan to all the local media.

The ACC had a lot to celebrate. They held a victory celebration at the end of the year. All of the leadership attended. They shared their stories with the membership. They took pictures and wrote articles about their stories for the state association's newsletter. Kaylan presented a certificate of appreciation to each of the board members, committee chairs, and local group leaders. Then, on the wings of enthusiasm, the leadership began regrouping and selling the membership on what they could accomplish the next year.

Daniel Wong Takes Action

Daniel found himself in a somewhat different position than Kaylan because he was not leading an organization. He decided that he would prefer to work on a smaller scale. So, instead of focusing on building coalitions among different interest groups, he decided to promote school counseling wherever he could and to build a network of individuals interested in his area of concern.

To promote school counseling, he prepared a half-page information card that listed the "10 Benefits of School Counseling." He asked the counselors in his pyramid to help him distribute it. He introduced himself as a school counselor at every meeting he attended, and he used "school counselor" as his title on his business cards and stationary. Whenever possible, he clarified the unique characteristics of school counseling, and distinguished these characteristics from those of school social workers and school psychologists.

Daniel also worked at building a network of individuals concerned about school censorship. He met with the president of the School Counseling Association (SCA) to discuss how school counselors could continue to provide quality programs in the face of threats of censorship. He asked them to take up the issue, and he volunteered to supply the SCA's board of directors with information he acquired. He also found other counselors who shared his concerns. He spoke with the counselors in his pyramid and with other pyramid directors and asked them to come up with ideas on how to approach the challenge. Some of the teachers also recognized censorship as a threat to needed counseling services. Further, the principals at several of Daniel's schools had received many complaints from religious parents and were thinking very carefully about how to handle them.

Initially, a small group of counselors, teachers, and a principal began meeting together at lunch to share their frustrations, to share ideas about how to nondefensively answer parents' complaints and demands, and to consider their options. The group grew as word of its informal meetings spread. The group gathered more information on what the concerned parents wanted and on the process by which they tended to voice their desires. Someone in the group noted that there were other parents who felt differently from the religious group, and he suggested inviting the president of the Parent Teacher Association (PTA) to have lunch with them. Someone else invited the president of the school board.

Daniel was surprised by and impressed with the cohesion of the group, with the support they found in each other, and with the benefit they all received from sharing information. He was also impressed with the boost in morale that came from talking openly with one another. He suggested that participants list their concerns and level of willingness to take action to rectify the problem. He also suggested that they begin documenting their experiences. The network of counselors, teachers, principals, PTA leaders, and school board members made a commitment to talk about school counseling, its role, and its benefits at every opportunity, in each meeting they attended (school board meetings, board of supervisors' meetings, departmental meetings, and PTA meetings). They also handed out Daniel's "10 Benefits of School Counselors." Daniel had the counselors in his pyramid hand out the list to parents and teachers, and he asked other pyramid directors to do the same. Each member of the group also began collecting anecdotes from students, parents, teachers, and others that illustrated very specific benefits generating from school counseling.

Daniel took the lists, commitments, and documentation to the SCA's board of directors so they could use it in their efforts. He encouraged the principal, the teachers, the PTA president, and the school board president to take the same information to their respective organizations. He also decided to present the information at the next SCA yearly convention so that other schools could develop the same methods and perhaps experience some of the same benefits. He formed a presentation panel for the conference, consisting of the principal, a teacher, the PTA president, and a school board member, so that all conference attendees could see the different individuals working together. The other members of the group decided to follow his example, and they organized panels to make presentations at five different professional conferences that year.

Of course, as more people became involved, and as their concerns became more public, the religious parents heard about what was going on. Initially they increased their efforts to require school

counselors to get parental permission before including children in counseling activities. Daniel's group was worried at first but decided that since meeting together had worked so well for them, perhaps meeting with some of these parents would also work. Daniel's group hired a mediator to facilitate the meeting. They also brought a potluck meal to share with the parents, and spent the time during the meal getting to know them. Daniel even offered a prayer before the meal. During the meeting following the meal, Daniel's group asked the parents to identify their main concerns, to state what they wanted, and to identify the changes that would satisfy them.

The primary activity of Daniel's group during the meeting was listening to the parents, making sure they clearly understood them and their desires. Daniel and his group came to understand that these parents disagreed with counseling because they saw it as the religion of secular humanism, and they thus felt that including counseling programs in schools was failing to separate church and state. They did not want the counseling programs in the schools, but they particularly did not want their children having counseling without their permission. Once Daniel's group had heard these concerns, they expressed gratitude for the parents' willingness to meet, and much goodwill was spread.

Daniel's group told the parents that they would carefully consider their desires, and they asked the parent representatives to take the results of the meeting back to the larger group of concerned parents. Daniel's group did not make any demands on the parents, nor did they express their position. Daniel put in writing all that these parents had expressed, and he asked the parents to correct any misconceptions before Daniel's group moved on to further action.

Daniel's group met again and discussed the results of the meeting. They struggled with the parents' demands and with what it might mean for their school to accede to these demands. They rediscussed the purposes of their school counseling program and tried to assess whether acceding to these demands would weaken the program or have other unwanted consequences. They then scheduled another meeting with the parents.

At the next meeting, Daniel and his group expressed to these parents the purpose of their counseling program, the benefits it had wrought for students and for the general atmosphere of the school. They particularly emphasized students' increased abilities to function in school and to plan for their future careers. They passed out Daniel's "10 Benefits of School Counseling"; had parents, teachers, and students share anecdotes about how they had benefited from school counseling; and passed out data and documentation to correct misconceptions the parents held about school counseling. Since the parents had requested that parental permission be required before their children received any counseling, Daniel explained the "opt-in" versus "opt-out" concepts. He said, "If legislation passes that requires all parents and children to 'opt-in' to counseling services, that means that before a student could receive any counseling services, a counselor would be required to get permission from the parents. If a student came to a counselor looking upset, before the counselor could ask 'What's wrong?' he or she would have to get the student's parents to sign a permission form. If a teacher's class was in trouble and the teacher requested some help from the counselor, the counselor would have to get permission from the parents of all those students before intervening. None of us likes bureaucratic delays, and none of us wants to risk a student's welfare on the basis of paperwork demands. Opting out, on the other hand, would give you the right to indicate that you don't want your child to participate in school counseling activities without your expressed permission."

Daniel and his group then let the parents know that they were willing to accede to their requests if they could all come up with ways to prevent children from being hurt and to ensure that acceding to the requests would not damage the morale of the school. Jointly they generated the following agreements:

1. The concerned parents were to send letters to the school counselors to identify themselves and to formally request that the school counselors obtain permission from them before including their children in school counseling activities.

2. The school counselors would obtain these parents' permission before providing counseling services, unless these parents' children approached them about an emergency situation, defined as risk of suicide, threats of harm to other children, psychosis, or child abuse.

3. The religious group's representatives would request that all parents refrain from making direct complaints to the school because of the time and emotional drain on the school counselors; they would submit their concerns to their representatives, who would then bring these concerns to the regular meetings scheduled with Daniel's group. The religious group's representatives agreed to resolve all conflicts using mediation or arbitration so that the school district did not have to worry about cutting programs to pay for litigation fees.

4. Should the failure of the concerned parents' children to participate in the school counseling activities cause problems in the overall school environment, Daniel's group would bring the problems to the meeting with the group's representatives so that they could work together to find a solution. The representatives would then discuss the solution with the involved parents and do their best to get the parents to comply with the agreed-upon solution.

5. Daniel's group and the concerned parents' representatives would evaluate continuously how this plan was working.

RESEARCH RESULTS AND THE LITERATURE ON TAKING ACTION

All advocacy activities can be considered a means of communicating information in such a way as to inform or persuade some public of counseling's position (Berry, 1989b; Heinz et al., 1993). Some activities are more appropriate to particular target publics; others are a means of gaining attention or access regardless of the particular target public. Figure 7.1 outlines the categories of publics and the categories of attention-getting activities. The figure will guide the discussion that follows.

Many possible advocacy targets exist, although those listed in Figure 7.1 are useful general categories. Because the courts and coalition building with potential allies are discussed extensively in later chapters, they are mentioned here only briefly. The remainder of this chapter will focus mainly on legislators, the White House, the public, and an interest group's membership.

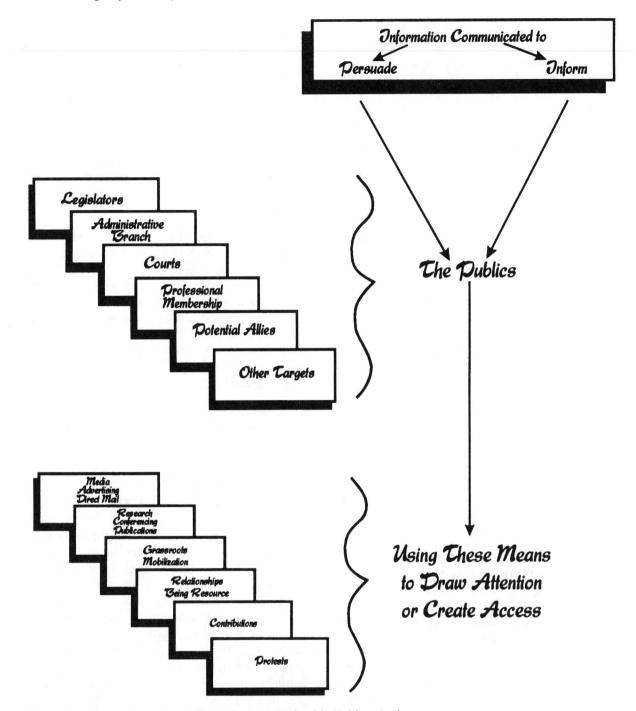

Figure 7.1. Stage Six: The Various Tactics Involved in Taking Action.

Legislators

Congress is the primary focus for groups trying to impact public policy. Congressional committees handle all of the legislation, which reduces the number of targets for counselor advocates. "Once you have established a good reputation, they will call on you" (Berry, 1989b, p. 141). Schlozman and Tierney (1986) and Berry (1977) did some of the initial research on the methods by which groups try to influence Congress. Schlozman and Tierney also found, by carrying on their research longitudinally, that groups were fairly consistent over time in the methods they used. Table 7.1 lists the activities that

Table 7.1. Tactics of Advocacy, According to Berry's Research

Tactic	Very Effective/ Effective	Effective with Qualifications	Not Effective	Use, but Cannot Evaluate	Do Not Use	Total
Personal presentation	53%	14%	7%	10%	16%	100%
Testifying at hearings	20%	16%	42%	10%	12%	100%
Litigation	29%	12%	5%	5%	49%	100%
Letter writing	47%	8%	4%	9%	32%	100%
Constituent contact	34%	11%	1%	16%	38%	100%
Demonstrations	8%	5%	5%	6%	77%	101%
Contributions	6%	—	—	—	94%	100%
Publishing voting records	18%	6%	4%	4%	68%	100%
Releasing research	30%	15%	6%	17%	31%	99%
Public relations	24%	6%	—	9%	62%	101%

From *Lobbying for the People* (p. 214), by J. Berry, 1977, Princeton, NJ: Princeton University Press. Copyright © 1977 by Princeton University Press. Adapted with permission.

Berry's respondents felt were effective. Table 7.2 lists, without attention to effectiveness, the methods that Schlozman and Tierney's respondents used. Heinz and his colleagues' (1993) research confirmed Schlozman and Tierney's findings while identifying slightly different subcategories. Cigler and Loomis (1995) indicated, however, that since 1986, when Schlozman and Tierney's research was published, lobbying efforts have changed, adding more technology, more grassroots efforts, and more public relations strategies.

Advocates who participated in the research for this book agreed with the public policy literature, which says that three of the top methods employed by groups are monitoring what is going on, making personal and letter-writing contacts with legislators, and testifying at hearings (Levine & Thurber, 1986; Petracca, 1992b). Interest groups devote considerable energy simply to monitoring a wide variety of issues and the activities of a number of government agencies, an approach that is contrary to the usual understanding of interest group representation as primarily advocacy. It seems that organizations need their Washington representatives more to stay abreast of issues than to advocate for their organization's issues (see also Berry, 1989b).

Personal and letter-writing contacts with legislators offer the clearest opportunity to present the substantive and political merits of a position (Tierney, 1992), and Berry (1989b) considered it most influential. According to Heinz and his colleagues (1993, p. 193),

Contacts between public officials and representatives of private interests may be very casual, or they may be highly stylized. Either party may initiate them. The motivation can be merely information, or it can be influence. Many contacts are private, but others are fully public, as in testimony before a congressional committee. The content of the communication sometimes consists solely of factual information, reasoned arguments, or a simple statement of interest group concerns and needs, or it may include an offer of a campaign contribution or a promise of electoral support.

Advocates need to go into the encounter with a clear idea of what they want to accomplish and the most effective way to make their case. They need to be very conscious of how they present themselves, verbally and nonverbally, so they can create a good impression of who they are. They must communicate that they are persons of character, because "if the messenger is suspect, the message will be suspect" (Berry, 1989b, p. 143; see also Wolpe, 1990).

Advocates need to build relationships and their sense of credibility with legislators. Cultivating a relationship with the legislator's staff may need to be the first line of attack. Advocates should not underestimate the importance of the staff. In fact, it is often better to see the staff first. They will analyze the issue and brief the legislator, and this "greases the skids" for counselors. The staff will be polite but realistic, and will want to know the pros and cons and who is against the issue (Wittenberg & Wittenberg, 1989). They will also want to know what is in it for their Congress member or congressional committee—in other words, they will want to know how the advocate can help them.

Table 7.2. Percentage of Organizations Using Each of Techniques of Exercising Influence

1.	Testifying at hearings	99%
2.	Contacting government officials directly to present your point of view	98
3.	Engaging in informal contacts with officials—at conventions, over lunch	95
4.	Presenting research results or technical information	92
5.	Sending letters to members of your organization to inform them about your activities	92
6.	Entering into coalitions with other organizations	90
7.	Attempting to shape the implementation of policies	89
8.	Talking with people from the press and the media	86
9.	Consulting with government officials to plan legislative strategy	85
10.	Helping to draft legislation	85
11.	Inspiring letter writing or telegram campaigns	84
12.	Shaping the government's agenda by raising new issues and calling attention to previously ignored problems	84
13.	Mounting grassroots lobbying efforts	80
14.	Having influential constituents contact their representative's office	80
15.	Helping draft regulations, rules, or guidelines	78
16.	Serving on advisory commissions and boards	76
17.	Alerting congressional representatives to the effects of a bill on their districts	75
18.	Filing suit or otherwise engaging in litigation	72
19.	Making financial contributions to electoral campaigns	58
20.	Doing favors for officials who need assistance	56
21.	Attempting to influence appointments to public office	53
22.	Publicizing candidate's voting records	44
23.	Engaging in direct-mail fund raising for your organization	44
24.	Running advertisements in the media about your position on issues	31
25.	Contributing work or personnel to electoral campaigns	24
26.	Making public endorsements of candidates for office	22
27.	Engaging in protests or demonstrations	

Chart from *Organized Interests and American Democracy* (p. 150), by Kay Lehman Schlozman and John T. Tierney, 1986, New York: HarperCollins. Copyright © 1986 by Kay Lehman Schlozman and John T. Tierney, Reprinted by permission of HarperCollins Publishers.

Timing these contacts is critical. Legislators and staff are always operating under pressure, so information needs to be timely, accurate, and concise, and needs to meet the needs of the moment. Advocates' efforts to lobby at the appropriate time are assisted by knowing when a bill is scheduled for markups, for floor votes, and for committee votes (Wolpe, 1990).

When writing letters, advocates need to keep their letters brief and to the point:

• Identify the subject clearly, providing the name and number of the legislation about which you are writing.

• State the reason for writing. Personal experience is the best supporting evidence.

• Do not be argumentative and do not engage in name-calling.

• Never threaten a legislator if the member of Congress disagrees.

• Avoid standard phrases that give the appearance of form letters (Schlozman & Tierney, 1986).

Other personal contact activities are numerous. Many participant advocates have instituted "adopt-a-legislator" programs similar to a suggestion made by Birnbaum (1992). Counselors or other advocates called and wrote their adoptee, took him or her to lunch, and otherwise built a relationship with the legislator. Organizations can provide instructions on how counselors can adopt a legislator. The instructions should clarify which legislators to target, emphasize how important these legislators are, and make suggestions of what to do. These suggestions might include inviting a legislator to tour the counselor's workplace, giving them the opportunity to talk with the local counseling association, finding and fostering reasons for them to back counselors' causes, and giving them the favor of publicity by writing a press release whenever they do something with the counselor's group. Counselors could also give their legislator an award for some service he or she has done, invite the local media, photograph the legislator receiving the award, and send photos and a press release to the newspapers, the counseling association newsletter, and the legislator. Counselors could couple this awards ceremony with a reception of some sort and invite people from similar groups to the reception. "Lawmakers need attention the way other humans need to breathe" (Birnbaum, 1992, p. 100). "They also have large but sensitive egos. 'If somebody's carried your water, it's important to acknowledge that as part of this whole process,'" said one lobbyist (p. 193).

Over and over, the literature and participant advocates stressed the need for constituents, *not* the organization's lobbyists, to contact legislators. "An organization's ability to convince policymakers that an attentive public is concerned about an issue and ready to hold them accountable for their decisions may be critical in determining policy outcomes" (Schlozman & Tierney, 1986, p. 185). Toward this end, organizations can

- arrange for members of the organization to meet with their legislators at home, so lawmakers can be educated on the organization's views (see also Birnbaum, 1992);

- have influential constituents meet with legislators in Washington;

- organize a strike force of constituents who can be called on short notice to lobby on an issue;

- find ways to produce huge floods of letters, telegrams, or phone calls on an issue all at once (Schlozman & Tierney, 1986); or

- do CEO fly-ins, bringing in the biggest names in the industry for a day of lobbying with the critical legislators at a critical time (Birnbaum, 1992).

Research shows that the constituents decisionmakers pay attention to are those who have independent views, who are active in state and community events, who have influence as local opinion leaders, who have status as large-scale producers, and who

are users of modern technologies. Decisionmakers avoid informants who are activists from national organizations (Browne, 1995).

The process of personal and letter writing contacts is accompanied by vote counting, according to Birnbaum (1992). Interest groups count the votes they think they have to get a bill passed, and so do legislators. Legislators and interest groups often confer with each other to find out who they can count on to support their measure. Both sides are constantly looking for people to "get the job done" (Birnbaum, 1992, p. 143).

Testifying at hearings is another widely used method of trying to influence legislators, although as Berry (1977) pointed out, it is considered necessary but not particularly effective. Hearings do, however, offer the chance to publicize an issue for a relatively low cost, as most hearings are reported somewhere in the press. "If we've got a case in the media, we've got a case in Congress. . . . Hearings show Congress at its theatrical best" (Wittenberg & Wittenberg, 1989, p. 110; see also Berry, 1989a). If interest groups can persuade committees to hold hearings, the result can generate a great deal of publicity for the issue, which can in turn influence policy.

Preparation for hearings is critical, both in the material presented orally and in that presented in writing. Groups need to coach their witnesses, rehearse, and anticipate possible questions. Sending committee chairs or committee members pertinent questions in advance may encourage them to ask questions that will help the witness emphasize the most important parts of the argument. James Fitzpatrick, made these suggestions for preparing for hearings:

- Keep it short.

- Do not read your statement.

- Do not be arrogant.

- Do not guess.

- Do not be hokey, but illustrate whenever possible (cited in Wittenberg & Wittenberg, 1989).

The Administrative Branch

Although rulemaking is discussed extensively in Chapter Eleven, contact with the White House is not. The White House's influence over agenda-setting and other aspects of policy making has increased. The president often wants to be responsive to interest groups or wants their support on policy. The Office of Public Liaison, established by the president, has the job of reaching out to various constituencies and building good relationships with them. It has thus "cultivated relationships with interest groups to supplement the coalitional benefits derived from party organizations and affiliations" (Peterson, 1992, p. 224).

Access to the White House is heavily influenced by the political views of the groups and by personal contacts (Berry, 1989b). The White House is responsive to a broadly defined national interest rather than to narrow interests. The president may need counselors to participate in presidential campaigns, to provide support or endorsement in campaigns, to help get Congress to support the administration's policy initiatives, or to assist in policy formulation, indicating costs, feasibility, and the consequences of proposed action (Schlozman & Tierney, 1986).

The General Public

The general public consists of consumers, referral sources, other professionals, and anyone who might have some interest in mental health issues. Participant advocates shared many examples of how to advocate with the public on behalf of the counseling profession. They suggested that counselors should simply "do what they do well," thus demonstrating their capabilities to the public. According to one participant advocate, "We need to show, not tell. We need to act the interventions, not wait for government legislation. We need to do things and ask forgiveness, not ask permission." Another concurs that the best way to advocate is "by example. The way you handle yourself professionally and the contacts you make. . . . Word travels more by word of mouth than by formal advertising." Counselor advocates can also identify themselves as counselors at every opportunity—in meetings, at social events, on their stationary—communicating their message everywhere to everyone (see also Birnbaum, 1992). They can correct those who introduce them as psychologists, using the opportunity to share information about the uniqueness of the counseling profession. One participant advocate urged counselors to politic a bit. "If you are invited to

something on The Hill, then by all means, go. Go shake somebody's hand and say who you are. Give them a name, give them an association, give them a title of who you are."

Counselor advocates might contact insurance companies, employers, and others who exclude counselors, educate them about counselors, and urge them to grant parity to counselors. One participant advocate said, "Any opportunity you get, you need to be adamant! You can talk with churches, clubs you belong to, networking groups, the National Association of Women Business Owners. You need to be constantly saying who you are and what you do."

Another participant advocate urged, "School counselors need to be encouraged to run for offices of various sorts at the local level." Gilchrist and Stringer (1992) concurred, suggesting the following as promotional activities:

- speak on various mental health topics;

- train other professionals (doctors, lawyers, principals, teachers), and

- inform others of available programs and services.

  Green (1988) added that school counselors could

- schedule "Consultation Days" in which they set aside a special time for consulting with other professionals or community members;

- do in-service programs at schools, hospitals, or mental health centers;

- sponsor a community seminar on a topical issue; and

- present case studies at professional conferences.

Another participant advocate suggested another twist:

> By the same token, I think that we should be taking each of the skills that each of us has and implanting them into other groups. I mean if, for instance, [I] were part of a civic association, I would gladly volunteer to do some type of an activity, or to suggest even a focus group for things that civic groups find themselves doing. It has nothing to do with counseling issues per se, but [I would] offer myself as a professional counselor to do A, B, C, and D, because it is using my skill outside of my discipline—which is going to teach another group something, and in the process I will be teaching them about me, too.

Yet another participant advocate concurred: "I believe that as mental health professionals we should involve ourselves in the community-at-large, provide programs to the public on various mental health issues, and promote our profession in the process." Most participant advocates agreed that counselors should "join everything out there," network, "be visible." One participant advocate reported, "I took our latest poster for mental health counseling week . . . to the library. They seemed so delighted to get it. This is just something I do." Another story was:

> When our program won the award for best counseling program, we got our dean to come to receive the award. We've worked real hard to educate our dean about who we are and what we do, and we brought him to a convention before, twice, to meet other political leaders and to really get a feel for what it is that we do. We took him around to all the meetings [at the ACA convention]. I don't know if he ever went to content sessions or anything, but he went to lots of receptions, met lots of the leadership. . . . He had all that face-to-face stuff, so that was a real major advocacy thing.

A participant advocate from Oregon noted that

> probably the single most effective thing we did to advocate for counselors was the professional disclosure statement. We were willing to put up front who we were, what we do, how much we charge, and that is public information. Our law requires the counselor to give that to the client before any money can be exchanged. It says what our education is, what techniques we use, how much we charge, the code of ethics, and the number and address for reporting. And we must give that to clients before we can do anything else. And it has to be on file at the licensure office. It is part of your application. And you have to swear to goodness that you will update it every time you make any change in it.

A public disclosure statement very clearly articulates who counselors are and what they do. It also demystifies the counseling process for those who are distrustful. Finally, making the statement available to the public says, "We are willing to be open to scrutiny and to be accountable."

Walt Seifert, public relations expert, has said that public relations is "doing good and making sure you get caught" (Seitel, 1984, p. 7). Newsom and his colleagues (1993) indicated that public relations includes press agentry, promotion, public affairs, and publicity, and is closely related to—though it does not include—advertising, marketing, and merchandising. The members of the Public Relations Society of America include as public relations activities the following: publicity, communication, public affairs, issues management, government relations, financial public relations, community relations, industry relations, minority relations, advertising, press agentry, promotion, media relations, and propaganda (Newsom et al., 1993).

Press agentry means staging events, not necessarily related to counseling, that will attract attention. For instance, school counselors might sponsor a dance for the parents of their students and have information on school counseling available at the door. Mental health counselors might sponsor a craft show at a fairground and hand out information on counseling to attendees. Birnbaum (1992) and participant advocates added that pro bono work and service projects help present interest groups well to advocacy targets. Seitel (1984) added the following ideas:

- hosting a speech by a politician or community leader;

- having a school official lead a community service drive;

- having a grand-opening ceremony or an open house;

- making a contribution to a minority enterprise;

- sponsoring a blood drive to benefit a local hospital;

- putting on a charity dinner; and

- starting an organization-wide graphics program that changes the look of stationery, signs, publications, and the organization's image.

Promotion also involves staging special events, but with the hope that the events will directly influence public opinion about counseling related issues. Promotion attempts to garner support and endorsement for a worthy cause. A promotion event staged by counselors would be related to mental health or the counseling profession: a stop-smoking day or booth at a local event, a conference for legislators or the public on managed care, or a "Counselors Care" rally in which participants would compete in doing caring, supportive activities. Participant advocates suggested finding a "Lee Iakoka, Audrey Hepburn, Walter Cronkite, or whoever . . . [to speak] on behalf of the kinds of counselors we have to provide services for the kinds of needs we have in our society." The purpose of promotional events is to shape opinion on a mental health issue or increase the occurrence of mentally healthy behavior, and to promote counseling in the process.

Public affairs is the equivalent of community and government relations. Later chapters draw a great deal of attention to how counselors can participate in these activities, so the discussion is not repeated here.

Publicity means calling attention to the special events or activities surrounding a promotion. Publicity is strictly a communications function involving placing information in a news medium. Publicists are writers. The public can only fully understand what counselors do and how they benefit society if each event, activity, or accomplishment of individual counselors or the counseling profession is publicized. Publicity merely means making sure that counselors tell newspapers, newsletters, television stations, radio stations, and other media what they are doing. Seitel (1984) indicated that putting together a brochure or developing an annual report are examples of publicizing what counselors do.

Group Membership and Other Counselors

Critical during Stage Six, participant advocates said, is providing constant, updated communication to a group's members to keep them informed about the issue, the progress being made, and the changing action needs. "We make sure everyone has the same information. We keep the flow of information constant, up-to-date, and factual." Phone trees, newsletters, and legislative alerts are among the means used to keep the membership informed. Several states have even hired an answering service that members can call at any time for updated information. During Stage Six, a continual feedback loop must operate, with members taking action, targets informing the core groups of the results of that action, and the core group regrouping, strategizing, and informing the general membership of further action needed.

Schlozman and Tierney (1986) concurred with the importance of communication. Their research indicated that groups spend as much time communicating with their membership as with members of government, in order to keep members aware of situations likely to affect them, to let membership know what the leaders are doing, and to communicate what members can reasonably expect from staff and leaders. Communications are a matter of "in-

telligence gathering and dissemination, . . . manipulation, and interpretive intermediation" (Schlozman & Tierney, 1986, p. 146).

A different slant is to inform the profession about the profession itself. Participant advocates suggested that counselor educators can try "to get [counselors in training] professionally involved, to get them committed to the profession, to help them understand what the issues are that are facing the profession, [to help] them take a stand on some of those, and to help them see the complexity and the implications of some of those issues." Counselor supervisors, while supervising, can contribute to the profession by upgrading counselor competencies. Smaller groups of counselors also can develop and put on quality training and continuing education programs for their own discipline and for other mental health disciplines to persuade all participants that, "We're here! We're legitimate!"

Other Publics

Any of the publics identified in the exercises in chapter 3 could become targets for advocates to phone, write, or speak with in person. Insurance companies and employers are clearly important publics. Political parties develop their party platforms after receiving input from interest groups. They often have committees and subcommittees on which people like counselors can serve (Bone, 1958). Counselor advocates need to review the publics they identified and decide which ones they need to communicate with to accomplish their goals.

MEANS OF GAINING ATTENTION AND ACCESS

Lobbyists and public relations experts have developed many means for gaining attention so as to persuade the various publics to listen and meet and talk. The following discussion stresses the importance of building relationships, mobilizing the grassroots, using the media and new technology, making contributions, and protesting. Using research to enhance the legitimacy of the group and its recommendations is not discussed here because it was discussed in chapter 6.

Building Relationships

As noted in chapter 2, participant advocates agree with the public policy and public relations literature that relationship building is critical to advocacy efforts. "The best of all possible worlds is to be in constant contact with policymakers, continually giving them information about the problems facing the group. When issues do have to be resolved, it can be done through quiet, informal negotiations between the principals (Berry, 1989b, p. 163). Participant advocates called this "greasing the skids." Birnbaum (1992) urged building long-term relationships; he claimed that relationship-building meetings are more important than issues meetings. "Every visit, every phone call, every research paper or issue brief they give to a staffer or legislator is part of their constant effort to build a trusting relationship" (Berry, 1989b, p. 146).

Authors and participant advocates suggested a number of relationship-building activities. One participant advocate said, "We did a legislative cocktail party one night. One day we set up a table at the state capitol with coffee and cookies. It worked really well. We weren't lobbying for any particular issue, just going for recognition." Schlozman and Tierney (1986) concurred that this type of social lobbying can provide relaxation and entertainment. To the list of possible activities, they added offering cocktail parties, lunches, dinners, and tickets to the theater or sports events. Birnbaum (1992) suggested hosting a birthday party for a member of Congress and inviting "well-placed friends" (p. 188). Another lobbyist described by Birnbaum "by careful design . . . managed to be a presence on behalf of those people who paid his fees. Sometimes loud, ever flashy, he was part host, part spy. His job was to know and to be known, and to always, always be there" (p. 34).

Birnbaum described a retreat that corporation lobbyists hold yearly for the Democrats in the House. They go to a very nice resort. Their families are invited. It is an issues conference at which top speakers talk on topics of interest to the legislators. The legislators contribute $500 per family. Then, for a whole weekend the lobbyists (and their spouses) hobnob with the legislators and their families. There are all kinds of activities, entertainments, and banquets. This is the most extended access lobbyists may ever get to the legislators. It is a time for building contacts and relationships, and for gathering information. "Only the smallest part of lobbying, at the very end of the process, entails directly asking members of Congress for specific favors"

(p. 25). The retreat-conference, "with its socializing and camaraderie, was more what lobbying is about most of the time: becoming part of the Washington network and, through it, learning the lay of the legislative landscape" (p. 25). According to Leon Panetta, "The most effective lobbyists here are the ones you don't think of as lobbyists" (as cited in Birnbaum, 1992, p. 40).

Access to legislators is gained by such unpressured social gatherings, by networking, by providing helpful information to legislators, and by promising to help legislators get what they want on their issues in terms of votes from the public and other legislators. "More specific lobbying contacts with those lawmakers would come later, on an as-needed basis, and usually they were quick and businesslike" (p. 40). The lobbyist who has a strong relationship with a legislator is never denied access. As one legislator said after taking action on a measure, "It was a question of friendship; it wasn't a matter of money" (p. 158). At an event such as the retreat, lobbyists may never bring up the issues. They may only focus on getting on the legislator's good side, and getting her or him connected with others who can be helpful to him or her.

Clearly, being a resource to decisionmakers is part of relationship building. Also, interactions between lobbyists and legislators should be reciprocal.

> Each participant has resources of various kinds—information, strategically placed allies, political support and the like—that the other needs. This mutuality of need binds legislators and lobbyists and draws representatives of organized interests into virtually every detail of both congressional politics and the legislative process. (Schlozman & Tierney, 1986, p. 290; see also Berry, 1989b)

Sometimes interest groups are approached by government officials because the interest group has something significant to offer. Government officials may want to solicit support for a particular policy effort. They may need political intelligence. They may need substantive information on the policy issue. Legislators may ask lobbyists to wage a propaganda war to line up more votes. They may ask for speaking points, arguments, and fact sheets to assist in this process. Sometimes lobbyists ghostwrite op-ed pieces to appear under the legislator's byline in newspapers (Birnbaum, 1992). According to Berry (1977, p. 281),

> It is probably every group's desire to become a known, trusted source of pertinent data. It is "cheaper" in resources

expended to have people come to solicit their views than for
them to have to attract the attention of those they want to
influence through various lobbying tactics.

Advocates can serve as a resource by functioning "as unpaid staff to the decision-makers, who
often don't have enough people on their own pay-
rolls" (Birnbaum, 1992, p. 6). They may draft legislation, plan legislative strategy, offer their contacts
with those who have the information or with those
who can form majorities, write speeches (Schlozman & Tierney, 1986), write position papers, or
demonstrate the consequences of the alternatives
under consideration (Bauer, de Sola Pool, & Dexter,
1963; Berry, 1989b; Birnbaum, 1992; Levine &
Thurber, 1986; Petracca, 1992b; Tierney, 1992;
Wolpe, 1990). Counselors' substantive knowledge
and skill in relationship building are critical to gaining access, and the importance of these abilities to
the advocacy process should encourage them to
involve themselves more in the process.

Grassroots Mobilization

Success in advocacy depends on grassroots involvement, as indicated in Chapter Six. The grassroots in counseling organizations are the larger group
of members that the core group of leaders wants to
mobilize for advocacy. They are the numbers that
have the impact. The Advocacy Institute (1990) and
Wittenberg and Wittenberg (1989) have indicated
that almost all campaigns are designed centrally by
Washington-based organizations; few arise from the
grass roots. Participant advocates agreed on the
importance of the grassroots, even though they
sometimes disagreed on where issues and actions
originate.

The grass roots are important legislatively because they are the constituents who get the legislators elected. As Birnbaum (1992) said, "Every
lawmaker's chief interest is getting reelected. So
lobbyists see it as their job to persuade lawmakers
that voters are on the lobbyists' side" (p. 6). "All
politics is local," former Speaker of the House Tip
O'Neill, a Democrat from Massachusetts, said repeatedly. "Voices back home are much more audible
in chorus" (cited in Birnbaum, 1992, p. 46). Jim
Wright, former Democratic representative from
Texas, said that mail from home is a barometer of
how intensely people feel about one side of an issue
or another (cited in Birnbaum, 1992). As a result of
the importance of involving the grassroots, "one of

the fastest growing businesses among Washington
lobbyists [is] the recruiting of non-Washingtonians
to help them do their jobs. The reason [is] simple: It
work[s]" (Birnbaum, 1992, p. 234).

According to participant advocates, when the
core group involves the larger membership, action
needs to be brief, intense, very coordinated, and
well-planned, because the attention span and time
available to busy professionals are limited. There
may need to be breaks between efforts, as sustained
effort by the larger group membership is nearly
impossible. Finally, a coordinated effort with a lot
of communication is necessary. Continual communication between Washington representatives
and the field is necessary, to reassure the representatives that their supporters are behind them and to
keep the field informed and solicit their input. It is
necessary for the grass roots to see Washington
representatives as real people, and for Washington
representatives to get a clear picture of the grass
roots. The Advocacy Institute (1990, p. 25) called
this "leadership with listening." The leadership
needs to bring the constituency along, not get too far
ahead of them, and to always seek approval. Leaders
need to keep 80 percent of the membership with
them, not just the most active or committed. The
Advocacy Institute indicated that grassroots meetings should be informational and action oriented.
The leadership should be knowledgeable and able
to answer questions. It is most useful for the local
leadership to meet in a small group with the Washington representatives so that more in-depth discussions can take place (Advocacy Institute, 1990).

The grass roots can be mobilized through action
alerts, direct mail (Tierney, 1992), and telephone
trees, and the focus of these is usually the constituencies of key legislators. Mailed alerts require special packaging and a pitch that will compel action
by conveying a sense of urgency, because grassroots
efforts work best when motivated by fear (Cigler &
Loomis, 1995). Alerts need to make it easy for
constituents to respond.

Sometimes groups use the grass roots in proxy
lobbying. They collect proxies from group members
so that when an issue arises, the organization can
send letters for them. The organization then does its
best to try to camouflage the fact that an organization has been orchestrating the effort. The more
unintelligible and ungrammatical the letters, the

better, said Schlozman and Tierney (1986). Some organizations they researched sent out letters that were all different, carefully prepared on colored paper with different letterheads. However, even if letter writing is clearly an orchestrated effort, if the letters arrive in sufficient quantity, then they will be heeded. "Although members of Congress may not be fooled by contrived constituency pressure, they do not feel free to ignore it" (Schlozman & Tierney, 1986, p. 196).

Other groups have a centralized phone bank that calls the organization's members, legislator's constituents, or other interested parties, informs them of the issue, and gives them the option of either being directly patched through to their legislator or sending a mailgram or voice-mail message (Cigler & Loomis, 1995).

To succeed in grassroots efforts, organizations need to train the grass roots. Birnbaum (1992) suggested that government relations training be done in a government room the morning before lobbying; that it include thanks to the people for coming, and lots of encouragement; that it prepare participants for some of the questions they might face, arming them with arguments and carefully dictating what the answers should be and what language should be used. The organizers might demonstrate the arguments with simulations, or at least with modeling. They need to present "scientific" evidence that constituents can use. They should encourage people to use common sense and to use the expertise gleaned from their own vocations. When speaking of making it easy for people she recruited to lobby, one lobbyist said that she included a folder that

> constituted a complete lobbying kit, much like the instructions many other professional lobbyists gave to their people from back home. [The] folder included a sample letter to lawmakers that argued for [the issue], with a place reserved to "insert your own story about your company." Another document listed "talking points" that the executives could use to make the case for [the issue].... The kit ... strongly recommended that the executives write editorials for local newspapers. Samples of such articles written by other business executives were included in the packet. She also told the executives that they need not worry about the wording of their columns. Her company in Washington could give them plenty of help with that: It kept three ghostwriters on its staff for that purpose. (Birnbaum, 1992, p. 233)

Wittenberg and Wittenberg (1989) indicated that all successful grassroots campaigns have the following in common:

- a cause that substantial numbers of people can rally around;

- access to lists of voters likely to be interested in the success of the cause;

- a Washington connection to supply current legislative information and advice on strategy and tactics;

- an education campaign aimed at keeping the supporters informed and willing to act;

- a concentrated effort to get the views of the voters to Capitol Hill in a timely fashion; and

- a cadre of members of Congress who are ideologically attuned to the issue and see substantial support for it in their districts.

Using the Media

Effective use of the media is essential to the success of any advocacy campaign, yet the media are seldom used by counselors. Counselors not only need to stage events, they need to publicize them by involving the media. The media focus public concern and spur public action; and legislators use the media as a tool for assessing public sentiment. To use media effectively, a campaign must catch and hold the media's attention, despite their notoriously short attention span. The media are the battleground on which each side seeks to secure for its cause the most powerful affirmative symbols and to attribute to its adversaries the most negative symbols. How issues are framed in the media-and how they can be strategically reframed-can determine the outcome of an issue campaign. Media advocacy promotes broad-based media coverage that frames and captures the symbols of public debate, thereby building public support for policy initiatives. "Framing the issue" is the process by which advocates convey their message to maximize the affirmative and minimize the negative values associated with it (Advocacy Institute, 1990). Because of cost considerations, counselors typically have more access to radio and written publications than to other media.

Counselors can get their name or the name of their organization in the paper by sending in a news release, getting their event covered, doing an interview, submitting a public service announcement (PSA), writing letters to the editor, doing a press conference about a newly completed study, or persuading an editor to do an article on a particular issue related to the counseling profession, a mental health program, or the particular counselor (Birnbaum, 1992; Newsom et al., 1993; Richards, 1990, Seitel, 1984; and participant advocates). To have any of these occur, relationships need to be cultivated with the media and reporters (Schlozman & Tierney, 1986).

When composing an article, news release, or PSA, it is particularly important to keep in mind the public interest side of things. In other words, why would anyone want to see this information in print (Richards, 1990)? If the issue involves lots of money or people, or if it threatens people's quality of life, the media will probably be interested. Articles need to be audience specific and have a local angle. Competition for media attention is fierce, but they do need stories. Op-ed pieces, in particular, amplify the effectiveness of the rest of an advocacy effort. Wittenberg and Wittenberg (1989) suggested providing news releases on a Friday afternoon, when the media have more need for input and less people on hand to find it.

Counselors can compile media kits and should keep in mind the following when they do so (Newsom et al., 1993; Wittenberg & Wittenberg, 1989):

1. Make sure the information is appropriate in content and style to the chosen medium; make sure it is timely. Counselors need to study the medium in which they want to be seen.

2. Check the facts for accuracy.

3. Give the name of a contact person for follow-up.

4. Include on any photographs the name, address, and phone number of the supplier, stamped or written in felt-tip pen on the back in such a way that the ink will not soak through. Attach captions with rubber cement.

5. Never call to find out why a story or photo did not appear, and do not ask when it will appear when you submit it.

6. Do not send out a note with mailed releases asking for clippings.

7. Do not call at deadline time.

8. Schedule press conferences carefully; sensational events can bury your press conference. Time and place are important. A rehearsed spokesperson is also important—he or she should not speak for more than 45 minutes. Do not hold a press conference on the weekend.

Counselors may not want to limit themselves to newspapers, particularly when other print media are more accessible. Organizational publications reach employees or stockholders. Industry publications are periodicals aimed at bettering an industry. Professional associations publish trade or association publications. Organizations or industries publish sponsored magazines. Internal or external newsletters provide a wealth of information to particular audiences (Newsom et al., 1993). Often these publications are hungry for articles and are a ready resource for counselors. Counselors could also publish their own newsletters, publish in professional journals, or do research the media needs for its stories (Linzer, 1988).

Radio is another medium through which counselors can gain free exposure. PSAs are carried on radio as well as in newspapers. One participant advocate said, "During National Child Abuse Prevention Month, I sponsor radio ads, which they write; but they say this is brought to you by [names her practice and location]. It's partly public service and partly advertising." Talk show hosts need a regular supply of experts on various mental health topics. Interested counselors can write a letter to the station about their knowledge of certain areas. They can then follow up the letter with a phone call. When on the show, counselors should be themselves, be aware of the listeners, and project strength and clarity (Richards, 1990).

In short, counselors can gain a lot of publicity for their advocacy efforts through information carried as editorial comment in a publication or news medium. This publicity also might consist of such things as a column in a local newspaper, a cover story in a national magazine, 30 seconds on the 6:00 evening television news, chatter by a radio disk jockey, mention of counselors once or twice in a long story about mental health, a talk show on mental health issues done at the local cable station, a single photo in a newspaper or magazine, a two-inch item in an association publication, an annual report, a house publication, or a film (Newsom et al., 1993). In general, more publicity is generated by the use of celebrity spokespersons, symbols and drama (for example, a "war" on drugs obviously merits attention), and large and official statistics from published works.

Advertising and Direct Marketing

Advertising. Advertising can assist counselors in promoting themselves or their clients' needs. Research shows that ads are more effective in increasing people's convictions and mobilizing action on current convictions than in changing people's beliefs. Ads may thus be useful to channel and strengthen current opinions and to provide information supporting preexisting attitudes. Some research suggests that in many cases public opinion has been swayed toward the opinion propagated by the group that spent the most money on their ad campaign. Advertising needs to be used cautiously, however, because broadening the scope of conflict by alerting and mobilizing the opposition may hurt counselors' cause (Schlozman & Tierney, 1986).

Six categories of ads are useful, although not all of them are likely to be used by counselors (Newsom et al., 1993; Schlozman & Tierney, 1986):

- Ads that aim to increase *name recognition* continually make the public aware of a counselor's name, practice, certifications, specialties, or discipline. These include yellow page ads, business cards, brochures, stationary, signs outside the office, listings in community resources, and putting one's name on and distributing inexpensive items (such as pens, mugs, or buttons).

- *Target marketing* has a specific goal, program, or service in mind. It is a way to directly generate clients for the practice or participants for a program, and includes advertisements or columns in local newspapers, announcements, flyers, open houses, workshops, or speaking engagements. Target marketing is time oriented and designed to have an immediate, measurable response (Richards, 1990). One participant advocate suggested that counseling groups advertise in journals read by people who buy services (benefits and personnel administrators, for example). "It's getting where they are. It's finding out what they read, getting in their publications."

- *Issue ads* allow an organization or individual to express opinions and views on a controversy currently receiving public attention. Advocacy ads go beyond offering general comment to urging support for a particular position that benefits the organization. They usually look like editorial copy. They do not push products directly, but some product goal or corporate ideology is expressed. The tone is restrained and civilized, and they are carefully placed and targeted. It is difficult to gauge the effectiveness of these ads, and they are very expensive (Loomis & Sexton, 1995). They are not typically done by groups such as counselors.

- *Image ads* symbolically associate a redesigned logo or a change in policy with an organization or individual.

- In *cooperative advertising,* groups combine for a common purpose in using one of the other types of advertising.

Because of cost considerations, counselors will be most likely to use target and name-recognition advertising.

Direct Marketing "Interests use direct marketing to raise money, recruit new members, lobby public officials, and publicize issues, programs, and candidates" (Godwin, 1992, p. 308). Direct mail, telemarketing, and television solicitation are the three mechanisms used to solicit letters and phone calls from voters in any district in the nation to particular legislators or committees. One company that specializes in this sort of thing was able to make calls to constituents; then, if the constituent was willing, they would immediately switch them over to the legislator's office (Birnbaum, 1992). Direct marketing such as this is more likely to be successful when tied to highly visible current events. It is, however, a risky enterprise; organizations are lucky if they receive a 2 percent response. Sabato (1984, p. 57) suggested the following formula for success: "pure emotion, lightning-rod issues, and 'hot' names."

Direct marketers begin with a prospect list of those who have shown themselves to be most responsive to an issue. The marketers' strategies use fear of immediate harm to motivate people; they make great use of negative information, stressing the darker side of politics. They use terms like "enemies" instead of "opposition," and other purposely provocative terms. They use positive symbols for their own side and negative symbols for the opposition. Fundamentalist ministers are the primary users of television as a marketing tool. Biznet, the Chamber of Commerce's television program, publicizes the chamber's positions, but it is very expensive and not widely used. Using the telephone is very personal but also very expensive. Using telephone trees is not expensive, and it encourages member involvement. However, the more steps in the chain, the greater the chance that the message will get altered (Godwin, 1992).

Godwin found that groups that use direct mail as a strategy limit their political options because they have to choose highly visible and emotional issues that maximize media exposure, issues that are very controversial and allow no compromise, and issues on which the leadership must appear innovative and radical in order to maintain their membership. Direct marketers are less substantive and expertise oriented than other attention-getters. If they use direct mail marketing, they cannot use the traditionally effective techniques of lobbying behind the scenes on narrow, less visible issues, or of working out necessary compromises with opposition groups. Ideological PACs use direct marketing more frequently than other methods and find it very effective in increasing attention to social and moral issues.

Making Contributions

Some have asked whether "social" lobbying or making contributions of some sort is not a form of bribery, and Tierney (1992) indicated that it is *indeed* legal bribery. Schlozman and Tierney (1986) pointed out that although direct payment is not legal and not common, it is also not necessary. There are plenty of legal ways to make contributions—such as free and favorable publicity; reelection and promotion; privileges and special favors; inside knowledge; tips on the stock market, real estate developments, and public contracts, future fees; jobs for relatives; business for the partner of the officeholder; election to clubs; invitations to dinner; visits to and from the elite; help for the children; fishing trips; and golf vacations to Florida. Fifty-six percent of organizations do this sort of favor. Other kinds of favors include providing technical information, serving as a resource, extending service to needy constituents, making life easier for policy makers, making PAC donations, sponsoring fundraisers, offering honoraria for talks in nice places, and offering conferences in exotic places to educate policy makers on the issues (see also Birnbaum, 1992). One legislator had honoraria distributed to his favorite charities. The result was that money dribbled "around the state" until he looked "like the great philanthropist of all time," said Republican Senator Alan Simpson of Wyoming (as quoted in Hook, 1989, p. 3421). Birnbaum (1992) urged organizing fund-raising events, not just making campaign contributions. "Fundraising of one kind or another [has] become virtually a way of life for both lawmakers and lobbyists" (p. 165). A lobbyist cited by Birnbaum urged showing up at fund-raising events with a checkbook.

> It's nice to be seen. It's important in a lot of ways. It's important that you be seen as being a player in the game. You show up, members see you there, and over time the cumulative effect is that you are seen as a participant in the process. You are a player. You're a contributor, a benefactor. And that leads to other things. (p. 111)

Protests

Protests may be effective with highly emotional issues. They are usually only used by organizations with roots in social movements. "If you have a cause that can become an emotional issue for a number of people anywhere in the United States, the cheapest, most effective way of forcing the government to deal with the issue is to organize a march on Washington" (Wittenberg & Wittenberg, 1989, p. 84).

According to Lipsky (1968, p. 1145),

> Protest activity is defined as a mode of political action oriented toward objection to one or more policies or conditions, characterized by showmanship or display of an unconventional nature, and undertaken to obtain rewards from political or economic systems while working within the systems.

It might involve histrionics, threats of exposure, picketing, or sit-ins (Berry, 1977). People do not march because they like marching, they march because the publicity alerts people on The Hill, and it makes people at home aware of the issues and activates them or persuades them that the organization is working for them (Wittenberg & Wittenberg, 1989).

Protests and demonstrations are used by very few groups, and they are usually used after more conventional means have been tried. They are ranked lowest by groups as a means of influence. Protests can be used to attract new members, motivate existing members, increase a sense of solidarity, and gain political leverage and credibility. They can also alienate and mobilize the opposition (Schlozman & Tierney, 1986). Minority and low-income groups have frequently resorted to protest in their political efforts.

Protest leaders have to appeal to four constituencies at the same time: They must nurture and sustain an organization. They must choose strategies that maximize their exposure in the media. They must maximize third-party involvement—in other words, they must influence certain other publics who have greater resources and influence to take up for them. And they must influence decision-makers capable of granting their goals. There are inherent tensions in manipulating these four constituencies (Lipsky, 1968).

Different types of leaders are necessary for different types of protests. Angry, militant leaders are more effective in groups that are ideological and that do not depend on the system for material rewards. This type of leader may also be needed to build cohesion in relatively powerless groups by questioning the rules of the game. Those groups that desire tangible benefits need more moderate leadership (Lipsky, 1968).

Protest activities are inherently unstable. They cannot maintain an organization or effort by themselves. Long-term success depends on a wide spectrum of political strategies in addition to protest activities (Lipsky, 1968).

STAGE SEVEN: VICTORY CELEBRATION, EVALUATION, AND REGROUPING

The advocacy process is ongoing, and provisions for continuous feedback and evaluation are important at every stage. Any decisions made today can be reversed tomorrow. Certainly the opponents of any legislation will be trying to overturn it tomorrow. So, rather than Stage Seven providing closure for the process, it provides a transition into the next level of an ever-escalating spiral. Whenever efforts are successful, participant advocates said, it is time to celebrate. "People need to pause and say, 'We've done a good job. Look what we've

accomplished,' before somebody says, 'What have you done for me today?' which really wears your folks down."

Too often counselors do not know what their professional associations have accomplished for them and therefore do not celebrate their successes. This can only limit future motivation for advocacy and for joining the professional association. So, successes need to be photographed, documented, published, and disseminated to complete the advocacy cycle. The core group needs to be honored publicly. Legislators, insurance company representatives, employers, and referrers need to be thanked, publicly if possible. Press releases honoring all involved will help to ensure continued support from advocacy targets.

One counseling association held a luncheon at a conference in honor of a legislator who had spearheaded passage of important legislation. The legislation allowed for counselors to appeal insurance company claim denials to an independent appeals board. This legislator had initially opposed the legislation but he did some personal research and as a result changed his position. Prior to the luncheon, the counseling association mailed out news releases to all the local news media to notify them of the award they planned to present to the legislator. They included with the news release information on counselors, on the counseling association, and on the legislator. At the luncheon, the government relations chair told the story of the legislator and counseling association working together to get the legislation passed. Then, the government relations chair introduced the two lobbyists who had worked with the organization and the legislator. Pictures were taken of the proceedings and sent to the local news media, to the legislator and lobbyists, and to the counseling association's newsletter.

Because it is sometimes difficult, as indicated previously, to define complete success, advocates need to build on small victories, sharing the credit, learning from defeats, and keeping their eyes on the longer term. They need to record and tell stories to motivate new advocates (Advocacy Institute, 1990). The Virginia Counselors Association (VCA) was successful in getting the state's board of education to pass a resolution mandating school counselors in elementary schools. However, the passing of this resolution met with a great deal of opposition. As soon as VCA "succeeded," the opposition mounted its attack, trying to get the legislature and the board of education to overturn the decision. A new governor then succeeded in changing the composition of the board significantly enough to put the resolution at risk. Rather than having time to celebrate their success, VCA continues to regroup, restrategize, defend their position, and never let down on their efforts for fear of losing what they have gained.

When counselors do receive a clear defeat they need to remember that advocacy is a long-distance race, not for the short-winded. Rarely are battles won or lost with a single effort (Wittenberg & Wittenberg, 1989). The Advocacy Institute (1990) urged advocates not to lose heart. "A loss in Washington does not mark the end of the fight, just the close of a round" (p. 136). If advocates are persistent, a new Congress, a new administration, or new political and economic situations may change their chances in the next round. Experienced lobbyists "don't even wait 24 hours before starting the next round with a new approach" (p. 137). They rebound quickly from their losses, never forgetting to protect their gains. Clearly this was true for the opponents of VCA's efforts to make sure that elementary students had school counselors. So, Stage Seven involves celebrating the successes, grieving the losses, and regrouping for the next effort. Whether counselors have won or lost, there is always more to do.

ACTION EXERCISE

Begin the action phase of your advocacy effort with the exercise shown here. Using the lists of possible activities from this chapter, answer the following questions:

1. What action plan fits your resources, your goals, your problem definition, and your research results?

2. What kind of organizational decision-making and communication structure do you need to develop to fit the plan?

3. Who will carry out the plan and with what deadlines?

4. What type of end-of-the-year evaluation, celebration/gratitude giving, and regrouping do you think would be most effective?

SUMMARY

Different advocacy strategies and methods of communication are necessary for different publics. This chapter has attempted to provide an inclusive—though not exhaustive—description of the possibilities, with examples given by participant advocates. Related to these activities are the actions necessary to gain attention from the various publics or access to decisionmakers. Many authors have developed lists of commandments necessary to lobbying campaigns. The ACA suggests the following *21 Steps in a Successful Legislative Process:*

1. Know who and what you are—develop and maintain **a consistent** voice for the profession.

2. Identify a **key person** to speak for you, and at a moment's notice.

3. Make sure that the key person speaks with **integrity,** and that his or her message is reliable.

4. Communicate in clear language so that the **direct professional interest,** the public interest, and the fiscal effect are evident. Make sure that every assertion is supportable.

5. Make sure there is a **logical basis** for your position, and be alert to the mood of the legislature—Is your proposal timed correctly?

6. Convey the **message** directly to the legislator, especially the sponsor. Make sure he or she knows the support and opposition.

7. Select the **introducer** carefully—make sure that he/she is on the appropriate committees where the bill might be sent. Make sure that he/she understands the subject matter.

8. Begin to **systematically contact** all committee members and determine potential support and opposition.

9. Secure a **majority of the votes** in the committee at hand to assure passage, or defeat.

10. Never veer from the stance that yours is a **legislative,** not a political, objective. Contacts and content must bear directly on the interests of the profession, not on partisan politics.

11. Make direct **personal contact** with all key legislators and with their staff, if there are any. Keep legislators informed.

12. Identify **constituent counselors** in your state who know their legislators personally, or who can get to know them. Mobilize this force.

13. Mobilize a **legislative network.**

14. Be certain that legislators acquire an **accumulating record** of positive contacts from constituent counselors. Do not wait until a crisis.

15. Be prepared for early **intervention.** Develop contacts which will serve as an early warning system.

16. Seek action at the **earliest stage** practical—preferably when the bill is in draft form or before it is heard in its first committee.

17. Attempt to ensure that committee reports, especially conference committee reports, convey the **intent language** to your satisfaction.

18. Monitor and be willing to work with state agencies responsible for implementing new laws and drafting the **regulations.**

19. Be alert to the **precedence** of new legislation—where favorable, seek its extension into related programs and codes.

20. Look for opportunities to attach counselor support to legislative concepts that are timely and in the **public interest.**

21. Say thank you to legislators, staff, your members—anyone who was involved in the effort, whether it was successful or not. Be a good loser as well as a good winner. (Reprinted from fact sheet, *21 Steps in a Successful Legislative Process.* © ACA. Reprinted with permission. No further reproduction authorized without written permission of the American Counseling Association.)

Wolpe (1990) urged advocates to tell the truth, to never promise more than they can deliver, to listen long enough to fully understand, to use the legislative staff, and to spring no surprises on legislators working with them. Wittenberg and Wittenberg (1989, p. 16) somewhat humorously claimed that all of the advice they have could be distilled into the following "Ten Commandments of Lobbying." They urged advocates to display them over their desk, on the photocopy machine, and near the water cooler.

1. Thou shalt speak only the truth, and speak it clearly and succinctly, on two pages and in 15-second sound bites.

2. Thou shalt translate the rustle of thy grassroots into letters, phone calls, and personal visits.

3. Thou shalt not underestimate thy opponent, for he surely packeth a rabbit punch.

4. Help thy friends win reelection; but in victory, dwelleth not on the power of thy PAC.

5. Thou shalt know thy issue and believe in it, but be ready to compromise; half a loaf will feed some of thy people.

6. Runneth not out of patience. If thou cannot harvest this year, the next session may be bountiful.

7. Love thy neighbor; thou wilst need him for a coalition.

8. Study arithmetic, that thou may count noses. If thou can count 51, rejoice. Thou shalt win in the Senate.

9. Honor the hard-working staff, for they prepare the position papers for the members.

10. Be humble in victory, for thy bill may yet be vetoed. (Reprinted from *How to Win in Washington.* Copyright ©1989 by Blackwell Publishers. Reprinted with permission.)

Clearly, underlying any advocacy effort by counselors are essentials that counselors should have no difficulty fulfilling: good timing, preparation, relationship building, being a resource, good communication, grassroots efforts, and respect for any advocacy target.

Part II
ADVANCED ADVOCACY

ROUNDING UP THE PLAYERS

The principal means by which [advocacy] is achieved in our society, and within our political tradition, is through advocacy networks and coalitions. . . . The term "coalition" encompasses a great diversity of institutional and individual alliances formed to advance a common goal. (Advocacy Institute, 1990, p. 3)

Coalitions vary in their structure and in their funding sources. They can be "formal or informal; permanent (dedicated to a complex, long-term agenda) or temporary (formed for the achievement of a single task or goal); they may be . . . staffed independently or collectively" (Advocacy Institute, 1990, p. 3). Most coalitions are informal, requiring members to contribute time, professional help, or clerical services. This informality minimizes power struggles and jurisdictional disputes. Coalitions vary in how much members have in common: some are homogenous, while others bring together "truly strange bedfellows" (Schlozman & Tierney, 1986, p. 48).

In the public policy literature, coalitions are generally alliances among differing interest groups (such as the coalition formed by Kaylan Sanders) or among groups and the executive and legislative branches of government. It seems apparent, however, that many coalition principles also apply to the collective action taken by individuals joining together in such groups as professional associations (note the activities of Daniel Wong). Both types of alliance are considered in this chapter.

THE NECESSITY FOR COALITIONS

The public policy literature indicates that "the exacting measure of success in congressional lobbying is the ability to create, join, or manage coalitions united behind a public policy proposal" (Wolpe, 1990, p. 35), that "coalition-building is a crucial part of any organization's strategy of influence" (Schlozman & Tierney, 1986, p. 278). Ninety

percent of the organizations in Schlozman and Tierney's research indicated that they enter into coalitions. Sixty five percent indicated that consulting with friends in other organizations provides an invaluable source of information when planning their organization's strategies.

Coalitions also are increasing in importance in Washington politics. Sixty-seven percent of the Washington representatives in Schlozman & Tierney's research had increased their commitments to coalitional activity, bringing joining of coalitions up to second on a list of 27 techniques of influence (Schlozman & Tierney, 1986). Although it is difficult to assess the efficacy of these efforts, it is clear that these organizations would not consider coalitions such a priority if they did not believe in their efficacy (Hula, 1995a).

There are many reasons for joining coalitions:

People who join coalitions do so out of enlightened self-interest. If your ox is about to be gored, warn the owners of the other oxen in the neighborhood and fight the threat together. Coalitions create a very useful product called clout. The more interests you can get to stand up for your side, the better the chance that legislators will consider the project. . . . [Lobbyists are] aware that they can seldom win all by themselves in a complex, interdependent society, so effective lobbyists line up whatever allies they can find, and the frequently shifting alliances make for odd bedfellows. . . . In building coalitions, you'll also be gaining strength in congressional districts where you previously may not have known a soul. (Wittenberg & Wittenberg, 1989, p. 128)

"Coalitions are essential to broaden support for a policy initiative, and to coordinate effective action to accomplish a common goal" (Advocacy Institute, 1990, p. 3). Further, unlike in market situations—where the more units of a product or the more businesses or businesspeople there are, the lower the price will be and the less will be the benefit to the participants—in nonmarket situations that supply collective goods, the more members there are, the better the chances of success. Coalitions do not decrease the benefits for participants; in fact, they contribute more clout. The supply of collective goods in nonmarket situations "automatically expands when the group expands" (Olson, 1965, p. 38). Strong coalitions gain the chance to define the terms of the policy debate and to have some control over policy outcomes (Hula, 1995a), and the adversarial process involved in forming coalitions gives rise to a degree of rationality that would otherwise be unattainable (Hayes, 1986).

"Washington representatives who join coalitions for strategic, legislative reasons frequently cite changes in government and the growth of organizational representation in Washington as key institutional explanations for the growth of coalitions" (Hula, 1995a, p. 243). Collaboration among interests has been necessitated by increased policy complexity, growth and decentralization of government, improved communication technology, and the growing politicization of interests that were previously either nonexistent, poorly organized, or relatively inactive (Loomis, 1986). Organizations find it necessary to present their case to more political actors than ever before. "Because even the largest individual groups find it difficult to reach all of the relevant congressional players, collective strategies may be necessary if groups wish to present their case in all the appropriate forums. A hallmark of coalition strategies is that membership enables the workload to be spread out" (Hula, 1995a, p. 243; see also Berry, 1989b; Heclo, 1978; Huntington, 1975; and McCool, 1989). Thus, because "the difficulty of passing legislation has increased exponentially, to make a common cause with people who would not be your traditional allies is important" said Cortech lobbyist Stuart Eizenstat (Hula, 1995a, p. 240).

Another key motivation for groups to join coalitions generates from the explosive increase in the number of interests active in Washington (Hula, 1995a; Mann, 1990; Schlozman & Tierney, 1986; Walker, 1983). This growth in organized interests has created a paradox: The creation of more groups has meant less clout for all of them (Salisbury, 1990). Thus, Burdett Loomis (1986) and William Browne (1988) have argued that the existence of coalitions has further pushed groups toward coalition strategies in order to compete. "As each new group joins the Washington melee, governmental capacity to process external demands is reduced. Groups are pressured to work out their differences before approaching Congress" (Hula, 1995a, p. 243) and to speak with a single voice on a given subject "rather than requiring Congress to sort out a seemingly infinite number of differences among groups. Congressional staffers, the Office of Public Liaison in the White House, and individual agencies all initiate coalitions to encourage groups to work out what Douglas Costain and Anne Costain label 'predigested policies' outside governmental institutions" (Hula, 1995a, p. 243; Costain & Costain, 1981; see also Berry, 1989b; Birnbaum, 1992; Peterson, 1992; Schlozman & Tierney, 1986; Wolpe, 1990). Loomis equates forming coalitions with constructing majorities, and indicates that coalitions have always been necessary. "Politics under the Constitution virtually demands coalition building among interests that seek new policies. Majorities must be constructed at a series of stages within the legislative process. . . . Broadly based coalitions . . . may well convince members of Congress that a consensus exists on a given legislative proposal, thus easing the way for its passage" (Loomis, 1986, p. 260).

Finally, along with the growth in the number of interest groups has been parallel growth in public criticism of "special interest groups."

> Public and campaign rhetoric creates a more hostile political climate for organized interests and generates another incentive for collective action. In order to avoid stigmatization as "special interest groups," individual organizations advocating particular policy outcomes turn to coalition strategies in an attempt to demonstrate varied support for their positions. A union leader stated: "The more diverse you can make your coalition, the better. . . . [It looks like] good government—you know, broadly held ideals, a broad array of citizens with perceived wide varying interests, all interested in this issue.". . . [Some coalitions, therefore,] are consciously structured to provide tactical cover for members of Congress who fear being linked by the public to "special interest group politics." (Hula, 1995a, p. 244)

In summary, coalitions have increased in numbers, and scholars believe they have become more necessary due to

1. the increasing complexity of government;

2. the need for clout in defining the policy debate and influencing policy outcomes;

3. the increasing numbers of interest groups and the resultant decrease in each group's clout;

4. the government's need for predigested policies; and

5. the legislators' needs to build majorities without being criticized for favoring special interests.

Advocates who participated in the research for this book primarily focused on the need for more clout as their rationale for forming coalitions. What was immediately apparent, however, in comparing the research responses with the public policy literature was that counselor advocates do not expend as much energy building coalitions as lobbyists and public policy scholars would recommend. The advocacy and government relations staff at the American Counseling Association (ACA) emphasized coalition building as a critical strategy, but other counselor advocates rarely did. The ACA staff pointed to a variety of coalition efforts:

> What we've been doing is more taking a philosophy of inclusion, playing the politics of inclusion. And I'm really finding that that is being well-received. Decisionmakers have even said to me, "So, you would be okay if we included social workers?" And we say, "Unequivocally, yes. There is no doubt in my mind that there are people trained as social workers that are trained to do this. I would go further and say that there are people trained as marriage and family therapists, that are trained as psychologists, nurses, psychiatrists, who may be qualified to do this." Whatever "this" may be. The idea [is] that while we're fighting to be let in, we don't have to come from that underdog mentality.

Nationally, said one participant advocate, counselors have formed coalitions with psychiatrists:

> Psychiatrists and the American Psychiatric Association have been much more supportive of professional counselors being included in things than ever before, recognizing our training, recognizing that we provide services across a continuum. And I think part of the reason is, we're the good children right now. Psychiatrists consider their discipline as the parent of mental health, and their firstborn, the psychologists, are now being very rebellious and asking for meds privileges, and privileges to commit, and so forth. And psychiatrists are getting very annoyed. And we capitalized on that, to some degree, saying, "Look, we're not touching that. We don't want to touch it. We want to be part of the team." And that's been well-received. So, we've gotten psychiatrists to write letters on our behalf.

One ACA staff member pointed out the power of coalition building when she said, "We were able to hand to Clinton's transition team, then to his administration, and now to Congress a statement saying that there are 35 different organizations that represent both practitioners and consumers of men-

tal health services, all saying we must have a continuum of services." Another participant advocate urges counselors to

> [network] and [go] outside of our own group. For example . . . if we had the Parent Teacher Association and/or the National Superintendents, or the Association of School Principals advocating collaboratively with us for positions in schools and for roles of counselors that would allow them to be more effective, I think we could do it a lot easier. We would be more effective if we were doing that.

Another national leader pointed out that coalitions can be formed with

> people like the Red Cross, with whom we have just signed a formal agreement, so that we will now be a part of their disaster relief programs. We were not trying to reinvent the wheel, but we needed to find an avenue in which we would be able to lend a service, as providers of services. So, we have just signed a formal agreement with Red Cross a couple of weeks ago so that members will be on the scene for the floods and the hurricanes.

A few coalition efforts at the state level were mentioned by participant advocates. In one state, all the mental health professions were linked by working with one lobbyist. In others, "omnibus bills" have been sought, which license social workers, marriage and family therapists, and professional counselors under the same bill and the same licensure board. In other states,

> We have put out the hand to say, "Look, we're going to go for this. We believe that you should have the same kinds of things. Why don't we do it together. And we'll help you fight your battles; you can help us fight ours. And we'll do this as a coalition."

The Virginians for Mental Health Equity joins together over a hundred organizational and individual members concerned about various mental health funding issues. Among other things, they persuaded the state of Virginia to include certain mandates in their managed health care plan; they maintained an ongoing dialogue with the state benefits manager to improve the quality of mental health care provided by the plan; and they currently monitor, testify, and lobby on legislation related to mental health care.

In short, coalitions are alliances between groups that feel they can accomplish more if they join together. While counselors frequently join together in professional associations in order to advocate for the profession, and sometimes join together with different groups to achieve a common goal, they demonstrate less propensity for using coalition strategies than lobbyists and public policy scholars would advocate.

COALITION THEORY

Hula's (1995a) research applies the incentive theory discussed in chapter 5 to coalition membership. When organizations join coalitions for strategic, policy-oriented reasons—reasons that Clark and Wilson (1961) called *purposive* and Salisbury (1969) labeled *expressive*—they are seeking collective, ideological benefits. Sometimes organizations join coalitions to obtain selective benefits that they would not otherwise have, such as information or timely intelligence about the policy process. These benefits equate to the *material* benefits described by Clark and Wilson (1961).

> Information benefits are particularly important as incentives for smaller groups with limited staff and resources. . . . In addition to monitoring the introduction of bills and proposed regulations, small staffs without significant contacts on Capitol Hill may find it nearly impossible to monitor activities in the relevant subcommittees, follow legislation between hearings and markups, and maintain contact with relevant congressional staff. For these groups, coalitions are a lifeline of information, scuttlebutt, and rumors about developments in the policy process. Coalition partners often function as an early warning system on issues that a representative had not been following. (Hula, 1995a, pp. 246, 248)

Coalitions also allow groups to brainstorm about strategies, coordinate lobbying, target particular Congress members, and capitalize on their strengths (DeGregorio & Rossotti, 1995). "The rational group recognizes that opportunities to shape . . . policy are closely tied to membership in the coalition" (Hula, 1995a, p. 242). Finally, group lobbying may also be responsible for achieving selective benefits (Salisbury, 1969). For instance, when marriage and family counselors successfully lobbied for clinical members of the American Association for Marriage and Family Therapy (AAMFT) to be reimbursed by the Civilian Health and Medical Program of the Uniformed Services (CHAMPUS), they made it attractive for practitioners to join AAMFT as clinical members.

Other groups join coalitions for symbolic, show-of-solidarity reasons—for example, to convince their members that they are active or to demonstrate solidarity with another organization.

When symbolic reasons predominate, appearance is more important than actually obtaining specific policy outcomes (Hula, 1995a).

> Photographs of organizational leaders testifying before a congressional committee or subcommittee frequently grace the front pages of their newsletters. Participation in a coalition can represent a low-cost trophy that group leaders can deliver to the membership to demonstrate activity on issues they may view as secondary, if not downright unimportant. The investment is small—perhaps no more than attending an hour-long meeting each month. (Hula, 1995a, p. 248)

"Any coalition probably contains members who have joined for each of these reasons" (Hula, 1995a, p. 241).

Incentives to join coalitions differ from incentives to join groups in that joining coalitions frequently means saving resources while joining groups means contributing resources. In other words, the potential member of a coalition is an organization represented by a staff member, a paid Washington representative. The potential member of a group is generally apolitical. Potential group members are thus more reluctant to expend resources for political action. For potential coalition members, "the already politically active representative is offered an opportunity to reduce his other resource expenditure on that issue and to increase the likelihood of policy success through a specific strategy, namely a coalition" (Hula, 1995a, p. 242).

Hula also argues that because different groups join coalitions for different reasons, they assume different roles within the coalition. Table 8.1 outlines these different roles. *Core members* are groups that join a coalition to accomplish broad strategic, purposive goals. They are willing to commit time and effort to the coalition's work. *Specialist organizations,* or "players," join coalitions for more narrow, strategic or material goals, but they are still important to the coalition. "These specialists are willing to commit time and resources to the coalition as long as it continues to emphasize their particular goal" (Hula, 1995a, p. 256). Players generally "bring specialized expertise to the coalition that core members may lack. . . . [This] is their key source of political capital within the coalition" (Hula, 1995a, p. 253). They thus shape the coalition's agenda and hone its position on the points that are relevant to them, and in ways that would not be possible on their own.

Table 8.1. Coalition Members, Their Roles, Their Goals, and Their Resources

	Core Member	Specialist or "Player"	Peripheral or "Tag-along"
Issue importance	High	High (specific)	Low (peripheral)
Organization's goal	Overall strategic victory	Issue honing	Coalition by-products
Degree and type of resources brought by an organization	High level: money, reputation, expertise, membership	Enough to buy a place at the negotiating table: expertise, reputation, membership, money	A name: perhaps a prestigious name, perhaps just another name for the list
Time commitment (work level)	High level for overall goal	High level for specific goals	Low level across the board

Source: From "Rounding Up the Usual Suspects" (p. 251), by Hula. In A. J. Cigler and B. A. Loomis (Eds.), *Interest Group Politics* (pp. 239-258), 1995, Washington, DC: Congressional Quarterly Press. Copyright ©1995 Congressional Quarterly Press. Reprinted with permission.

> Organizations that join a coalition for symbolic reasons or solely in order to gain benefits such as information are generally unwilling to expend significant resources to further the coalition goal. Although they support the goal in principle, coalition membership is an end in itself, and they will remain on the periphery of the coalition, welcome all the same. (Hula, 1995a, p. 256)

Very large, politically active organizations may become peripheral members. Their reputation, resources, and perceived clout within an issue domain make them critical. These "big guns," or "tag-alongs," are *sources* of intelligence in a coalition and do not join to gain information. The peripheral member may be merely lending its name to coalitions as a favor, and other coalition members do not expect them to actively participate. In fact, "the asymmetries in membership are generally acceptable to all concerned. . . . Not a single group leader suggested that the tag-alongs were not welcome in the coalition. While their contribution might have been merely to add another signature to joint letters, that was a welcome addition" (Hula, 1995a, p. 254-255).

Hula's research (1995b) also tried to determine why groups would join coalitions in some situations and not others. He found that in *policy* activities, groups are far more likely to join coalitions, whereas in *political* activities, groups are far more likely to remain independent. *Political* activities are "those that deal specifically with the selection of individuals for public office: political endorsements for elective office, publicizing candidates' voting records, attempting to influence political appointments, campaign work, and PAC contributions" (Hula, 1995b, pp. 24-25). Interest groups participate in political activities in order to keep communication channels open, to curry favor, or to buy access. These involvements are opportunities to build the group's reputation and are not likely to fail. Hula thus discovered that reputation building by an organization conflicts with the incentive to build coalitions.

"*Policy* activities are those that are directed at shaping legislative or regulatory outcomes: various forms of lobbying (influencing the drafting of legislation or regulations, supplying information about the effects of a bill on a member's district, stimulating grassroots mail to policy-makers, contacting government officials), and filing suit" (Hula, 1995b, p. 25, author's emphasis). These are riskier ventures than political activities, and they require more cooperation, coordination, and collective action. "To summarize, groups cooperate when necessary for policy outcomes. Reputation enhancement stands in tension with this policy cooperation, because group self-differentiation must be pursued independently" (Hula, 1995b, p. 23). Interestingly, Hula claimed, most groups do policy, not politics.

THE DOWNSIDE OF COALITIONS

The political activity of reputation enhancement is not the only contraindication for joining coalitions.

Time spent in a coalition is often the best of times and the worst of times of any advocacy effort. . . . When effective, coalitions mass and focus the collective skills, resources, and energies of their constituents. When ineffective, they can drain energy and resources, exacerbate institutional and personal rivalries and conflicts, paralyze flexibility, and deaden initiative.

Coalitions are inherently fragile. It's in their nature to be slow and cumbersome, and achieving agreement on even minor objectives can be time- and energy-consuming. And that can hamper the coalition's ability to respond to crises and opportunities [see also Loomis, 1986]. Group rivalries inevitably erupt, along with the understandable reluctance of organizations and individuals to subordinate their individual identities to the coalition. Hard feelings can fester and grow, especially when some groups or individuals work harder than others, and still others show up in time for the victory celebration to claim an unfair share of the credit. (Advocacy Institute, 1990, p. 3)

According to Hula (1995a, p. 239), "an interest may find itself in a minority position, with its issue preferences submerged under those of other groups. Or it may not receive credit for whatever success the coalition achieves. Group leaders must continually evaluate the trade-offs between autonomy and the potential for enhanced influence."

Groups may have very important political reasons not to join coalitions. DeGregorio and Rossotti (1995, p. 228) found that with respect to judicial appointments, "rather than reducing conflict and reconciling differences . . . coalitions . . . seem to expand the conflict, raise public awareness, and put senators on alert." Groups may find it unhelpful to expand the scope of conflict in this way.

In summary, counselors need to be aware that groups join coalitions for a wide variety of reasons. If group and coalition organizers expect levels of involvement to differ and do not expect collective benefits to motivate everyone, they may not become so frustrated when some participants contribute very little and other potential beneficiaries do not even join. Also, knowing a party's level of motivation may help coalition leaders use their resources more effectively. Further, counselors and their professional associations should probably choose coalition strategies for policy activities and independent action for political activities.

THE PRACTICE OF COALITION DEVELOPMENT

As Loomis (1986) pointed out, coalitions do not simply emerge. Rather, during the mobilization stage they are assembled by an individual or small group of individuals who play a role more like that of a broker than a group entrepreneur. "The explosion of interest group advocacy, along with the increasing reach and complexity of policies, has generated a great demand for lobbyists who can bring diverse interests together. . . . This is a long-term fight, and brokers are crucial to maintaining the coalition's visibility and standing. . . . Coalitions require organization . . . and law and public relations firms increasingly act as the brokers for the building of coalitions" (Loomis, 1986, pp. 270–271). The broker provides the initial stimulus and capital to organize the coalition. At a minimum, this includes hosting, chairing, or co-chairing the coalition, as well as providing clerical support for organizational tasks (Hula, 1995a). Brokers offer flexibility, speed, and often access that traditional coalitions may lack. They can organize as broad or as narrow a set of interests as the particular issue requires. They may provide useful services without the baggage of interest groups being forced to make long-term commitments (Loomis, 1986).

Most coalitions are started by staff lobbyists in large organizations that have strong, broad interests in particular legislative issues within their policy domain (Loomis, 1986). This is good news for ACA staff and members. Reputation, centrality of the issue to the group's self-identification, and political resources all enhance the likelihood that a given organization will successfully found a coalition (Hula, 1995a). Brokers spend many months developing a policy goal or agenda for the coalition that will draw people in. Careful problem definition and buzzword development are part of this initial strategizing (Birnbaum, 1992; Hula, 1995a).

Brokers are not certain about the potential group or market. Generally, a market is selected on the basis of a leader's experiences and contacts, or by emulating other, similar organizations. The broker might purchase or borrow mailing lists of similar groups or publications in the policy domain (Salisbury, 1969).

The initial 50 members of a coalition are the most difficult to recruit because at first people are not sure they want to be bothered, and there is no list of members with which to impress them (Wittenberg & Wittenberg, 1989). "As a minimum we may assume that, so long as the entrepreneur desires to maintain the organization as a going enterprise, he must get a sufficient return in the form of membership support to enable him to continue to provide the benefits which attract members," and sufficient return to pay overhead costs "and keep him sufficiently satisfied so as not to shift his energies to some other enterprise" (Salisbury, 1969, p. 25).

As coalition development progresses,

> the general policy stance becomes more formalized, . . . details are added, and the coalition's platform is fleshed out. A large, proactive coalition's platform often profoundly influences the terms of the ensuing policy debate; therefore, there is a strong incentive for sympathetic organizations to join the coalition in order to influence that platform with their own particular policy goals before the chorus begins to sing it in public. A teachers' union representative put it this way: "We prefer to be in the coalition early. When you see things forming, you want to be in it before the concrete sets." (Hula, 1995a, p. 244)

When the initial issue around which a coalition has organized has been resolved, the passion dies, just as it does in any organization (see chapter 5). At this point, brokers must decide whether to disband the coalition or to reorganize and maintain it.

MAKING COALITIONS WORK

Advocacy manuals and "how-to-lobby" books espouse many "rules" for making coalition efforts work. Anne Wexler (quoted in Wittenberg & Wittenberg, 1989, p. 14), a specialist in creating legislative coalitions, identified ten rules for a successful coalition that are very similar to the rules discussed in chapter 6 as essential for effective advocacy.

The Advocacy Institute (1990) developed its own set of basic rules, although it stressed that these cannot replace the constant "care and feeding" of coalition members:

> 1. The goals and objectives of the coalition must be clearly stated, so that organizations who join will fully comprehend the nature of their commitment. At the same time, coalition members must openly acknowledge their potentially differing self-interests. [Trust and respect generate from stressing common values and vision and from openness about differences.]
>
> 2. Coalitions can be formal or informal, tightly organized or loose and decentralized. The type of coalition chosen will depend on the kind of issue as well as the styles of the people

and organizations involved. Coalitions evolve naturally, and should not be forced to fit into any one style.

> 3. Coalitions should reach out for broad membership. . . . The most effective coalitions are composed of a solid core of fully committed organizations, which can draw together shifting groups of allies for discrete projects or campaigns [see also Birnbaum, 1992]. . . .
>
> 4. Interim objectives should be chosen carefully. They should be significant enough for [a broad coalition of] people to want to be involved, but manageable enough so that there is a reasonable expectation of results. . . . Interim objectives should be chosen so they build relationships and lead toward work on other, more encompassing objectives.
>
> 5. A coalition must be able to work with a great diversity of advocacy groups, but all groups need not belong as formal members. Organizations whose goals are more radical, or whose tactics are more extreme, are often more comfortable and effective working outside the formal coalition structure and informally coordinating their activities.
>
> 6. Yet the coalition's leaders must have strong ties to the major organizations within the coalition. And the commitment of those organizations and their leaders must be strong. This commitment must be communicated within the organization, so that its staff members clearly understand that coalition work is a high priority.
>
> 7. Coalition tasks and responsibilities should be clearly defined and assignments equitably apportioned. If a member is falling down on the job, that should be dealt with promptly. Meetings should allow opportunities for members to report on their progress. (Reprinted with permission from *The Elements of a Successful Public Interest Advocacy Campaign* (pp. 4–6), 1990, Washington, DC: Advocacy Institute.)

Lawmakers are seeing fewer and fewer individual pressure groups.

> Instead what they saw was a coalition of interests that claimed to care about the public good, often led by organizations that, politically speaking, were less offensive to an elected official than were the self-interested corporations that tended, in reality, to bankroll such efforts. Lobbyists call this creating coalitions of nontraditional allies. . . . The idea behind these odd couplings was to raise the comfort level of lawmakers when they were being hit up for some taxpayer-paid benefit. . . . Most voters [are] working people, not corporate chieftains, the theory [goes]. So the front man for each coalition had to be close to the people and not even remotely associated with the executive suite. Indeed, effective coalitions had to possess a public profile far prettier to the average legislator than the relatively ugly countenance of the corporate interests that lurked not far in the background." (Birnbaum, 1992, p. 36)

One example Birnbaum (1992) gave is a coalition of many major corporations with university researchers. The corporations wanted a tax break for research and development. They paired up with underfunded university people engaged in "virtuous" endeavors that were respected by everyone. Their strategy had academicians and scientists as the front people. Corporations are frequently viewed as "black hats," as only self-interested, while universities are viewed as the "white hats." Black hats finance many of these types of coalition efforts (p. 83).

Hula's (1994) research addressed "maintaining networks." He claimed that in forming coalitions, groups need to ask three questions:

1. How can groups identify other organizations that might be interested in the policy?

2. How can they determine who might be potential allies?

3. How do they establish collective action with these allies.

It takes an inordinate amount of time to address the first two questions before coalition founders can address the third. Groups who have a way to answer the first two at less cost have a "leg up" on groups who do not have a way because, in fact, groups spend more time in information gathering than in actual lobbying.

Hula's research showed that institutional linkages are critical to answering the first two questions. These linkages arise from three sources: the career paths of organizational staff members, group interlocks, and third-party links.

1. *Career paths:* Organizational staff members move around from organization to organization, and may have moved from government into organizations. They maintain contact with their previous employing organization, and they consider those contacts critical to their "intelligence." "Beyond communication, a representative brings knowledge of past positions held by other groups, and enhances the ability of an organization to anticipate the position that representative's former employers will take on new issues" (Hula, 1994, p. 16).

2. *Group interlocks:* These are created by staff or board members who serve in positions of responsibility in more than one organization.

3. *Third-party links:* Third parties, such as attorneys and lobbyists, link the variety of organizations they service. According to Hula (1994, p. 7),

These institutional linkages can provide effective conduits for the coordination of information exchange and group strategy, vastly simplifying the intelligence-gathering efforts that would otherwise be required of organizations desiring to pursue collective strategies. If organizations are structurally or institutionally linked to each other, they do not face great challenges "finding" each other, and there is a lower cost of discovering what preferences are.

These linkages are not used on every issue, but their presence provides a loose and generally stable framework of relationships. "Organizations that have institutionalized mechanisms for gathering this information have an advantage in coordinating action with other organizations, in part because they can identify potential partners and adversaries more efficiently" (Hula, 1994, p. 32). Institutional linkages provide groups with greater ability for collective action, but in general those linked do not find it necessary to form formal, long-term coalitions. Groups with fewer linkages find it more difficult to establish formal coalitions, but they need it more (Hula, 1994).

Participant advocates indicated that consensus-building language is critical to coalition effectiveness. "We're trained to listen, but don't always use it for ourselves. We need to keep the dialogue open. Legislators get tired of bickering professions. They do want to see professions working together." Another advocate said, "I think you have to come to being of one mind, even if that's not really the case . . . [to] identify what our differences are and then come to some common understandings." Counselors have to believe that "we are one profession. We have practitioners who are trained in specialty areas, but that we have a common core of knowledge, that we share, and that those decisionmakers can, in fact, accept our credentials." According to another advocate, "Each specialty is worthy of equal consideration." We have got to say, "Look there is no one right training, and there's no one right way to do anything. We have yet to prove that any one way of doing [counseling] works, so why should any one discipline be the only one." We need to "speak in one voice, and one voice internally as well as externally, recognizing that it really takes a collaborative effort to advocate. You can't have one person, one group. You really need to be a cohesive unit."

Wolpe (1990, p. 36) drew similar attention to the importance of delivering one message on The Hill: "This is good for us, it is good for America, and the common good must not be frustrated by the objections of a relative few." This is the message he feels every legislative coalition ought to be sending.

One participant advocate described her methods as follows:

> I want to use inclusive definitions for health care providers, look for commonalities across specialties and across disciplines. I try to explain to people that when such an enormous amount of energy goes into diversity, it keeps us from accomplishing anything. I look for ways to cooperate and see different points of view. I try to dialogue with these [different] groups, use language showing understanding of their profession, to try to express that we are kindred. I try to show them how we fit into the bigger picture of health delivery systems. How could we work together? We particularly suggest language which is "inclusive" of us, *not* exclusive of others. I take the point of view of the common good, rather than distinct identity. I look for "consensus items," and sometimes they are few and hard to find. In other words, how much can you give up and still agree to statements? That people would be open to looking for common motivation for what they are doing, then look for ways to accomplish these goals together, by appealing to reason and praying a lot.

> People call with their objections or challenges, and I suggest that they send the language they would like included and the research to back it up. I then rework everyone's ideas into a further draft. I think it is important not to be wed to the original ideas you come up with, but to be open to the feedback these other groups give, to try to look at the whole spectrum.

Other participant advocates offered further suggestions:

> "I think you need to get as much input as possible from those invested, present evidence, weigh the arguments, and decide on the greatest good for the greatest number."

> "[You need to] involve those the change will affect, . . ."

> "[You need to understand] other attitudes, and [show] in your arguments that you can meet the needs of other decisionmakers. No one view catches it all. So I think you need other views."

> "I think you need to have had some kind of a battle plan that was decided on collectively, so there is multiple, in terms of entity or person, support for an agenda that you are pursuing."

> "It is [also] important to have people in positions of advocacy leadership who can reach across broad spectrums. We were very conscientious and respectful of the divisional desires. We tried to foster legislative activity which would benefit everyone."

> "We need to work together, talk together, travel together. We can't do it as an individual person."

> "Obviously part of [this] process [is] a great deal of compromise, and part of compromise is watering down some of what many of us would like to see."

Counselor advocates need to know their compromise points and be willing to let go of parts of a plan in order to bargain for other parts.

Coalition leaders also need to recognize that coalitions have differential usefulness based on what stage of the policy process they are in. The *formulation stage* is probably characterized more by entrepreneurs than by coalitions (Kingdon, 1984). During the *decision-making or legislative stage,* coalition activity is greater. The power of cooperation comes into focus here as "impending decisions often prompt cooperation among interests, especially when they feel an imminent threat" (Loomis, 1986, p. 265). However, interests have less clout at this stage because legislators are more open to influence from large numbers of interest groups.

"Once interests develop some history of cooperation . . . they become increasingly involved in the assessment of how policies are put into place" (Loomis, 1986, p. 266). Loomis thus claimed that involvement in *policy implementation and evaluation* may motivate coalitions to stay together. Hula (1995b) indicated, however, that the common wisdom is that coalitions are more active during the *legislative phase* than the *implementation phase.* He hypothesized that this is because legislation needs to be more generally stated in order to gain enough consensus to pass. When the *regulatory phase* arrives, groups feel very strongly about the specifics and try to push their own agenda. "Many groups identify the regulatory arena as a place where the specificity and detail of proposed regulations drive communications and information gathering inward to membership rather than outward to other organizations" (Hula, 1995b, p. 11). Hula's research demonstrated a slight trend in group activity from working in "coalitions" toward working "alone" as policy moves from the legislative to the regulatory phases. The significant difference was away from working in coalitions and toward working "alone, but consulting friendly groups" as groups move into the implementation phase. So, groups find it necessary to remain in contact with other groups, even during the implementation stage.

SUMMARY

Coalition building at its simplest is merely the formation of relationships and the sharing of information, activities that are well understood by counselors. The following list consolidates the principles of the experts. Notice the similarity of this list to the discussion on essential elements for advocacy in chapter 6:

Eriksen's Five Rules for Making Coalitions Work for Counselors

1. Use all of the communication skills you use in counseling:

    • Clearly articulate and dialogue on needs, views, goals, responsibilities, and conflict areas.

    • Negotiate and compromise to build a consensus.

2. Be inclusive and value diversity:

    • Frame the issue in inclusive language that potential members can rally around.

    • Carefully frame interim objectives so as to draw in more members.

    • Aggressively identify and court all who could be affected by an issue.

    • Mobilize the grassroots.

    • Use and "carefully feed" all of your networks.

    • Remember that careful management of greater diversity means better, more saleable solutions in the long run.

3. Use your education skills on everyone.

4. Work with a small directorship of leaders who have the ability to speak for their organizations and the status to rally their members behind the cause.

5. Be a resource to those you seek to influence.

Much of the focus in this chapter has been on influencing public policy through coalition building, because the public policy field is the only one that has researched and written about coalitions. It is clear, however, that health care change will not be accomplished merely by changing laws and regulations. Nor will finding support when a school counseling program is threatened. So, counselors are heartily encouraged to use the principles presented here in building coalitions to achieve other advocacy goals. There is strength in numbers.

Chapter **9**

CONFLICT AS FRIEND, NOT ENEMY

Madeleine Kunin, who served three terms as governor of Vermont and is now deputy secretary of education in the Clinton administration, claims in her book *Living a Political Life* that "she wanted to believe that if she found the 'right' answer, she could satisfy all parties to a controversy. She had to learn over and over that 'conflict is the essence of politics'" (Garment, 1994). Counselors share a similar struggle with conflict, even though they help others learn to manage conflict and have historically valued diversity, with all of its political implications. Although the American Counseling Association's (ACA) pencils bore the statement "Unity Within Diversity," some counselor advocates "think we have too much diversity and not enough unity." This diversity translates into conflicts over organizational priorities and how to spend resources that are by nature limited. Different divisions within the counseling parent organizations have disputed over where to draw the line when establishing standards and credentials. For instance, how does one ensure quality while seeking not to be exclusive? Divisional needs have often been in conflict, and power struggles have ensued. What does this mean to the advocacy efforts of professional associations of counselors, efforts that are largely political?

This chapter presents the participant advocates' responses to the question "How does conflict impact counselor advocacy efforts?" Their answers are compared with the literature on conflict management and resolution and with the public policy literature. Initially, definitions and levels of conflict are explored. Then, the negative and positive impacts of conflict are discussed. Later, effective conflict management is examined in terms of theory, identifying factors that lead to productive or destructive conflict results. Finally, the literature is used to explore people's styles of approaching conflict, and the appropriateness of different styles or strategies.

DEFINITIONS AND LEVELS OF CONFLICT

For the purposes of the research done for this book, conflict included disagreements between or among groups or individuals resulting from a diversity of goals, priorities, or needs. To allow a broad interpretation of the concept, when advocates who participated in the research for this book asked what was meant by conflict, the answer they received was "whatever you feel conflict is." The literature defines conflict in several ways. Hocker and Wilmont's (1991, p. 12) definition combined the best of the other definitions: "Conflict is an expressed struggle between at least two interdependent parties who perceive incompatible goals, scarce resources, and interference from the other party in achieving their goals."

Conflict occurs at different levels, according to both the participant advocates and the literature. There are three levels of conflict: interpersonal, within-group, and intergroup. In *interpersonal conflict* there is an ongoing, interdependent relationship, and this interdependence is usually broad: parties depend on one another for a wide range of emotional, psychological, and material resources (Folger, Poole, & Stutman, 1993). For this reason, when need frustration occurs, anxiety and conflict may arise. Anxiety can increase the parties' rigidity and inflexibility during the conflict. Further, the parties may struggle internally when this occurs, and according to psychoanalytic theory, this struggle creates energy that needs to be released. Psychoanalytic theory thus helps explain the role of aggressive or anxious impulses during conflicts. "That these impulses build up and can be redirected into other activities, including attacks on a third person, is crucial to most conflict theories" (Folger et al., 1993, p. 17). In particular, conflict managers need to know that becoming aware of what is driving conflicts can give individuals control over them.

In *within-group conflict,* the parties share long-term interdependence; however, this interdependence is much more limited than it is in interpersonal conflict. The parties are not involved in meeting very many of one another's needs. For instance, "a number of people who are members of some larger unit . . . know each other, have interacted with each other in meetings or work settings, and attempt to reach decisions as a group. The divisive issues in these conflicts are central to the group as a whole" (Folger et al., 1993, p. 7). The narrower range of interdependence means conflicts tend to be "just business" and are not taken so personally. Conflicts may be over group priorities, how to spend resources, or what group actions ought to be.

Intergroup conflicts "involve two or more large groups of people who represent some political or ideological stance or who are members of cultural, community, action or neighborhood groups" (Folger et al., 1993, p. 7). It is more likely that spokespersons will speak for the collective. Again, there is a narrow range of interdependence, because the parties are only dependent on each other for achieving the collective goal the groups have set for themselves. "The roots of intergroup conflict lie in the basic human need for identity" (Folger et al., 1993, p. 34), which is defined by the groups to which a person belongs, and does not belong. This identification may in turn create oppositions among people. "When people accept social categories, they are likely to act toward those in other groups on the basis of these attributions. This sets up a self-reinforcing cycle that preserves theories about other social groups (Cooper & Fazio, 1979) and increases "the polarization between groups and the attendant stereotyping of other groups that triggers conflicts" (Folger et al., 1993, p. 35). Intergroup conflicts may arise from a wide range of events: economic and political problems; natural disasters; wars; population movements; the structure of society, economic opportunity, or the political system; changing demographics; or long-term shifts in economic fortunes. "When this happens, groups tend to attribute responsibility for their problems to other groups and to unite against them" (Folger et al., 1993, p. 36).

Some participant advocates attributed differential impact to these three levels of conflict, while others did not. Putnam and Folger (1988, p. 350) indicated that "theoretical principles apply across [conflict] contexts because interaction processes form the foundation of conflict management." In other words, because all conflicts are made up of actions and reactions, moves and countermoves, planning of communication strategies, perceptions, and interpretations of messages that directly affect substantive outcomes, the level of conflict is irrelevant to discussions about impacts or about conflict management. It will be interesting to remember these conflicting views as the literature and the research responses are compared.

NEGATIVE IMPACTS OF CONFLICT

When participant advocates were asked what happens to advocacy when conflicts exist, they were for the most part quite expressive about the negative effects of conflict on their advocacy goals and on their functioning as individuals.

Within-Group Conflict

Within-group conflict expresses itself most often in the counseling profession between divisions or cohorts in an organization or among professional association board members. The conflict between the American Counseling Association (ACA) and the American Mental Health Counselors Association (AMHCA) is one example of within-group conflict. In this conflict, AMHCA basically said to the ACA, "You have abused our trust by mismanaging our money. You have not taken enough action on issues pertinent to our membership. Therefore, we want to disaffiliate. Furthermore, we want to do so immediately (instead of following the rules requiring disaffiliation to be a two-year process) because you are bankrupt and we don't want to go down with the ship." ACA agreed that they had serious financial difficulties, which they were trying to remedy. They did not agree with the accusation that they were not attending enough to AMHCA issues, and they were against the immediate disaffiliation because, as it turned out, so were most of the AMHCA members who voted in a special referendum.

The ACA-AMHCA conflict had negative effects on the organization and the people within the organization. One ACA staffer repeatedly declared, "This job is going to kill me," and "I think I'm getting ulcers." She reported having nightmares regularly and looked exhausted. Others said similar things and also looked stressed. Surreptitious meetings were held in hallways and behind closed doors, and strong statements were made about how inappropriately the "other side" was handling things. The conflict dominated conversations and meetings for months. Staff worried about whether they would lose their jobs.

I personally felt tension as a result of the ACA-AMHCA conflict. I found myself thinking and talking about the conflict often—while at ACA events and while at home. I found myself seeing this conflict as a major event, and wondering what my role in it ought to be. Many people called me from my own state association, asking for information. I worried about losing access to the informants I needed for my research, and I wondered how much I could get away with saying before I alienated a potential participant advocate.

Participant advocates had much to say about within-group conflict even beyond the ACA-AMHCA struggle. During the interviews, they made strong negative statements about conflict:

"People cuss and discuss. The inability of this profession to unify around key concepts has slowed its progress tremendously. . . . [When people cuss and discuss,] they begin asking questions about whether their interests are being represented, or they begin feeling left out when they want to participate."

"[When this type of disenfranchisement occurs,] we can't get the numbers we need to lobby and to advocate for the changes we need."

"[It] makes it hard to go out and present a unified voice, [which] confuses the people we are trying to deal with."

"I think [this] stops us from getting laws passed, licensure laws specifically."

"I try to explain to people that when such an enormous amount of energy goes into diversity, it keeps us from accomplishing anything."

"You can't reach a goal for the betterment of your clientele when you are too busy fighting among yourselves, with regard to division rivalries, misunderstandings, personality clashes. . . .

I think any time you have divisions within any organizations . . . you have people who feel slighted, either rightfully or wrongfully. . . . Anytime you focus your energies upon internal conflict, it detracts from the ability of an organization to focus outwardly toward bigger goals."

"I think the core thing for me is if we can't agree among ourselves, who we are, what it is that we do, and how we're going to work together and allow for differences among us internally, how are we ever going to go out and advocate?"

"Everything is focused on the present when things are in turmoil. Then the whole focus becomes money and the future goes to hell in a handbasket. It has kept the organization tied up in the now and [it] ignores the future."

Yet another advocate claimed that she spends more than 50 percent of her time negotiating within-group conflicts and that it depletes her energies more than anything else. Divisional battles are particularly fierce over agenda priorities. "There are a lot of needs that we have as a profession," and different groups advocate attention to their needs exclusively. This splits the efforts of the organization, or results in summit meetings that "are not pretty," because they turn into a "sort of pissing contest."

These "splits" result in distrust and failure to work together as a team. This distrust was reflected in a kind of guardedness in the ACA and AMHCA informants. Self-protective statements and lack of openness in responding to some questions were apparent. One informant specifically asked about confidentiality with respect to names and positions, which she had not seemed concerned about in previous interviews. Another gave short, clipped answers on conflict questions, while being vociferous about nonconflict tangents. Many times she seemed hesitant to answer, as though the information was privileged; or she would indicate that she was not the one "to comment on that history."

The ACA-AMHCA conflict, the view of its seriousness, and the fact that "it is perceived as [a] livelihood issue" may explain this guardedness. The interviewer's tension in broaching questions because of not knowing what the forbidden territories were matched staff members' reports about their high levels of tension.

Overall, it seems that counselor advocates view within-group conflicts as a waste of time and energy that could be better spent on accomplishing important organizational goals. Many advocates reported that internal conflicts demand great expenditures of time and money to resolve, and result in tremendous frustration, sadness, and burnout on the part of the advocates (see also McFarland, 1992).

Intergroup Conflict

Intergroup conflicts or "turf" battles are exemplified by the conflicts between the associations representing counseling and those representing other mental health disciplines, such as psychology, psychiatry, social work, and marriage and family therapy. In policy domains where there are peak associations (large organizations trying to organize and speak for many smaller member organizations), there is more intergroup conflict. In the health domain, there is relatively little conflict, but what does exist generally results from competition for the same funding dollars (Heinz et al., 1993).

Intergroup conflicts have resulted in decision-maker confusion. Decisionmakers often do not know that there are differences among the mental health disciplines, so when two people from seemingly the same profession are presenting different views, the decisionmakers get confused. Even when varied mental health groups come up with one position paper, they later seem to splinter. Said one participant advocate, "What happens in reality . . . are still individual organizational lobbying efforts that may, in fact, conflict with that general message of 'We are one, we are together, and here's what we feel the citizens of the United States need.'" Another counselor advocate told of a conversation with an insurance company representative: "She said, 'You know, we really don't know who speaks for you. If AMHCA does or ACA does. We're not sure around the country if the LPCs [Licensed Professional Counselors] are the same as mental health counselors or different.' A representative from NIMH asked the question, 'Are you one group or are you a group of groups?'"

This confusion hurts all the mental health professions, but particularly the newcomers, like counseling. "I've heard more and more legislators turning around and going 'Oh, come on. Are you telling me that nobody else is qualified to do this?' when one profession has attempted to testify against another in a hearing." And yet despite legislators' reluctance to believe turf declarations, when the mental health disciplines do not agree, it is "those who yell the loudest, who have the most PAC money, and the strongest lobbyist . . . [who] get heard." Particularly troubling is that "confusion, even without somebody speaking loudly, results more in moving toward the traditional or comfortable, instead of something new." This keeps "an orientation in our health care system towards treating pathology, rather than preventing pathology where it can, in fact, be prevented." The message Congress is getting is that treating pathology should be health care's priority, which is contrary to counseling's values of seeing mental health care on a continuum.

According to participant advocates, these "turf wars" have resulted in a cycle of abuse. One participant advocate said:

> I did this article and it gives a wonderful analogy of how psychiatrists try to block psychologists, and psychologists try to block social workers, and so forth and so on. And rather than when psychologists finally got in and they were allowed to do the things that they wanted to do, rather than turning around as an older sibling and saying to the social workers or counselors, "Well, come, we will show you the ropes. Let us help you," they turned around then and said, "Well, . . . tough." So rather than being that helpful older sibling, it was almost like the cycle of abuse. They became the abuser after being the abused. And I think that we have been oppressed for so long that internally what we do is we look within and set up our own pecking order within counseling. We go from being the oppressed to being the oppressor—but we have nobody left to oppress. I mean, if you are lowest down on this well-perceived hierarchical chain, who do you repress? You don't have a younger kid to pick on yet, you know, so you turn around and pick within your own family. I see that a lot. And while many of us honestly believe that there's a continuum of counseling services, of working with people very functional to very dysfunctional, of primary prevention through intervention, and of specialties on a continuum, not a hierarchy, what I still see out there is this pecking order that has been established . . . that . . . the more clinical specialties . . . are perceived as being more skilled.

So, intergroup conflict results in counselors being blocked from inclusion in "job classification systems, insurance reimbursement, programs in schools, training monies. . . . It's every discipline for itself as a number of groups . . . [try] to block the newer or . . . more up-and-coming professions, such as counseling." Counselors have been sued for practicing psychology without a license. The public has generally been perplexed, not fully knowing or understanding the differences between the mental health professions. As a result of turf wars, counseling associations have suffered surprise setbacks when advocating. A great deal of time and energy gets spent correcting messages that other groups have given to legislators and other decisionmakers about who counselors are. And finally, intergroup conflicts do not "help the consumers, who ultimately are the ones that we are supposed to be caring about and working [for]."

Literature on the Negative Impacts of Conflict

Interestingly, participant advocates were much more vocal about the impacts of conflict than was the conflict management and resolution literature, while the literature was much more vocal about management of conflict. The literature does confirm many of the participant advocates' views and researcher observations of their behaviors. Hocker and Wilmont (1991, p. 5) pointed out that "many people view conflict as an activity that is almost totally negative and has no redeeming qualities." And "when parties are in an interpersonal conflict, internal conflict usually occurs within each of the parties" (p. 14). Folger and colleagues (1993, p. 4) added that "entering a conflict is often like making a bet against the odds: you can win big if it turns out well, but so many things can go wrong that few people are willing to chance it." Other authors point to the destructive impact of a "we-they" polarization in conflict (Blake, Shepart, & Mouton, 1964; Sherif, Harvey, White, Hood, & Sherif, 1961). When groups are put into competition, "in-group messages . . . slant positions in favor of the group and demean the claims and validity of the other group" (Folger et al., 1993, p. 36). This prevents reflection on the merits of the other group's claims. It moves the in-group toward a narrow, oversimplified view of the other group and creates stereotypes. "Discussions in the in-group minimize similarities between the in-group and other groups and exaggerate differences between the groups' positions. . . . Polarization is heightened by suppression of disagreement in the in-group" (Folger et al., 1993, p. 37). Clearly,

> conflict is often felt as a crisis, whether the crisis appears internally, in a two-person relationship, in a small group's work, or in an organization. But conflict also presents a chance for growth, new life, and change at the same time that it affords potential destruction, death, and stagnation. (Hocker & Wilmont, 1991, p. 4)

In fact, as Hocker and Wilmont pointed out, "the Chinese character for conflict is made up of two different symbols superimposed: one indicates *danger* while the other signifies *opportunity*" (p. 3).

POSITIVE IMPACTS OF CONFLICT

What, then, are the opportunities inherent in conflict situations? According to participant advocates, conflict situations have resulted in an increased sense of professional identity, the development of political savvy, increased motivation for advocacy, increased advocacy activities, the formation of coalitions with other underdog groups in fighting for a common cause, and increased alertness on the part of legislators to what the real issues are. One participant advocate urged, "We need to seek it out, resolve it, and then grow in the process." Others claimed that conflict informs us of where we need to advocate, and clarifies what is really important to the organization. "Conflict keeps individuals on their toes and alerts them to the need for personal involvement. I believe conflict and competition need to be handled carefully, however, so they don't become the focus of too much attention and result in fragmentation." The conflict between ACA and AMHCA, noted another participant advocate, has created enough of a crisis that the membership has finally awakened, become involved, developed strategies to fix problems, and made constructive suggestions.

Madeleine Kunin said that conflict is the "essence of politics" (Garment, 1994). Peltason (1955, p. 2) said that "politics is the process of group or interest conflict" (see also Madison, 1987; and Mansbridge, 1992). Petracca (1992c) took the discussion a step further when he said that politics is "the resolution of group conflict" (p. 5). Latham (1952) indicated that the purpose of the U.S. government's structure "was not to avoid friction, but by means of the inevitable friction incident to the distribution of government powers among three departments, to save people from autocracy" (*Myers* vs. *United States,* 1926). Clearly, if conflict plays such an important role in politics, it plays an important role in advocacy.

Increased Motivation for Advocacy

When other mental health provider organizations write laws, job classification systems, and insurance policies that exclude counselors, counselors get busy trying to prove that they are as capable as these other organizations at providing mental health services. They look for research backing up their qualifications. They create ethical standards, standards of practice, accreditation standards, and model licensure laws. When counselors nationwide accept and incorporate these standards and credentials more uniformly, it becomes easier to say to the world, "This is who we are!"

Further, when livelihood issues are involved because another mental health provider organization says "You can't do this!" counselors become much more motivated to take action, to become involved in advocacy. They band together more strongly, and develop more of a group sense. Coser (1956) also indicated that a "we-they" relationship contributes to high levels of cohesion and turns attention away from conflicts or dissatisfactions within the group. One participant advocate said:

> I think that the inter[group] conflicts were the driving force with our licensure laws. If the American Psychological Association had not changed their model licensure law in the seventies [to prevent everyone but psychologists from providing mental health services] . . . I'm not sure we would have had the court battles that we had in Virginia, and in a couple of other states, that got us our first licensure laws as a separate profession.

Increased Political Savvy

Counselors have also, as a result of intergroup conflict, become more politically savvy, and they now approach decisionmakers from a position of strength, not as an underdog. Counselors have adopted the "politics of inclusion" in their problem definition, in their attitudes toward other mental health groups, and in building coalitions with other groups that feel similarly. They realize that trying to exclude other providers only perpetuates a "cycle of abuse" that is unnecessary and politically unwise. Rather than urging legislators to "let us in," or saying to legislators that counselors are "better than" other providers, counselors now try to demonstrate to legislators that they can be part of solving a problem, and that they feel that all qualified mental health providers should be included as part of solving the problem.

Increased Legislator Wisdom

Finally, because many mental health organizations have expressed their views to legislators, legislators are getting wise to what the real issues are. Instead of falling prey to turf battles, legislators are seeing through them to concerns about consumer protection. One participant advocate said:

> There's a growing realization in dealing with decisionmakers at a variety of levels. . . . One of the things that's become very apparent to me is they're starting to see through turf even when . . . [issues aren't] presented as turf issues. And no organization in their right mind presents something as turf. Psychologists don't turn around and say "we're the only ones who can do this because we want our guild to stay intact." They say [that] only doctoral level clinicians . . . can do this, so it can help protect the consumer. Now, when [psychologists] are pushed to bring forth any kind of data . . . to support that, they can't. . . . Nobody turns around and talks about their guild, and that they are there to support their university structure, and their association dues. I've heard more and more [legislators] turning around and going, "Oh, come on," even directly to people presenting things—which is, I must say, amusing to watch. Thank God it hasn't been me on that seat who's had to turn around and fluster something back. But I've heard testimony stopped, going "Are you telling me that nobody else is qualified to do this?"

Developmental Growth

Counseling organizations go through developmental stages, and they approach conflict differently depending on the stage they have reached. Young organizations often feel threatened when faced with opposition by other organizations: "We've been the underdog for so long that we'd plant our feet and get just as rigid as anybody else, declaring our superiority to other mental health groups. . . . We collectively have felt the need to defend so much that we often [came] off sounding like 'Oh, please let us in. We'll be good.'" This seems to be the natural response of those being threatened with extinction.

But "the continuing struggles between us and other organizations may have helped us move along in our own development, to feel stronger about who we are." As already noted, the increased sense of identity expressed in accreditation standards, ethical standards, and credentialing have helped to distinguish different groups of counselors from one another. Conflicts have forced counselors to choose more effective advocacy strategies, rather than throwing temper tantrums.

And most of all, greater organizational maturity has resulted in "taking a philosophy of inclusion," cooperating, and being more proactive. Those people with greater self-esteem and identity can tolerate differences and see themselves as more in control. "If you look at internal and external locus of control, [a defensive posture] puts us at a real early developmental stage," a participant advocate said, laughing. "Do we really want to present ourselves to the world as children?" Growing up clearly has its benefits in the advocacy process.

Despite Putnam and Folger's (1988) declaration that theoretical principles apply across all levels of conflict, participant advocates primarily described the impacts of within-group conflict negatively and saw the impacts of intergroup conflict more positively. The general sense was that counselor advocates plan for and anticipate intergroup conflict as part of the political process, while they are shocked, disappointed, and set back by within-group conflict.

Literature on the Positive Impacts of Conflict

Again, the literature is limited on the positive impacts of conflict. According to Folger and his colleagues (1993, p. 1), "conflicts allow important issues to be aired; they produce new and creative ideas; they release built-up tension; they can strengthen relationships; they can cause groups and organizations to reevaluate and clarify goals and missions; they can also stimulate social change to eliminate inequities and injustice." The literature implies, however, that the impact of conflict depends on how conflicts are handled. A great deal of literature addresses theories of conflict, understanding the process of conflict, how to use conflict to achieve one's goals, the role of power and climate in conflict management, and face-giving (allowing another to save face). The remainder of this chapter addresses these issues.

EFFECTIVE CONFLICT MANAGEMENT

Effective conflict management, according to the literature, requires an understanding of the conflict process and the ability to use power, face-giving, climate control, and communication effectively. Folger and his colleagues (1993) claimed that there are five key properties of conflict interaction:

1. "Conflict interaction is sustained by the moves and countermoves of participants; moves and countermoves are based on the power that participants exert" (p. 69). For conflicts to maintain a constructive direction there should be a bal-

ance of power, meaning that parties must reverse the usual flow: weaker parties should build their power, and stronger parties should share theirs or at least not use it to force or dominate the weaker ones.

2. "Patterns of behavior in conflicts tend to perpetuate themselves" (p. 70). Conflict interaction gains a momentum or life of its own and tends toward repetitive cycles.

3. "Conflict moves are embedded in larger interaction sequences" (p. 80), a context, or sequence of behaviors. Conflict moves through phases of differentiation to integration (Walton, 1969).

4. "As senseless and chaotic as conflict interaction may appear, it has a general direction that can be understood. . . . Conflict interaction is any exchange of messages that represents an attempt by participants to address some incompatibility of positions" (pp. 89-90).

5. "Conflict interaction affects relationships among parties" (p. 92).

What Contributes to Negative Outcomes?

Participant advocates felt that conflict becomes destructive for a number of reasons. "I think the organizational structure we have fosters the differences, as opposed to the commonalities. Literally, the divisions foster competing interests and foster different points of view, which is an advantage and a disadvantage, both." This view stems from a belief that "conflicts and disagreements are the same phenomena" (Hocker & Wilmont, 1991, p. 8); the literature calls this view a myth. Simons (1979, as cited in Hocker & Wilmont, 1991) explained that many people refer to conflict as a communication breakdown or lack of communication. Referring to conflict as disagreement implies that if you just work hard enough at communicating, you will resolve the conflict. Hocker and Wilmont believe, however, that conflicts are more serious than disagreements, and cannot be resolved just by better communication. One advocate, referring to the ACA-AMHCA struggle, agreed: "I don't think of this as conflict. I think of it as differences, not conflict. I see conflict in capital letters, as being to a greater degree than differences. I think that being alert to differences helps me avoid head-on conflicts."

It is critical to understand the differences between diversity and conflict. People can have different faiths, participate in different counseling work settings, and be interested in working on different issues. These only become conflictual when one party's interest, desire, or need and the action they desire to take on it will hamper another party's ability to attain what they want or need. When wealthy people want a tax break on capital gains, there is less tax money available for other government functions. Frequently that money seems to be taken from social programs for the poor. So, the conflict is often framed as one between the haves and the have nots.

Counseling associations are not different. When AMHCA says that health care reform is the most important legislative issue to focus on because of its potential impact on the livelihood of the membership and that therefore all the government relations staff's time should be spent on it, this conflicts with the position of the American School Counselors Association (ASCA). The ASCA said "No! The Elementary and Secondary Reauthorization Act is most important. We've worked on the Elementary School Counseling Demonstration Act for eight years, and we now know that if we do not amend it to the Elementary and Secondary Reauthorization Act, it will not pass on its own. Elementary schools are without enough counselors. We need this passed." Because there were a limited number of government relations staff and very limited funding dollars, time spend on one division's project took away from or inhibited time spent on the other. This is not just diversity or a disagreement. This is conflict.

Participant advocates also felt that people's beliefs about conflict affect conflict outcomes. Negative results stem from seeing conflict as bad and as involving anger and meanness. When people view conflict this way, they "draw lines in the sand"; winning becomes everything, anger and defensiveness result in "telling people off," "deflaming [sic] people's character," and making derogatory comments. Dishonesty and lack of respect further inflame these problems. Beliefs are often influenced by culture, and our culture has confusing and contradictory messages about conflict: "Sports are all right, random violence is not. Conflicts with peers are all right if you have been stepped on and you are a boy, but talking back to parents when they step on you is not all right" (Hocker & Wilmont, 1991, p. 7).

This complicates people's attempts to have helpful beliefs about conflict.

The literature agrees with the participant advocates that beliefs affect conflict outcomes. Hocker and Wilmont (1991) listed the following as assumptions that prevent positive conflict outcomes:

1. "Harmony is normal and conflict is abnormal" (pp. 7–8). Hawes and Smith (1973) described an alternate perspective that harmony is lasting and conflict is temporary. Coser (1967) and Simmell (1955) both believed that conflict is a normal state of affairs in a relationship that endures over time. As one participant advocate said, "Conflict is an inevitable part of change. People need to get used to it. They need to understand it. They need to understand that it is something that is part of the process."

2. "Conflict is pathological" (p. 8).

3. "Conflict should be reduced or avoided, never escalated" (p. 4). Hocker and Wilmont preferred the term "conflict management" to "conflict resolution," because they believed that sometimes making the conflict bigger, more important, or more crucial draws important attention to important issues.

4. Conflicts result from "clashes of personalities," and therefore cannot be resolved by people changing. Hocker and Wilmont claimed that this assumption results in separating people in conflict, which in turn results in factions being created, resentments simmering, and a lessening of the effectiveness of the larger group. Interestingly, participant advocates did not agree with this assumption. They felt that "ego and self-aggrandizement," personalities, an unwillingness to compromise, and strong, contrary beliefs prevented dispute resolution. Unfortunately, some of them said, these characteristics seem to correlate with some people's rise to national leadership.

5. Aggression and peaceful conflict resolution cannot coexist. Whitmont (1986, p. 17) pointed out that "Ares, the God of war and strife, and Eros, the God of love and desire, are twin brothers psychologically. . . . The absence of fighting experience makes for a wishy-washy personality

devoid of . . . motivation and self-confidence. Differentiation from others, and hence self-definition, occurs through struggle" (p. 17). He urged people to transform aggression into assertion, to direct and responsibly enact and moderate aggression, and to maintain enough energetic connection to struggle together. Peace and aggression are not opposite forces. Peace requires enough energy to keep people connected in respectful struggle. "Love without strife readily results in boredom and indifference because the challenge needed for growth is lacking. Love is not static peace but active involvement with and against one another" (p. 25). Preservation of the other, and of the relationship, is the key to a productive and creative conflict. When the other is cut down or destroyed, a relationship dies, and with it dies the part of the self invested in that relationship.

6. "The primary emotion associated with conflict is anger or hostility" (Hocker & Wilmont, 1991, p. 10).

The literature directs attention to other sources of destructiveness in conflict situations. Hocker and Wilmont (1991) identified two forms of conflict that are destructive: escalatory conflict spirals and deescalatory conflict spirals. *Escalatory conflict spirals* have only one direction, upward and onward. They involve overt power manipulation, threats, coercion, deception, more and more damaging ends, self-perpetuating misunderstanding, discord, and destruction. One party unilaterally attempts to change the structure, restrict the choices of the other, and gain advantage over the other, often involving efforts to "get even" and derogatory labeling (Deutsch, 1973; Folger & Poole, 1984; North, Brody, & Holsti, 1963; Wilmot, 1987).

Deescalatory conflict spirals are more subtle. The parties slowly lessen their dependence on each other rather than openly fighting. This conflict is more covert but no less damaging than escalatory conflict. The dynamics include less direct interaction, active avoidance of the other party, reduction of dependence, harboring resentment or disappointment, and complaining to third persons about the other party (Swensen, Eskey, & Kolilheps, 1981, pp. 850–851, as cited in Hocker & Wilmont, 1991).

In both escalatory and deescalatory conflict spirals, the situations become tense and threatening, involve a great deal of uncertainty, and are ex-

tremely fragile. These situations can result in terminating a conflict by force, uncomfortable suppression of the issues, or exhaustion after a prolonged fight—all outcomes that leave at least one party dissatisfied. Deutsch (1973, p. 17) claimed that conflicts are destructive "if the participants are dissatisfied with the outcomes and feel they have lost as a result of the conflict." But Folger and colleagues (1993, p. 9) felt that "it is not the behaviors themselves that are destructive—neither avoidance nor hostile arguments are harmful in themselves—but rather the inflexibility of the parties that locks them into escalation or avoidance cycles."

Participant advocates pointed out that negative results also ensue when people see no need for change or have no desire to resolve conflicts. One participant advocate pointed out that some people engage in conflicts merely to stop a particular policy from being adopted. "I think [you need] motivation for success or change. We have lots of conflict on the Governing Council. We have some motivation for change." Coser (1956) would call this a nonrealistic climate for conflict. In this type of climate, aggression is expressed in which the sole end is to defeat or hurt the other. Force and coercion are the only means for resolving the disputes. Much less flexibility is demonstrated because the goal is narrowly defined. The result is protracted, uncontrolled escalation cycles or prolonged attempts to avoid issues. The belief exists that one party must win and the other must lose. This belief stems from the fear of losing resources, self-esteem, or the respect of others; or the fear that working through a conflict is too risky. A win-lose orientation results in the loser trying to even the score. Parties often become polarized, and "the defense of a nonnegotiable position becomes more important than working out a viable solution" (Coser, 1956, p. 10).

What Contributes to Positive Outcomes?

Participant advocates felt that what is important in preventing or turning around negative impacts "is conflict resolution. That needs to be the focus." "People don't like conflict, confrontation, dissention. But this is the real world, and if we teach people about change and conflict, we need to listen to ourselves."

A Philosophy of Inclusion. Perhaps most important to achieving a positive outcome is the creation of a supportive climate for conflict management. A philosophy of inclusion can create just such an environment by valuing many different points of view. "Creative conflict management assumes there are multiple truths and realities, rather than only one right way to do things" (Hocker & Wilmont, 1991, p. 23). As indicated in chapter 8, participant advocates agreed that a philosophy of inclusion underlies efforts to create a consensus-building climate. One participant advocate claimed, "There's room for all kinds of counselors in treating the whole person. Wouldn't it be good if we could adopt the team approach?" Another said, "'Counselors first, divisions second,' has been a very successful model in [our] state."

The literature agrees with the philosophy of inclusion and valuing diversity. "Empathy can form the basis for all productive conflict management" (Hocker & Wilmont, 1991, p. 39). Understanding another person's position and seeing through their eyes provides the motivation for taking care of the relationship, which in turn leads to the active maintenance of connections in the midst of conflict. This creates an environment of safety, which is critical to creative, growth-producing conflict. "Without connections, the possibility for growth is lost" (p. 39). And, after all is said and done, the "overall purpose of human communication is—or should be—reconciliation" (Peck, 1987, p. 257).

Coalitions. Clearly, inclusion means valuing what each discipline or type of counselor has to offer. That valuing is most helpful if expressed in joining together with differing groups to form alliances and coalitions, and in working together, not, as one participant advocate said, "getting off in camps." (See chapter 8 for more information on coalition building.)

Developing a Constructive Climate. Hocker and Wilmont (1991) encouraged the development of a positive belief system about conflict. "Without some breaking apart, no new growth is possible. Out of conflict come new patterns of relatedness; out of new patterns comes new conflict. The cycle of birth and death, disintegration and renewal repeats itself in all of life" (p. 49). "Also necessary to productive conflict management are recognition that the actions of each person make a difference and that we are radically responsible for our own actions" (p. 41). Hope, along with skill development, can make miraculous changes, while despair adds to destruction and chaos.

Gibb (1961) pointed out specific behaviors necessary to creating constructive climates. He compared defensive and supportive environments on the basis of what it takes to create each. In a defensive environment, communication is evaluative and controlling. Statements are strategic, manipulative, certain, or dogmatic. Participants are apathetic or neutral, or they convey a sense of superiority. In a supportive environment, communication is descriptive and problem-oriented. Statements are spontaneous and sincere, provisional, and open to change and experiment. Participants are empathetic and communicate an attitude of equality between parties.

Mansbridge (1992) urged advocates to use conflicts to fuel a climate for collaborative deliberation. Deliberation can "illuminate both conflict and commonality" (p. 36) and involve both self-interest and altruism. It does not assume a zero-sum game, that there must be winners and losers, but that better solutions can be generated for all if all sides are represented. It allows debate of all important alternatives and refinement of the issues and solutions. It recognizes that in market-type competition, the "chorus sings in an upper-class accent" (p. 50), so decisionmakers need to provide some way of balancing power.

Assessment of Problems and Goals. When a conflict becomes apparent, assessment is the first priority. Participant advocates claimed, "You need to know all the ramifications in a conflict, all the parties involved, their views, their potential reactions, and be prepared." Assumptions need to be explicitly identified. Boundaries between competing groups need to be clearly defined. Counselors could benefit from developing language that differentiates without implying inferiority.

The literature agrees that people must assess how much is at stake in a conflict (Folger et al., 1993). Parties have to decide how interdependent they are. Then they "must enter into the process of determining who they are as a unit" (Hocker & Wilmont, 1991, p. 16). These concerns must be addressed before successful negotiation on any issue can be undertaken. Because incompatible goals form the foundation of conflict, working with and making explicit each party's goals is critical to conflict resolution. Relationship and content goals need to be clarified and collaborative goals built (Hocker & Wilmont, 1991).

Scope of Conflict. As mentioned in chapter 6, political strategy must always decide on the desired scope of conflict. "The structure of interest groups in the United States may be characterized in terms of the extent and shape of conflict among participants" (Heinz et al., 1993, p. 248). Schattschneider (1960) said that all fights have an audience and that "the outcome of every conflict is determined by the extent to which the audience becomes involved in it . . . by the scope of its contagion" (p. 2). There is nothing inherently good or bad about a broad or narrow scope of conflict. It depends on what the contestants want. "The distinctive quality of political conflicts is that the relations between the players and the audience have not been well defined and there is usually nothing to keep the audience from getting into the game" (p. 18). In small conflicts, the relative strength of the combatants is known, and the stronger side may not have to fight overtly to impose its will on the weaker, since the weaker will not fight if it stands to lose. However, the weaker side's strength comes from its ability to draw in spectators, or the potentially involved. The spectators do not remain constant and are not representative, but "a free society maximizes the contagion of conflict; it invites intervention and gives a high priority to the participation of the public in conflict" (p. 5). If parties can resolve conflict privately, they will. However, when they cannot, democratic government offers access to those who need to appeal to government. It could be said that politics is the socialization of conflict. "Private conflicts are taken into the public arena precisely because someone wants to make certain that the power ratio among the private interests most immediately involved shall not prevail" (p. 38). It could further be said that the only way to keep the powerful powerful is to keep conflict out of the public arena.

Essential Elements. After assessment and clarification, participant advocates considered a number of elements essential. *Communication* is time-consuming but essential. In addition, according to one advocate, "part of [any coalition] process [is] a great deal of *compromise*, and part of compromise is watering down some of what many of us would like to see." For instance, another participant advocate described a situation in which "the clinical people [AMHCA] . . . have had to be willing to give up the word 'clinical' as a modifier for legislative purposes . . . and ACA's also had to . . . be willing

to give up the word 'professional' in front of the word counselor. . . . All [the legislative proposals] say is 'counseling' now." The current position is, "We are one profession. We have practitioners who are trained in specialty areas, but we have a common core of knowledge that we share."

Coser (1956) underscored the need for *flexibility* in conflict management strategies. He indicated that realistic conflicts are oriented toward the resolution of some substantive problem and thus foster flexibility and a wide range of resolution techniques—force, negotiation, persuasion, and voting. In a constructive conflict, groups change direction often and are guided by the belief that all factions can attain important goals (Deutsch, 1973). People are open to movement when such movement will result in the best decision. There is an effort to bridge the apparent incompatibility of positions. Constructive conflict produces solutions satisfactory to everyone and a general feeling that everyone has gained something. Sometimes constructive conflict is competitive. When both parties stand up for their own positions, tension and hostility may result. However, needs for power, saving face, or making the opponent look bad do not stand in the way of change.

According to Folger and colleagues (1993, p. 230), "*self-regulation* refers to behavior that checks destructive conflict interaction and turns it in a constructive direction." Parties continually need to diagnose emerging problems, and "determine the possible power resources in the situation and identify who holds them" (p. 230). They need to use their diagnoses and quickly alter destructive conflict interaction patterns. Changing these patterns may require a structural change in the parties' relationships, groups, or organizations.

Other Suggestions. What counselors already do with families was suggested as a means to help conflicts move more positively: improving communication skills, reframing, recognizing face-saving, finding a way for one's image to be okay while disagreeing on an issue, or making small changes in interactions so as to make major changes in climate.

Both participant advocates and the literature indicated that using a group processor may be helpful or necessary. One counselor advocate said, "We had meetings of all the people involved so we could help correct invalid assumptions. We set these meetings up in neutral public places, and then people respond differently, better. We also had a person who was really good at listening, letting people vent fears and anxieties." Another said, "Do not get defensive. . . . It's a counseling issue, folks. Work it out!" If counseling organizations have difficulty using their counseling skills, "get a group processor in. . . . Fight it out. But don't present anything publicly until you've done [that]." An outside expert, a "well-placed legislative counsel, used sparingly," can be an additional tool in achieving consensus.

Counselors also need to be models of how to resolve conflicts, and they can do so by being other-concerned, keeping the "big picture perspective," not "deliberating things to death." And finally, those who can agree can "individually persuade the people [who are] guarding particular positions that this is what [has] to be done." Often a smaller group has an easier time achieving consensus and persuading the larger group to join.

Results of Constructive Conflict Management. "Productive conflict takes place within and helps to create productive relationships. Indeed, we may assert that the ability to bear the tension of conflict while pursuing a productive transformation of the conflict may be the most important description of a productive long-term relationship" (Hocker & Wilmont, 1991, p. 39). The results of productive conflict should be what Miller (1986, p. 3) considered the results of growth-producing relationships:

> Each person feels a greater sense of 'zest' (vitality, energy). Each person feels more able to act and does act.
>
> Each person has a more accurate picture of her/himself and the other person(s).
>
> Each person feels a greater sense of worth.
>
> Each person feels more connected to the other person(s) and a greater motivation for connections with other people beyond those in the specific relationship.

Overall, people should experience more cooperation between parties and more satisfying exchanges, and they should use and hear more positive personality attributions about the other party.

STYLES OF APPROACHING CONFLICT

Although the participant advocates did not specifically address people's styles of approaching conflict, or what the benefits and problems associated with each style are, the literature is quite helpful on this. Folger and colleagues (1993, p. 4) claimed that "we believe that the key to working through conflict is not to minimize its disadvantages, or even to emphasize its positive functions, but to accept both and to try to understand *how* conflicts move in destructive or productive directions."

The human relations perspective on conflict (Blake & Mouton, 1964; Hall, 1986) identifies five types of conflict behavior, varying on the dimensions of assertiveness and cooperativeness: competing, avoiding, accommodating, compromising, and problem solving.

Competing

In competing, the

> primary emphasis [is] on satisfying the party's own concerns and disregard of others' concerns. It is a closed style, low to moderate in disclosiveness; parties make their demands apparent but often hide their true motives and any other information that might weaken their position. Competers are quite active and highly involved in the conflict. Competers aggressively pursue personal goals, taking any initiatives necessary to achieve them. Flexibility is generally low in the competing style. Competers attempt to avoid sacrificing any goals, instead using any effective means to compel others to satisfy their concerns. This requires that competers attempt to control the situation and to deny others power or control (Folger et al., 1991, p. 187).

The pattern goes like this: start high, concede slowly, exaggerate the value of your concessions, conceal information, argue forcefully, and be willing to outwait the other (Lax & Sebenius, 1986, p. 32). Threats, confrontation, argumentation, and manipulation are used. A competing style should be used when there is not much time, or when the superior's needs or position are very important and agreement seems unlikely.

The disadvantages of this style are that resistance and resentment may develop. The use of power may ultimately undermine one's power base. This style is hard on relationships; it breeds mistrust and feelings of separateness, frustration, and anger; and it may result in more frequent breakdowns in negotiations, distortion of communication, misinformation, and misjudgment. It restricts access to joint gains, and creates many opportunities for impasse. It increases difficulty in predicting the responses of the opponent because parties rely on manipulation and confrontation to control the process. The focus is not on a relatively objective analysis of the substantive merits, so there may be an overestimation of the payoffs possible through alternatives such as litigation (Murray, 1986, p. 184).

Avoiding

In the avoiding style, parties "show low levels of concern with both their own and other parties' concerns" (Folger et al., 1991, p. 189). Folger and colleagues (1991) further indicated that while parties are avoiding, issues are not aired, addressed, or resolved and may resurface destructively in the future. Parties who avoid demonstrate apathy, a low level of activeness, and a low level of disclosiveness, and they attempt to disempower others by denying them the possibility of dealing with the conflict.

Three tools used by avoiders are protecting, withdrawing, and smoothing. When *protecting,* parties are determined to avoid conflict at all costs, as though conflict automatically means crisis. *Withdrawing* is a softer, more subtle, flexible, way to keep issues off the table by being apologetic or changing the subject. *Smoothing* involves playing down differences, emphasizing common ground, emphasizing the positive, and spending time on other issues besides those involved in the conflict.

Avoiding is helpful when chances of successful problem solving or compromising are slight and when parties' needs can be met without surfacing the conflict. Avoiding may also be necessary if a party has a very weak position or faces a formidable opponent. It may enable a party to save face. But avoiding can impede the development of relationships and result in "walking on eggshells." It may anger others, encouraging them to compete.

Accommodating

According to Folger and colleagues (1991, p. 189), accommodating "permits others to realize their concerns, but gives less attention to the party's own concerns. Accommodators basically give in to others." Accommodating is useful to relationships in that it can improve a bad or shaky relationship or preserve a good one. Accommodators are highly flexible, demonstrate a low level of activeness, and are not involved in the issues but in the relationship. They demonstrate a low to moderate level of dis-

closiveness and learn a great deal about the other party's concerns. They empower the other party and suspend their own control. Accommodating is useful when one party is weaker than the other and will lose in any competition.

Compromising

Compromising requires moderate levels of assertiveness and cooperativeness, and requires "both parties to give up some of their needs in order to fulfill others" (Folger et al., 1991, p. 190). Compromisers demonstrate a moderate range of flexibility, are moderate to high in activeness, are moderate to high in disclosiveness, and attempt to empower themselves and others for the purpose of shared control. *Firm compromising* is a tough approach and involves limited flexibility in position and low to moderate disclosure, but offers trade-offs. *Flexible compromising* is more cooperative. Positions are less well-defined, so parties share thoughts and positions in order to evolve compromises. "Compromises often attain a low level of commitment from parties because they force parties to give up something they value" (Folger et al., 1991, p. 191).

Problem Solving

In problem solving, the "goal is to develop a solution that meets all important needs of both parties and does not lead to any significant disadvantages" (Folger et al., 1991, p. 191). Burke (1970) stated the following characteristics of a problem-solving approach to conflict:

- Both parties have a vested interest in the outcome.

- They believe that they can resolve [the problem] and find a better solution through collaboration.

- Conflict is in the relationship, not in each person separately.

- Parties are concerned with solving the problem, not accommodating different points of view.

- They explore and test alternative solutions.

- They are problem minded instead of solution minded, maintaining fluid instead of fixed positions.

- Both positions in the controversy have potential strengths and weaknesses.

- The parties try to understand the problem from the other's point of view.

- They look at the conflict objectively, not taking it personally.

- They examine their own attitudes.

- They understand less effective methods of conflict resolution.

- They allow people to give without attributing it to weakness.

- They minimize the effects of status differences and defensiveness.

- They are aware of the limitations of arguing or presenting evidence in favor of one's own position while degrading the opponent's position.

Collaborative negotiation, part of a problem-solving approach, assumes that the parties have both diverse and common interests, and that bargaining can gain something for each party. Collaborative negotiation assumes that (a) the negotiating world is controlled by enlightened self-interest, (b) common interests are valued, (c) interdependence is recognized, (d) there are limited resources with unlimited variations in personal preference, (e) the resource distribution system is integrative, and (f) the goal is a mutually agreeable solution that is fair to all parties and efficient for community. In collaborative negotiation each party tries to maximize its own returns, including any joint gains available; to focus on the common interests of the parties; to understand the merits as objectively as possible; to use nonconfrontational debating techniques; to remain open to persuasion on substance; and to stay oriented to the qualitative goal of achieving a fair, wise, and durable agreement, efficiently negotiated (Murray, 1986).

The disadvantages of collaborative negotiation are that it requires a great deal of time and energy and enhances hopes that might not play out. Further, it requires "a high order of intelligence, keen perception and discrimination . . . [and] brilliant inventiveness" (Follett, 1940, p. 45). It requires specific training. It is strongly biased toward cooperation,

creating internal pressures to compromise and accommodate. It avoids strategies that are confrontational because they risk impasse, which is viewed as failure. It focuses on being sensitive to the other's perceived interests, increasing vulnerability to deception and manipulation by a competitive opponent, and it increases the possibility that settlement may be more favorable to the other side than fairness would warrant. A problem-solving approach increases the difficulty of establishing definite aspiration levels and bottom lines because of its reliance on qualitative goals (Murray, 1986).

Research results point to the benefits and deficits of particular conflict strategies, styles, or tactics. Jones and White (1985) found that problem-solving groups confronting conflict were more effective in task accomplishment than accommodating groups. The more group members differ in their preference for a confrontational approach, the less effective the group is. Phillips and Cheston (1979) found that a problem-solving (collaboration) approach yields fewer bad results than does forcing. Lawrence and Lorsch (1967) found problem-solving endorsed as most effective in six different types of organizations. Competing was a useful backup. Burke's (1970) study agreed but also found smoothing to be useful sometimes. Wall, Galanes, and Love (1987) found that open recognition and expression of conflict tended to increase the quality of outcomes. Spitzberg (1990, as cited in Folger et al., 1993) found that parties' perceptions of their own competence and effectiveness positively correlated with use of collaborative strategies and negatively correlated with use of competitive strategies.

What is very clear in the literature's discussions of various styles or tactics that can be used in conflict situations is that experts in conflict management encourage different approaches. Flexibility is advocated. The approach should depend on the context, the participants, the issues, and the stage of the conflict. No one "right" way exists. Although a problem-solving approach has been supported by research as most effective, it is not always possible or appropriate.

SUMMARY

The results of the research done for this book made it clear that counselors have many ideas on the negative impacts of conflict on advocacy, and a few ideas of the positive impacts. They indicated that the negative effects of *within-group* conflicts are

- stress, tension, fatigue, and somatic complaints;

- secrecy, distrust, polarization, and decrease in respect;

- domination of the conflict in meetings, conversations, and staff time, and exclusion of other agenda items;

- worries that one's interests will not be represented or that staff will lose their jobs;

- no unification on goals and priorities and difficulty achieving these, difficulty presenting a unified voice to decisionmakers, and not enough numbers to make an impact on issues (no teamwork);

- loss by consumers because there is no energy or time left for their issues; and

- an internal focus that detracts from external focus and that distracts from concern about the future because the focus is on now.

The negative impacts of *intergroup* conflicts were identified by research participants as

- loss of status with insurance companies, legislators, and funding sources, as well as exclusion, lawsuits, and a cycle of abuse

- decisionmaker confusion;

- winning by those with the most PAC money, so policy tends toward the traditional and no progress is made; and

- public confusion.

The literature added that intergroup polarization

- causes a closed view toward the other group, which is viewed stereotypically;

- minimizes similarities between the in-group and the other group;

- results in no reflection on the merits of the other groups' views; and

- suppresses disagreements in the in-group.

The positive impacts of conflict identified by the participant advocates were

- an increased sense of professional identity and unification as an organization;

- the development of political savvy;

- an increased motivation for advocacy and increased advocacy activities;

- the formation of coalitions with other underdogs;

- an increased alertness of legislators regarding real versus turf issues;

- the knowledge of which issues the group needs to advocate about;

- a clarification of what is really important;

- keeping people on their toes; and

- an increased maturity, adopting the politics of inclusion and approaching advocacy targets from a position of strength.

The literature agreed that conflict helps individuals and groups know what the issues are and clarify what is important. It added that conflict

- is a chance for growth, new life, and change;

- produces new and creative ideas;

- releases built-up tension;

- can strengthen relationships; and

- can stimulate social change to eliminate inequities and injustice.

What is particularly notable in comparing participant advocates' views on conflict with those of the literature is that participant advocates focused primarily on the negative impacts of conflict while the literature focused on effective management of conflict. This difference reflects an inherent value differential between counselor advocates and conflict experts. That is, counselor advocates seem fairly intent on preventing or reducing conflict. The existence of conflict implies some sort of failure on their part, or not having reached the "ideal." Perhaps this attitude accounts for the levels of stress experienced by counselor advocates in the midst of the ACA—AMHCA conflict. Further, advocates seem to experience greater stress as a result of within-group conflicts. They seem to expect, plan for, and strategize about existing intergroup conflicts.

Conversely, both conflict experts and politicians stress the inherent value of conflict, and that the management of conflict determines its end results. According to these experts, counselor advocates operate from a belief system that hampers effective conflict management and thus results in negative outcomes for participants. Counseling coursework currently stresses communication and negotiation as the methods for overcoming conflict, but it rarely imputes any positive value to conflict. Since conflict is inevitable and since counselors are so stressed by it, perhaps coursework during counselor education needs to include conflict management.

Conflict is a natural and inevitable part of most interpersonal involvements; it is particularly inherent in the American political process, of which advocacy is a part. As in a family, conflict can either be characterized and played out as abuse *or* as disagreements that lead to greater growth. If counselors expect and plan for conflict, and develop their skills in managing conflict and building consensus, perhaps they will find conflicts less personally threatening. Certainly the gain in the sense of personal powerfulness vis-à-vis conflict situations should decrease the sense that conflict means crisis.

Chapter 10

CHANGING PUBLIC POLICY LEGISLATIVELY

"Anyone who views lawmaking in Congress as a precise, neat process of drafting, debating, and approving legislation overlooks the dynamic forces at work on Capitol Hill. It is not a static institution" (Oleszek, 1989, p. 283). In fact, John Dingell (D-MI) said, "Legislation is like a chess game more than anything else. It is a seemingly endless series of moves, until ultimately somebody prevails through exhaustion, or brilliance, or because of overwhelming public sentiment for their side" (Maraniss, 1983, p. A-1). Counselors often feel intimidated by the political process. They feel hampered by not knowing the rules of the game and by the overwhelming size of government. And yet, according to the research done for this book, legislative change is most frequently that change which counselors view as necessary. Gaining licensure or certification, instituting freedom-of-choice legislation, pursuing legislation to fund school counseling programs, or including counselors in such legislation as the Public Health Services Act occupies a great deal of advocacy and government relations time at the American Counseling Association (ACA) and in its state branches.

The professional association's government relations training, designed to reduce counselors' feelings of intimidation, inform counselors about the legislative system, and motivate them to take action, is necessarily brief and narrowly focused. It focuses primarily on the particular legislation currently being targeted, and on the very specific "how-to's" for talking with or writing to legislators. It rarely encompasses the broader field of policy making, and the procedures and politics involved in adopting legislation.

The purpose of this chapter is to comprehensively describe the process by which legislation is adopted, specifically drawing attention to the political strategies and procedural tactics used. The goal is to increase the sophistication of counselors' understanding so that they can increase the effectiveness of their strategies and become influential players in this "game." To do this, counselors must see policy making as more exciting and maneuverable than a dry set of rules and regulations; they must understand the mechanics and political uses of those mechanics; and they must be more adept at questioning and challenging their lobbyists, rather than solely relying on lobbyists to tell them what to do. Counselors need not become experts in the legislative "game of chess" (Maraniss, 1983, p. A-14) to be effective. However, they must be aware of the number of legislative decision points on which they can take action.

The focus here will be on national legislative processes, so the guidance given should not be applied carte blanche to state processes. It should instead be used to stimulate discussion within the state counseling association, and with any lobbyist the association chooses, about possible actions that might be taken. The chapter begins with a review of the principles presented in Kingdon's (1984) and Oleszek's books, and then specifically analyzes these books with respect to potential counselor action.

POLICY FORMATION

Counselors can be instrumental in influencing public policy during the policy formation stage. Among other things, they can influence the problems on which legislators focus and they can help define problems in ways most likely to draw legislative support.

As indicated in chapter 6, Kingdon (1984) asserted that three streams—the problem stream, the policy stream, and the political stream—must converge simultaneously for a policy window to be opened and an issue to be acted on favorably by

Congress (see Figure 10.1). The policy stream involves interest groups, scientists and academics, policy entrepreneurs, and others who are continually stirring around a "policy primeval soup" (p. 222) of favorite solutions and possible programs. They watch for the right problem and politics to arise to bring their preferred solution into the foreground. The problem stream means that certain conditions or events occur that raise problematic situations to the government's decision agenda by making them valid problems on which to focus. National crises or evaluation data from existing government programs might be two of the conditions that draw legislators' attention to a particular problem. The political stream is equivalent to the political environment. Kingdon indicates that the national mood or

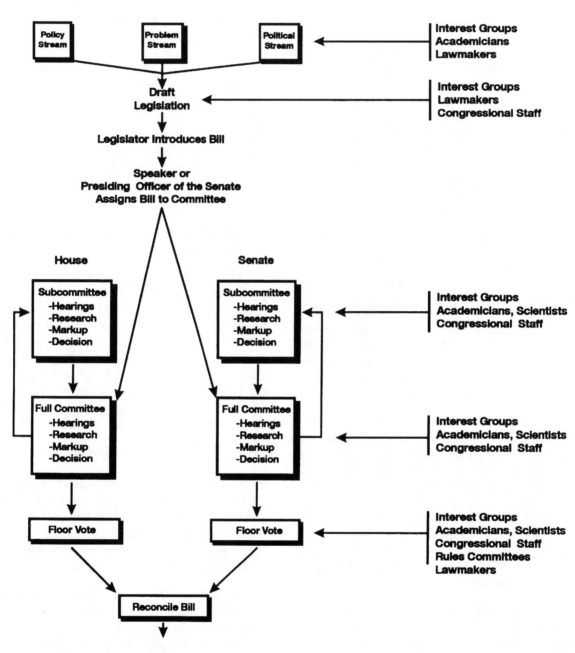

Figure 10.1. The Legislative Process.

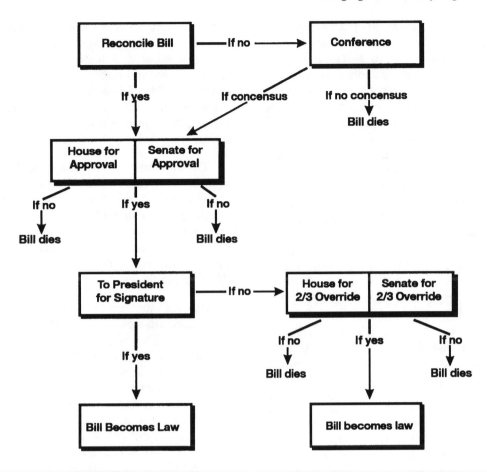

Figure 10.1. The Legislative Process (*Continued*).

the administration's agenda need to be right for legislators to take action. Action, said Kingdon, requires the "confluence" of these three streams.

The inclusion of counselors in the Public Health Services Act provides a perfect example of Kingdon's assertions. Counselors believe that they should be included as core providers in the Public Health Services Act and the Federal Employee Health Benefits Program (FEHBP), just as psychiatrists, psychologists, social workers, and nurses are (Public Health Services Act, section 303.(d)(1)). This solution—that is, counselor inclusion—is what Kingdon would refer to as the policy stream.

Why should legislators care about counselors' desire for inclusion? And even if they think it is a nice idea, what would make them care enough to take the kind of action necessary to get the desired legislation passed? Kingdon claimed that policy

entrepreneurs would find a problem to which to attach their solution—this is the problem stream—perhaps something the legislature recently has identified as a problem, or something a powerful legislator considers a problem. In the case of counselor inclusion in the Public Health Service Act and FEHBP, a suitable problem existed. Congress has identified a shortage of mental health service providers willing and available to work in rural areas and competent to provide services to children, the elderly, the seriously mentally ill, and minorities (Wohlford, Myers, & Callan, 1993). This became the problem that counselors could offer to help solve, if legislators would legitimize—by inclusion in legislation—the 350,000 master's-degreed counselors nationwide.

Kingdon claimed that if the political climate—that is, the political stream—is not right, legislators will still not take action; but a number of factors combined to make the climate right in this situation. First, the stigma associated with mental health problems and services has decreased over time. Second, health insurance coverage, including coverage for mental health care, has become more standard. In fact, the federal government's insurance coverage has lagged behind private coverage, putting federal employees at a disadvantage with respect to using counselor services. Further, mental health coverage was spotlighted when Tipper Gore championed its inclusion in the Health Security Act. Finally, and perhaps most important, the Minority Health Improvement Act, Title VII of the Public Health Services Act, needed reauthorization in 1993. Because the Public Health Services Act served as the guide for including mental health care providers in other federal legislation, counselors focused on it as the prerequisite to getting other federal legislation to be even more inclusive. Counselor inclusion in the Public Health Service Act was added as an amendment to the proposed Minority Health Improvement Reauthorization Act, the reauthorization of which was considered an easy pass.

The confluence of these three streams resulted in the launching of counselor inclusion in the Public Health Services Act through a policy window onto the decision agenda. The Reauthorization Act passed both houses in Spring of 1994. Unfortunately, the House and Senate bills differed enough to require conferencing. The bill produced in conference passed the House. However, at the last hour of the 103rd Congress, three senators put a hold on the bill. Their disagreement was with other portions of the bill, not with counselor inclusion. Nevertheless, counselors needed to find another vehicle for their "solution" during the 104th Congress.

POLICY ADOPTION

Introducing the Bill

After congressional members, interest groups, the executive branch, or others agree on the problem, the solution, and the timing, they draft and introduce a bill. The most important action counselors can take at this stage is drafting or assisting with drafting the bill. This assistance might include providing language for the part of the bill with which they are particularly concerned.

Introducing a bill involves a House member dropping the bill into the "hopper," the box near the clerk's desk, or a Senate member submitting the bill to the clerk or introducing it from the floor. The bill is then numbered, sometimes associated with a name, printed, and made available to the members and to the public (Oleszek, 1989; all further legislative information is from Oleszek's book, except the analysis of counselor's roles, or unless otherwise indicated).

The bill is referred to the appropriate standing committee. Officially, the referral is made by the Speaker of the House and the Presiding Officer of the Senate, but actually the parliamentarian of each chamber makes the referral. Decisions about referrals are generally straightforward, and are made on the basis of precedent, law, and jurisdictional mandates.

Although they are the exception rather than the rule, certain strategies can alter the standard referral process. A bill can be drafted ambiguously, so referral is less clear-cut, in order to set up the possibility of review by a less hostile committee. Or the bill can be framed as an amendment and added to statutes over which a friendly committee has jurisdiction. The bills must be referred to a primary committee of jurisdiction, but additional referrals may be made to other committees; the additional committees may only consider those items falling under their jurisdiction. The Speaker controls when these additional committees receive legislation and how long they have to act on it (Evans & Oleszek, 1995). In the House, an ad hoc committee can also be formed of members from different committees. In the Senate, the referral or multiple referral is usually decided prior to the bill's introduction.

Although in most circumstances, counselors can have little impact on the referral of the bill, in exceptional circumstances, they may be able to draft or amend a bill in such a way as to have it considered by the most favorable committee. Lobbyists or legislators, experts in playing the game, would be the best advisors in these circumstances.

Committee Work

The committee stage is one of the most important to counselors trying to influence public policy. There are many, very public decision points of which counselors must be aware, and many actions they can take at these decision points. First, counselors can educate, lobby, and otherwise build relationships with all of the players: the committee chair, the staff, and the members. Second, counselors can help the committee do its research, preparing and supplying documentation on an issue. Third, counselors can suggest expert witnesses or prepare themselves to be expert witnesses at the hearings. Finally, counselors can draft the questions to be used in the committee hearings.

Committee work is open to public observation and a committee has recourse to several actions. It can (a) consider and report (approve) a bill, with or without amendments; (b) send the bill to the House or Senate for a vote; (c) rewrite the bill entirely; (d) reject the bill; or (e) fail to consider it, which effectively "kills" the bill. The committee and its staff become the experts on the issue, and therefore the House or Senate will generally accept the committee's recommendations for the bill. As a result, committee work is critical to the legislative process, and counselors need to be particularly knowledgeable about how to impact this process.

The chair of the committee has considerable power in the process. He or she decides the committee's agenda, refers bills to subcommittee, and manages both the committee's staff and its funds. If the chair opposes a bill, he or she can decide not to schedule a bill, to let the hearings drag on forever, to have the staff "stack" the witnesses, to ask those in favor of the bill to send statements while those opposed appear in person, to recognize committee members who oppose the bill (i.e., to allow them to speak), and/or to instruct staff to disregard the bill. Likewise, if the committee chair is in favor of a bill, he or she can mobilize staff resources, compress the time for hearings and markups, achieving a lot very quickly, influence powerfully the course of the bill, and time testimony so as to have the desired impact. If the bill is major or controversial, the chair will generally refer the bill to a subcommittee. Hearings may be held in subcommittee as well.

Hearings serve a variety of purposes. They can be used, as one would generally expect, as a fact-finding instrument, to explore problems and issues. Committees may thus use hearings to determine if the legislation is actually needed or if it is the best action. Hearings often have more political purposes, however. They can be used to educate and elevate the awareness of the media, other legislators, and the public. Hearings also provide a permanent, pub-

lic record of the issues and the members' positions, as well as legitimizing the members' decisions. Finally, hearings allow legislators to assess the intensity of the support or opposition to a bill. Sometimes private "prehearings" are held for the same purposes, allowing for private questioning and assessment of the information.

Committee staff play a significant role in the hearing process. They decide who should testify at the hearings so as to generate public support for the desired position. They decide what witnesses should say. They preinterview and prepare the witnesses, and they do all the preparatory work, researching the issues thoroughly, compiling documentation, and drafting the questions to be asked at the hearings.

Hearings can be conducted in Washington or in the "field." During the hearings, witnesses present prepared talks and committee members ask prepared questions. No extended interchanges and no in-depth analyses take place. Anything in-depth generally takes place off the record, privately.

Following the hearings, the bill is "marked up." This means that line-by-line consideration is given to the bill by committee members, any desired amendments are debated, and parts of the bill may be rewritten. During the markup, the chair attempts to generate consensus, because the greater the consensus, the greater the bill's chances of passing on the floor. As a result, a great deal of bargaining and compromise over language and inclusions occurs at this stage, and the greater the importance of the bill's passage, the greater the compromise. Although the markup is held publicly, the bargaining and compromising may not be.

A variety of strategies may be used during the markup phase. Amendments may be added to strengthen the bill. Strengthening some bills weakens their chance of passage on the floor; strengthening others may increase chances of passage. Sometimes a flurry of amendments is generated to confuse and complicate the issue and make the bill unworkable. Other times, amendments are specifically sought and added to increase each committee member's stake in the bill. Again, expertise is necessary to play this game successfully. Counseling's presence during this phase may be quite important. It may serve to remind a staff member of counseling's interest or to enable counselors to offer advice or suggestions on improving a proposed amendment.

Once the bill has been marked up, the subcommittee or committee votes on it. The committee can vote to recommend revisions, can report the bill unfavorably, or can report out the bill (approve the bill and send it on) with recommendations. They can also vote to have the chair introduce a "clean bill." This means that if a bill has extensive revisions and amendments, the chair can introduce all of these as a completely new bill. There is then less chance that portions of the bill or certain amendments will be voted down on the floor. Finally, the committee can choose not to take action, killing the bill. If all of the above action has taken place in subcommittee, the bill is then reported on to the full committee. The full committee can choose to repeat the whole process, or they can simply accept the subcommittee work as their own and report out the bill as the subcommittee has recommended.

Following the vote, the chair instructs the staff to prepare a report. The report includes the committee's decisions and recommendations, and all the reasons for these. Dissenters can add their own statements. The report is the principal means to inform the remainder of the legislators of the committee's decision and to persuade them to support that decision.

Once reported, the bill is assigned a number and both the bill and accompanying report are assigned to a calendar to await scheduling for a floor vote. During this wait, committee members try to raise support for or against the bill.

The committee chair, staff, and members play powerful and important roles in the committee process. Counselors should never underestimate the power of phone calls and letters to these people. Also, as is probably clear from what's been stated so far, legislators play the game so as to accomplish what they want, while pleasing as many of their constituents as possible. Sometimes they will be able to satisfy their constituents with certain actions, despite knowing full well that these actions will actually hamper constituent goals in the end. However, when failure occurs, they still point to these positive actions on behalf of their constituents in trying to persuade their constituents to be pleased with them. Again, expert lobbying advice can some-

times preempt this. Also, as a past president of the American Mental Health Counselors' Association said, "It's not over 'til it's over!" In other words, counselors need to keep pressing and lobbying on all fronts, regardless of what appears to be a success.

Floor Action in the House

Of all the steps in the legislative process, floor action is probably that with which counselors most associate the whole of the legislative process, and with which they are most familiar. Most counselors have been asked at some time in their career to write their representative and ask him or her to vote in a certain manner on a bill on the floor. As in the committee stage, in the House floor process there are many decision points with which counselors need to be concerned. A review of Oleszek's work draws attention to some available strategies that counselors would likely overlook.

Reporting a bill out of committee does not guarantee action on the floor of either chamber. In the House, scheduling a bill for action is a political process in and of itself. Bills are placed on one of five calendars—the Private, the Consent, the House, the Union, or the Discharge calendar—by the Speaker of the House, the majority leader, and the majority whip. The Private Calendar is for bills of a private nature. The Consent Calendar is for noncontroversial measures. The Union Calendar is for legislation dealing with raising, authorizing, or spending money. The Discharge Calendar lists bills removed from committees through special procedures (Walton, 1969). The Private and Consent calendars expedite the legislative process. Scheduling is influenced by House rules; budgetary timetables; bicameral considerations (i.e., action needed in both houses during the same time frame); election year activities; national and international events; the leadership's policy and political preferences; the administration's programs; actions of the Rules Committee; the scheduling of recesses and adjournment; the need to coordinate floor and committee action and provide a steady, predictable weekly agenda; and *mystery.*

Suspension of rules is another way to expedite the legislative process. On Mondays, Tuesdays, and the last six days of the legislative session, any bill can be brought to a vote by "suspending the rules"— if the Speaker recognizes the representative offering the motion. Suspension of the rules is usually used on bills that can easily draw a two-thirds majority vote; those requiring fast, emergency action; and those that have not been reported out of committee. Nevertheless, this procedure can be used on any bill. Bills brought to a vote in this way are protected from floor amendments and points of order, which makes this procedure advantageous. The vast majority of bills are passed by suspension of the rules or by placement on the Private or Consent calendars.

Bills placed on the House and Union calendars are theoretically acted on in chronological order. However, in reality, six committees are considered "privileged"—Budget, Appropriations, Ways and Means, House Administration, and Rules of Standards of Conduct—and thus have immediate access to the floor. Further, committee chairs can ask for a "rule," which means a ruling from the House Rules Committee. The Rules Committee can decide when a bill is scheduled, what the parameters of debate are (how many people, how many minutes), what precedence will be given to the bill's amendments, and whether points of order can be waived. Clearly, because the Rules Committee's procedures can be used for political ends, it plays a critical role in the legislative process.

The Rules Committee holds hearings and operates much like the other standing committees. It serves several purposes. First, it is an agent of the leadership, preventing delays and encouraging the orderly consideration of legislation. It also "takes the heat" for the rest of Congress, drawing fire away from the leadership, members, and committees if most are opposed to a bill, by preventing legislation from reaching the floor. It resolves jurisdictional disputes between committees, decreases fights between committees, and simplifies floor decision making.

Rules Committee members are positioned well to get their own proposals attached to bills. They can delay rules, and thus floor action, by "failing" to have a quorum present at the committee meeting, by scheduling a parade of witnesses to testify against issuing a rule, by strict observance of rarely used procedures, and/or by scheduling votes so that certain members are there and others are not. Because of this delaying power, they can bargain for amendments or changes to bills in exchange for desired rules.

After a rule is granted by the Rules Committee, it must be adopted by the full House. Although one hour of debate is allowed, the rule is rarely rejected. If it is rejected, it amounts to a procedural "kill," without members having to oppose the bill itself.

If a committee fails to report out a bill or if the rule is rejected, the House has several other options for acting on a bill. On a noncontroversial bill, suspension of rules can allow for expedited action. On a major bill, four possibilities exist. First, 218 members can file a discharge petition after the bill has been in committee 30 days. The motion is put on the Discharge calendar for 7 days, and then becomes "privileged" on the second and fourth Mondays of the month. If the discharge motion is approved, any of the 218 petitioners can bring the issue up for consideration immediately. Although the discharge petition focuses attention on important issues, it is very difficult to use successfully because most members feel they need the committee's expertise and because 218 member signatures are hard to acquire.

A second method of overriding a committee's failure to report out a bill is the Rules Committee's extraction power. The Rules Committee can make rules for bills the committees have not reported yet, thus forcing floor action. This occurs very rarely, but its threat can help break committee logjams. Third, if the Rules Committee fails to take action after seven days, the discharge petition can be applied to the Rules Committee itself. And finally, on Wednesdays, standing committees can call up nonprivileged bills that are on the House and Union calendars. This final method is of limited usefulness because alphabetical calling of committees results in some bills waiting weeks. Also, if action is not finished during one Wednesday, the bill must go through the alphabetical process all over again the next Wednesday.

When a rule is adopted, a Committee of the Whole debates the bill. The Committee of the Whole is a small segment of the House whose quorum is 100 and who debates the bill briefly. The floor managers—the committee's chair and ranking minority leader of the committee—direct the debate. Usually, debate consists of one hour of prepared speeches. The debate has symbolic value and places positions on public record, but few opinions are changed by the minimal give-and-take involved.

The fate of much legislation is in the hands of the floor managers. During the Committee of the Whole, bills can be killed by various delaying tactics, such as adding trivial amendments, raising numerous points of order, or making scores of parliamentary inquiries. The delaying process can also be used strategically to allow more time to raise support.

The amending process is the heart of the decision-making process in the Committee of the Whole. The rationales for using amendments are diverse. Some amendments are enormous and are only used because reading them will delay the process. Some are added in deference to pressure groups or constituents. Amendments can be added to amendments, but these have limitations and a specified voting order, so much strategizing goes into the amendment process. The goal is to maneuver oneself into the right position at the right time for the right vote.

The Committee of the Whole then votes, "rises" (dissolves), and reports back to the full House. No further debate is allowed, although parts of the bill can be voted on separately and a variety of pro forma questions are asked before final passage.

Knowledge of the floor process suggests several strategies for counselors. For instance, a noncontroversial bill can be expedited by being placed on the Consent calendar; thus, drafting a noncontroversial bill can be an advantage. If a noncontroversial bill related to mental health care has been introduced, a counselor might be able to persuade their member of Congress to add to that bill an amendment favorable to counselors, allowing the bill to pull the amendment through. Further, if a counseling-related bill has gotten bogged down in a committee, it is good to know that a member of Congress could bring it to the floor by suspension of the rules. Cultivating relationships with legislators on the Rules Committee is thus a good idea. A Rules Committee friend could be in a position to bargain for inclusion of a counseling amendment or to set up favorable rules for floor action on a more major bill.

It is particularly interesting to note how few representatives must actually be present for House business to take place. Counselors would generally consider 218 members a lot to persuade. But it seems that if no one calls for a quorum, only a few representatives are required to make decisions.

Finally, it is interesting to observe the expertise that is necessary to play the game in the rules and amending processes. One wonders how freshman members manage to succeed at the game at all. It certainly would behoove counselors to have an experienced member on their side.

Floor Action in the Senate

By virtue of being less than one quarter the size of the House, the Senate has a completely different atmosphere and manner of operating. It seems, however, that counselors can utilize many of the same strategies in approaching the Senate as have been suggested for approaching the committees.

Some specific differences in the Senate floor procedures are worth noting. Historically, the Senate has been more responsive to individual senators' needs than the House is to the needs of individual representatives because of the greater demands on senators' time. Further, what actually occurs in the Senate relies on informal rules with very little resemblance to what the formal rules specify. Overall, the Senate operates in a more flexible manner and has a tradition of cooperation.

Other specific differences are that votes in the Senate are held on Mondays and Fridays, and the Senate works for three weeks and is then off one week. Votes on important bills are scheduled according to what is convenient for the key senators. Scheduling thus requires a great deal of discussing and pressuring. Only two calendars exist in the Senate, and action can be taken on either calendar on any voting day. There are no procedures comparable to the House. In fact, the Senate rules that do exist are so cumbersome that they are ignored.

Perhaps the most important difference in the way the Senate operates is what is called "unanimous consent." Ninety-eight percent of all bills and all noncontroversial bills are called up by unanimous consent. This means that in almost all legislation, a single dissent blocks the entire process. The principle of unanimous consent requires a great deal of private negotiation, and requires that everyone protect everyone else's interests. Otherwise, if one senator is mistreated, he or she could eventually block most legislation. Before most legislation is brought to the floor, therefore, discussions, negotiations, and bargaining take place privately until unanimous agreement is reached.

There are many ways in the Senate to block a motion, delay action on a bill, or put pressure on others to act in one's favor. A senator could threaten a filibuster, stopping all activity on that bill. He or she could take the measure off the calendar. Or as alluded to before, he or she could object to all unanimous consent motions until his or her measure is scheduled. Quorum calls also can be used to delay action so that unanimous consent can be reached. Finally, a hold can be placed on a bill. A hold is an informal and private process that stops floor discussion with very few people knowing who arranged for the hold. On bills that only two or three senators care about, holds are a particularly effective blocking device and are used to encourage bargaining.

Floor managers in the Senate are great strategists and have privileged recognition. They rely heavily on staff assistance, even while on the floor. In general, however, strategic moves are not observed during the floor debate. Extended give-and-take in the floor debate is the exception rather than the rule, similar to House floor debates. The strategies are more procedural and behind the scenes.

The amendment process in the Senate differs significantly from that of the House in that there is no Rules Committee to determine how many amendments can be added or how long amendments can be debated. Amendments can be added by a motion at any time in any bill brought to the floor. The precedence principle can affect the number of amendments pending simultaneously and the order of voting on them. This principle is used strategically by senators.

The primary lesson for counselors with respect to Senate operations seems to be to get as many senators as possible to agree to a counseling-related bill prior to a floor vote, or to nurture relationships with senators who are able to build the kind of consensus necessary to garner unanimous consent.

Reconciling the House and Senate Bills

Before a bill can be forwarded to the president to be signed into law (or vetoed), it must pass both houses in identical form. So, after initial passage of the Senate and House bills, the two bills must be reconciled. Reconciliation is a very important step in the legislative process, and one during which counselors need to keep lobbying their members of Congress, using methods similar to those used dur-

ing the committee and floor stages. In particular, counselors need to keep their members of Congress informed about why one chamber's bill is better than the other's, or why certain amendments are critical.

Reconciliation can be accomplished in several ways. A request for a conference can be made, the purpose of which is to allow members of each house to negotiate until agreement can be reached on the bill. The majority of bills are reconciled without a conference, however. In nonconference reconciliation, one house can adopt the other house's bill verbatim, or the bill can be sent back and forth between the houses, with amendments being made until agreement is reached. Usually, informal and private strategy sessions are held to develop ways to achieve reconciliation. Congress tries to avoid conferencing a bill because of the risk of a time-consuming deadlock, and the risk of weakening the bill.

About 6 percent of bills are conferenced. It is clear ahead of time which bills will be conferenced, and legislators use strategies during floor action to set themselves up well for winning in the conference. For instance, legislators will stake out absolute and extreme positions on the floor that they can then back away from in conference. They might add many expendable amendments on the floor to use as bargaining chips, and in conference put up a fight before dropping them. They might deliberately leave out some measure they know the other house wants so they can "offer" it during the conference. These strategies make it difficult to tell which chamber "won" the conference based solely on the number of issues "given up."

Reconciliation occurs as follows: After the House and Senate pass companion bills, one chamber sends their bill to the other chamber. If, for example, the House sends its bill to the Senate, the Senate could accept the House version verbatim or amend it and return it to the House. The House then has several choices: It can refuse to take action, in which case the bill dies; it can approve an entirely new version of the bill and return it to the Senate; it can agree to the Senate amendments; it can amend the bill further and return it to the Senate; or it can request a conference. If the Senate bill begins the process, the same possibilities exist, except that an entirely new version of the bill requires returning the bill to the appropriate standing committee.

If the Speaker of the House or the presiding officer of the Senate decides that a conference is necessary to resolve differences in the bill, he or she ask for and receives unanimous consent from the chamber to request a conference. Selection of the conferees is sometimes critical to the conference outcome, so attempts are made to select conferees who will best represent that chamber's views.

Once the conferees are selected, the bargaining begins. A chair is selected in an ad hoc fashion, and he or she sets the pace of the bargaining, proposes compromises, recommends tentative agreements, sets the agendas and order of the disagreements to be negotiated, and arranges the time and place of the meetings. The conferees' goals are to sustain their chamber's position and to achieve a result acceptable to the majority of their chamber—since the conferenced bill will have to be passed by their chamber. Staff research and information, outside pressures from interest groups and party leaders, timing, leadership, fatigue, the impact of threats, and an investment in upholding the prestige of their own chamber all critically influence conferencing.

Once the conferees reach consensus, a conference report that details the decisions made and their justifications is prepared by the staff. The report is printed in the *Congressional Record* and then brought up for action on the floor of each chamber. Conference reports have privileged status and so are acted on immediately. Each house must accept or reject the bill in its entirety, and it is seldom rejected.

Upon adoption by both houses, the papers are returned to the originating house, its clerk prepares the final "enrolled" bill, and the Speaker and the Senate's Presiding Officer sign the bill. The bill then moves on for presidential consideration.

The president has four choices: He or she can approve the bill outright, in which case it becomes law. He or she can let it sit on his or her desk for 10 days during a Congressional session, in which case it automatically becomes law. If it is fewer than 10 days before the Congressional session ends and the president does nothing by the time the session ends, the bill dies. Finally, he or she can veto the bill outright.

If the president vetoes the bill, it is returned to the originating chamber. If two-thirds of that chamber vote to override the veto, it is passed on to the other house. If not, the bill dies. If it is passed on and two-thirds of the other chamber votes to override the veto, the bill becomes law. If not, the bill dies.

IMPLEMENTATION

One final phase of the legislative process is worth mentioning. Once a law is passed, there is no guarantee that it will be implemented effectively. "Whoa!" you say. "After all that?" Unfortunately, this has proved to be true enough that many Re-organization Acts have been passed to require Congress to continually review how the executive branch is implementing laws. Implementation of laws begins with rulemaking—that is, determining how nonspecific laws will be specifically implemented. The rulemaking process is discussed at length in chapter 11. As you will see, interest groups such as counselors can profoundly influence the rulemaking process.

SUMMARY

The point of all this detail is not to overwhelm counselors into doing nothing. It is to help counselors realize the art of politics and to add sophistication to their understanding of the legislative process. Congress is currently more open to scrutiny than ever before because the vast increase in numbers of lobbyists in Washington makes it imperative for counselors to participate, and the revolution in technology (such as C-Span and CNN) makes the processes of Congress more accessible. However, actual decision making is taking place more and more in closed, informal settings, despite more open, formal processes. There are "more people than ever watching Congress, and fewer secrets that can be kept hidden" (Wolpe, 1990, p. 5).

Counselors must realize that policy change is a dynamic and incremental process. "It's not over 'til it's over" refers not only to the multiple decision points of which counselors must be aware and which they must act to influence, but also to the fact that policies are continually being made and unmade. The policy process does not end. At each step of the process, a new winning coalition must be formed to continue the process, and coalitions must continually change to meet new needs. If opponents fail once, they can always come back and try again

(Oleszek, 1989). If counselors fail or only gain part of what they want, they too can always come back and try again.

Do counselors need to be experts themselves in playing this game? No. Legislators and their staffs do not expect their constituents to be experts. Yet, counselors can know enough to "play" instead of be "played by" the experts. They can know enough to choose an effective lobbyist. And they can use their expertise as counselors.

Chapter 11

CHANGING PUBLIC POLICY THROUGH RULEMAKING

Congress rarely spells out the specifics of how legislation is to be enacted. Instead, it delegates these responsibilities to administrative agencies in a process called "rulemaking." "Rulemaking . . . refines, and in some instances defines, the mission of every government agency. . . . Rules provide specific, authoritative statements of the obligations the government has assumed and the benefits it must provide" (Kerwin, 1994, p. xi). Rules can affect private behavior, the way people can approach the government, or the way the government must act. The scope of a rule can be broad or narrow, but rules affect every aspect of human life. Therefore, every known profession can be affected by, and hence has an interest in, influencing the creation of rules.

Rules are created by bureaucrats, and thus rulemaking is sometimes considered inferior to the activities of the president, the Congress, or the judiciary. However, "the rules issued by departments, agencies, or commissions are law; they carry the same weight as congressional legislation, presidential executive orders, and judicial decisions" (Kerwin, 1994, p. 4; all of the following material is from Kerwin unless otherwise specified).

Administrative agencies perform quasi-legislative, quasi-executive, and quasi-judicial functions. Shapiro (1986) indicated that rulemaking is when agencies act like legislatures, adjudication is when agencies act like courts, and the classic bureaucratic tasks of executing, administering, and otherwise delivering programs and policies to the public are the more executive functions of agencies. For counselors, rulemaking might include the development of licensure regulations, Department of Education certification requirements for school counselors, regulations for implementing the Improving America's Schools Act, or regulations determining which mental health providers are qualified to be reimbursed by federal health insurance plans. Counselors might become involved with an agency's adjudication processes if ethical complaints are filed against them with the licensure board or certifying body, or if they appeal a denied health insurance claim. Finally, counselors are very aware of the executive functions agencies perform, such as processing licensure and certification applications, recredentialing counselors, keeping track of continuing education requirements counselors have fulfilled, paying insurance claims on federal employees and military dependents, running school districts and schools, and funding school counseling programs. Rules are involved in all three of the quasi-legislative, quasi-executive, and quasi-judicial processes.

Because of the obvious influence of rules in their lives, professions, and counseling programs, counselors should seek to play a role in the rulemaking process. Further, because the rulemaking process involves fixed procedures that allow for calmer, more predictable policy making, counselors may prefer the rulemaking process to the legislative and judicial processes. This chapter seeks to inform counselors about rulemaking and the potential for influencing rulemaking, so they can participate in the rulemaking process more effectively.

THE ADMINISTRATIVE PROCEDURE ACT

The Administrative Procedure Act (APA) of 1946 is the foundation in law of the rulemaking process. It defines "rule" as "the whole or part of an agency statement of general or particular applicability and future effect designed to *implement, interpret,* or *prescribe* [italics added] law or policy"

(5 U.S.C. §551(4)). When law or policy has been fully developed in a statute enacted by Congress, an executive order of the president, or a judicial decision, rules merely *implement* that law. When law and policy are well-established but confronting unanticipated or changing circumstances, rules *interpret* how the principles should be adapted to the new reality or specific instance. For instance, when school counseling programs have been challenged by the religious right, counselors have asked state departments of education to change the language of rules regulating school counseling programs to meet the new demand. When Congress establishes the goals of law or policy in statutes but provides few details about how they are to be put into operation or how they are actually to be achieved, rules *prescribe* the details of how to deal with the differing situations under which the law applies. Mental health counselors are very aware of how licensure regulations (or rules) spell out licensure laws. Vague licensure laws are purposely sought, with the expressed intent of specifying them through regulations. Vague licensure laws generate less controversy than precise laws would, so they are easier to pass; regulations are easier to change and can therefore be adapted as times and practices change.

The APA further indicates that a general notice of proposed rulemaking shall be published in the *Federal Register* with statements of time and place, the nature of public participation, the legal authority under which the rule is proposed, the terms or substance of the proposed rule, and a description of the subjects and issues involved. The APA mandates that the agency shall give interested people the opportunity to participate in the rulemaking through submission of written data, views, or arguments, with or without the opportunity for oral presentation (5 U.S.C.§552(1)). The publication of a rule in the *Federal Register,* according to the APA, shall be not less than 30 days before the effective date of the rule.

Rules may be classified according to three types: *legislative* or *substantive,* which are rules that amount to a new law; *interpretive,* which are rules that explain law and policy to the public; or *procedural,* which are rules that mandate certain organizational processes of agencies. All three types have the same authority, however. The *Code of Federal Regulations* (CFR) organizes rules into 50 subject categories, called titles, which correspond to specific public programs, policies, or agencies.

Counselors or mental health functions are named in 16 of these titles.

THE HISTORY OF RULEMAKING

Rulemaking was limited in early American history, but by the late 1930s, it was a major governmental function. The growth of rulemaking started when Congress began focusing on domestic issues and problems in the late 1800s. During the New Deal, however, the magnitude of rulemaking expanded exponentially. In 1934, the creation of the *Federal Register* provided the first authoritative vehicle for making rules and other federal decisions public. In 1938, 15 volumes of rules with 50 titles were published in the CFR, the summary of the results of rulemaking up to that point. By 1949 the CFR had grown to 47 volumes; in 1995 it contained 209 volumes.

The character of rulemaking changed dramatically during the 1960s and 1970s. Because of a lack of faith in the ability of government to understand or properly respond to what the public wanted, legislation was passed that mandated that government decision making involve citizens in more direct ways. This "participation" was seen as a way of empowering the disenfranchised and unrepresented. Congress passed the Freedom of Information Act, which allowed private citizens to review how agency officials made their decisions; the Privacy Act, which allowed people to gain access to information that the government had about them, to correct errors, and to prevent unauthorized disclosures; the Government in the Sunshine Act, which opened meetings and deliberations to the public; and the Federal Advisory Committee Act, which required that membership on these committees be balanced with regard to affected interests. In addition, many of the Great Society programs required some form of citizen participation.

Procedural requirements were also changed, allowing and encouraging greater public participation. Authorizing statutes more often required advance notice of proposed rulemaking to encourage early input by the public, a procedure that effectively weeded out unnecessary provisions. They also suggested innovative approaches to encouraging participation and maintaining communication, such as direct mail, television surveys, and other types of literature providing information about the rulemaking process. Some provisions "authorized nongovernmental groups and organizations to develop and propose rules to agencies" (Kerwin, 1994, p. 173). The new procedures required extended periods of public comment, giving the public more time to gather important information and build coalitions. The procedures mandated the dissemination of important agency information, and they often mandated public debate in legislative-style hearings. This meant that transcripts of the hearings became part of the "docket," or record of the rulemaking.

As a result of these changes, rulemaking authority swept broadly across the economy in a manner that it previously had not. Agencies felt pressured from above (by Congress) and below (by interest groups). Agencies that previously had extended periods in which to develop working relationships with those they regulated or served did not have this luxury in the 1970s, because authorizing statutes began mandating deadlines and specificity. Rulemaking became characterized by an increasing volume of work, an accelerated pace, and increasing conflict. In addition, agencies were expected for the first time to create information, and there was increasing need for coordination. Finally, accountability drew greater attention as Congress became increasingly concerned with the process by which rules were being written.

The last years of the Carter administration "represent the high water mark for participation in rulemaking as a public policy concern" (Kerwin, 1994, p. 180). By then, most of strengths and weaknesses of different types of participation were well-understood. What became very clear was that participation is costly. The design and maintenance of mechanisms to solicit input and incorporate it into rules takes time, which may ultimately postpone the flow of benefits to affected parties. It also requires resources on the part of the public that wants to participate.

WHY RULEMAKING?

Why has the rulemaking process expanded so significantly, and why is it considered so important? According to Kerwin, rulemaking has increased because it serves an essential role in implementing what the three constitutionally established branches of government mandate. Congress escapes politi-

cally difficult situations by delegating authority to rulemakers. The president, judiciary, and interest groups gain the opportunity to rise above their usually limited policy-making power through the rulemaking process.

There is simply too much to be done for Congress to do it all. Thus, "Congress has always chosen to cede crucial elements of the design and virtually all implementation of thousands of programs to rulemaking. . . . A symbiotic relationship exists between the growth of government and the role of rulemaking" (Kerwin, 1994, p. 273). Further, rulemaking provides advantages over the legislative process, which is overloaded by demands for action but impeded by lack of time and expertise. Rulemaking allows for flexibility and quick response in emergencies; the legislative process does not. Finally, Congress gains another group onto which to "shift responsibility" (Fiorina, 1982). "Whenever they suspect that the decisions made during the course of these types of actions could stimulate controversy, criticism, and adverse political consequences" (Kerwin, 1994, p. 274).

"Rulemaking . . . provides both the president and the courts, institutions with limited capacities, something that no other common form of administrative action provides: an opportunity to observe and supervise the bureaucracy." The president and the judiciary "encourage rulemaking because it broadens their oversight powers" (Kerwin, 1994, p. 276). For the president, both review by the Office of Management and the Budget (OMB) and executive orders allow for powerful impact on all rules made, providing a vehicle for the president to obtain his or her agenda and accomplish the policies promised to the American people. The judiciary also finds rulemaking "the more cost-effective path for . . . [pursuing] personal power and institutional influence or merely [fulfilling] their constitutional responsibilities" (p. 33).

Finally, rulemaking is important in limiting the power and discretion of bureaucrats. It sets limits on the authority of public officials in some areas of their work, to a certain degree "identifying what they can know, how they can learn it, when they must act, what they must do, when they must do it, and actions they can take against those who fail to comply" (Kerwin, 1994, p. 31). Agencies may not always consider it beneficial to use rules to take away the discretion of agency personnel, but they may also sometimes give personnel too much discretion. It is certainly true that the rulemaking process guides the behavior of bureaucrats who are attempting to make bureaucratic decisions fair to all interested parties (Davis, 1969).

STAGES AND ELEMENTS OF RULEMAKING

Table 11.1 outlines the stages of rulemaking as delineated by Kerwin (1994). The asterisked items represent areas in which counselors can have some impact. The discussion in the rest of this section draws attention to the essential elements of rulemaking and who is involved.

Not all rulemaking follows this process exactly or includes all of these stages. The determination of which stages are included is influenced by the subject of the rule and the scope of its potential impact. The subject and scope in turn determine the types and amounts of information needed, the size and type of the populations and activities affected, and therefore the legal requirements of the rule; the technical, administrative and political dimensions of the rule; and the extent and intensity of political attention and oversight. As Davis (1969) pointed out, agency personnel exercise a great deal of discretion in making these decisions.

It is apparent that, throughout these stages, agencies respond to information supplied by various actors; gather, generate, and manage information in order to develop a good rule; and keep various actors informed about the various stages of the process. Participation is the involvement of the public in the rulemaking process. Accountability is the oversight of the rulemaking process by other governmental entities.

Information

Agencies developing rules must distribute, collect, manage, and resolve apparent conflicts in information. "Information is the currency of politics. . . . The various parties use technical, scientific, economic, administrative, and attitudinal information strategically to influence the content of rules. The collection and analysis of information dominates rulemaking management systems" (pp. 278–279).

Agencies distribute information during Stages 8 and 10, and sometimes during Stage 4. In other words, they provide notice to the public-at-large about the rulemaking. Agencies must publish notice of proposed rulemaking in the *Federal Register.* Included must be the full text of the rule and a preamble that informs nonexpert readers, states the results of reviews that agencies are required to conduct, and summarizes the agency's basis for making decisions.

Agencies collect information during Stages 1, 2, 5, 7, and 9. The information collected is of five distinct types: legal, policy, technical, political, and managerial. In Stage 1, *legal information* comes from the specific statute that "establishes the substantive goals and procedural requirements for rulemaking" (Kerwin, 1994, p. 278). In other words, the legislative statute originally determines what rule needs making and how it will be made.

Policy information generates from more general statutes (for instance, information that agencies are required to collect regularly as specified in executive orders or information statutes, such as the Freedom of Information Act and the Paperwork Reduction Act), or is received during Stage 2 from agency leadership.

Technical information forms the substance and content of the rule and provides the basis for the various impact analyses that may be required. Agencies generally gather this information from industry, from in-house research offices, from outside experts, and from public interest groups during Stages 2, 5, and 9. The information and types of analyses needed are determined by the subject of the rule. Analyses consider the various alternatives that could be included in a rule, and the impacts of each alternative. Other analyses are also conducted: "Paperwork, regulatory flexibility, and regulatory impact analysis are all common" (Kerwin, 1994, p. 143). Sometimes these analyses are done by specialized units and sometimes by the group writing the rule. Contractors are used for these analyses in 70 percent of agencies, although not usually on a regular basis.

Political information impacts the rulemaking process at almost every stage. It consists of the views and positions of the internal and external interests (including counselors) affected by the rule

Table 11.1. Stages and Elements of Rulemaking

1. *Lawmaking by Congress.** The statute may indicate mission, number and timing of rules, degree of discretion, procedural requirements, and hammers (provisions that will take effect if deadlines are not met). Rules spell out more specifically how a law is to be implemented.

2. *Other Originators of Individual Rules*
   - *Internal sources:*
         Political leadership of agency
         Advisory committees attached to agency* (on which counselors can serve)
         Program administrators who see need for new or revised rules
         Office of general counsel
         Field staff
         Enforcement officials
         Participation as a result of advance notice of proposed rulemaking*
   - *External sources* (anyone can petition an agency to make a rule):
         White House
         Congress
         Other agencies
         Public action*

3. *Authorization to Proceed with Rulemaking.* Since there are multiple sources and a large number of potential projects, it is usually senior level management that decides which rules to work on and in what priority.

4. *Planning the Rulemaking.* Agency personnel

   - decide who will be responsible for developing the rule,
   - decide on the objective of the rule based on the statutory language and legislative history,
   - decide what information is needed and how to obtain it,
   - allocate monies for tasks,
   - decide how the public will be involved, and what sites and formats will be used, and
   - access guidance from senior management.

5. *Developing the Draft Rule.* During this stage,
   - content of rule is decided;
   - procedural requirements are determined and complied with;
   - extensive internal and external consultations are conducted;*
   - key constituencies are kept informed;
   - actual language is developed;*
   - studies and reports are completed;*
   - a preamble is drafted to explain how the rule was developed; and
   - consideration is given to how the rule is to be implemented, administered, and enforced.

6. *Internal Review of Draft Rule:*
   - *Horizontal review:* by other departments, program offices, general counsel, policy analysts, field and enforcement offices, advisory groups*
   - *Vertical review:* by supervisors and senior officials

7. *External Review of Draft Rule.* This review is conducted by
   - a wide variety of agencies,
   - the Office of Management and the Budget (OMB),

(Table continued on next page)

Table 11.1. Stages and Elements of Rulemaking (*Continued*)

- congress, and
- interest groups*

8. *Revision and Publication.* The draft rule is reviewed and published in the *Federal Register* so that interested parties can comment on the rule.

9. *Public Participation.** The kind of public participation depends on the amount and intensity of interest the proposed rule is likely to generate. Decisions about participation have to do with politics and public relations. The agency must manage receipt of comments. Participation opportunities may include written comment, hearings, and so on.

10. *Action on the Draft Rule.* Once feedback on the draft has been received, the agency responds by
    - making no changes,
    - making minor revisions,
    - initiating another round of participation if all questions were not answered,
    - making major revisions and returning to Stage 5,
    - choosing to abandon rulemaking and start over, or
    - abandoning rulemaking completely.

    The final rule is published in the Federal Register and becomes effective after 30 days.

11. *Post-rulemaking Activities.** If rulemaking works perfectly, this is not a necessary stage. If it does not, then the process of attempting to undo or revise the rule begins immediately after its publication in the *Federal Register,* through petitions for reconsideration, technical adjustments, and litigation. There will probably be an ongoing process of perfecting the rule.

---

under development. Many times this information is couched in technical terms and is difficult to distinguish from the technical or policy information.

How information is managed, how decisions are made about what information to collect, and how internal and external influences will be balanced is determined by the agency's organization and culture, which also affects all stages. Included in the management systems of agencies are "the capacity to set priorities, to control the initiation of new rules, to provide early guidance on important policy matters to the rule writers, to ensure horizontal and vertical concurrence, and to maintain a degree of discipline in the rulemaker's dealings with the OMB on proposed and final rules" (Kerwin, 1994, p. 145). Delays occur when the layers of these management systems do not operate effectively or efficiently.

Some agencies have formal processes for resolving conflicts in information and priorities, and some do not; but how well conflict is managed and resolved is critical to the rulemaking process. The purpose of horizontal concurrence, which is secured

prior to vertical concurrence (see Stage 6), is to work out conflict among the government departments and agencies early in the process. "When the net is cast broadly across an agency during rulemaking, the likelihood of conflict increases" (Kerwin, 1994, p. 146).

Management of public participation requires deciding on the mechanisms by which the public can participate (Stage 6) and evaluating the material the public submits (Stages 5, 7, and 9). These decisions are made in a variety of ways, sometimes involving the agency staff, sometimes involving an outside office. Regulatory negotiation (reg neg) is a relatively new method of resolving conflict among the interests likely to be affected by the rules, and it operates on the same principles as mediation. It represents participation at its most intense. "Reg neg . . . offers the public the most direct and substantial role in rulemaking of any reform of the process ever devised" (Kerwin, 1994, p. 185).

Clearly, in order to be fully informed by and to provide information to the rulemaking process, counselors need to be alert to available information on rules that affect the counseling profession or consumers of counseling. Reading the *Federal Register* regularly—or the state equivalent—is fundamental. The *Federal Register* will identify what kinds of information an agency is required to collect, so that counselors can develop and provide it. Kerwin's research found that interest groups also use professional newsletters, networks of colleagues/ coalitions, and contact with the agency both before and after notice of a proposed rulemaking to keep informed of rulemaking that might affect them. Because in some cases an agency will announce its intention to develop a rule, counselors can participate in the earliest planning stages of rulemaking, advising agencies on the type of information needed, on how to acquire this information, and on the type of participation that would be most useful and fair. They can build relationships with agencies so that the agencies will come to them for information on rules related to counseling concerns. Counselors are also in an ideal position to serve as contractors for the collection and analysis of information, to conduct original research, and to serve on advisory committees. Counselors can "mobilize political pressure and bring it to bear on agencies" (Kerwin, 1994, p. 280), because politics influences the information that is used in rulemaking and affects the environment of rulemaking. Counselors and counseling professional associations can serve as participants in regulatory negotiation on such issues as managed care, financing mental health care, and appropriate roles for school counselors. They might even want to suggest that an agency use reg neg to achieve the best policy outcomes.

Participation

The APA requires that agencies facilitate the participation of interested and affected parties and use the information acquired. This lends an element of democracy to the rulemaking process. Rulemakers may exercise considerable freedom, however, when structuring public participation, and the APA says nothing about how the information received must be used. Nevertheless, opportunities for participation have increased and become more varied. They are formal and informal. They stretch from written comments to conferences of affected parties, hearings (legislative or formal, trial-type proceedings), and advisory committees.

The purpose of the mandate for participation is to add to the quality of rules developed by adding to the accuracy and completeness of information on which the rule is based, and by enhancing the authority, credibility, and standing a rule enjoys. As Kerwin stated, "Stupid rules do not beget respect" (p. 162). Further, the content and tone of expressions from the public help agencies plan for what they will face when the rule is written and implementation begins. Finally, participation helps agencies to determine the degrees of acceptance and resistance they can expect from affected communities, so that a lawsuit need not come as a surprise.

In addition to providing technical information and political pressure, as stated above, counselors have the opportunity to participate formally and informally in many rulemaking functions. They can approach an agency about the need for a new or changed rule. They can draft the actual language of a rule. They can submit written comments and present oral arguments at public hearings on a rule. They can bring the rule up for internal or external adjudication by filing a complaint about the rule. To do these things effectively, counselors need to be aware that a rule is being developed; they need to understand how the rule will affect their interests; they need to be familiar with the opportunities available for participation, the resources, and technical expertise needed to respond; and they need to have the ability to, when necessary, mobilize others to join the effort to influence agency decisionmakers. These are the types of participation in which groups and organizations usually are the most effective.

Kerwin's research on public participation in rulemaking indicated that notices of proposed rulemaking are infrequent, and even when notices were issued, participation was not as frequent as case studies would lead readers to believe. Although 80 percent of the groups surveyed by Kerwin participated in rulemaking and ranked its importance as greater than lobbying Congress and other forms of political activity, participation in rulemaking is a relatively untapped policy-making resource.

Groups do not rely on only one tactic for influencing rulemaking, although some tactics are preferred. They consider informal mechanisms and difficult-to-observe mechanisms for communicating views to agencies to be as or more effective than traditional means. They consider coalition formation and informal contacts before and after notice of proposed rulemaking to be most effective. Groups do not perceive that filing petitions, serving on advisory committees, or participation in public hearings are very effective, although they do not feel that these activities are entirely useless. Because 50 percent of the time agencies are proactive in soliciting contact with interest groups, such groups may merely have to respond to requests in order to impact rulemaking.

The monitoring and influencing of agencies by groups is clearly multidimensional. Groups that participate in rulemaking do so to get what they want, and they continue because they perceive that they are succeeding.

Accountability

"Those who write rules are expected to be responsive to multiple superior authorities, each of which wields considerable but different power over the agency. . . . There are profound differences in the priorities and objectives of each of these authorities" (Kerwin, 1994, p. 71). The specter of judicial review and congressional and presidential oversight profoundly influences the rulemaking process. The threat of litigation fosters a healthy respect for legal principles and issues, and is a "powerful force pushing agencies to consider more seriously the views of those who might challenge the rule in court" (p. 252). The threat of having these rules challenged is one factor that motivates rulemakers to develop quality rules, follow procedures, and encourage public participation.

The public has a variety of choices if it decides to challenge rules. People can challenge rules directly, in which case the agency's administrative law judges—an independent corp of hearing examiners—hear the case. The public can challenge the rule through the courts, in which case the judiciary becomes involved in reviewing the rule. Or the public can complain to the president, the governor, or their legislators, in which case these people might review the rule. The review process occurs in various degrees of formality, although the trend has been toward increasing judicialization.

The Judiciary. "Our most passive and least responsive branch of government will, in many instances, be the most aggressive and influential

overseer of the rulemaking process" (Kerwin, 1994, p. 266). Rules affect large numbers of people. When the effects are adverse and groups are motivated and have the organization and resources to do so, they challenge the legality of these rules. "Their authority thus invoked through litigation, the judges are presented with the opportunity to review and influence rules in a manner analogous to that used by the White House, albeit for very different reasons" (p. 275).

For instance, one advocate who participated in the research for this book found that after practicing counseling successfully for more than 20 years and serving in the leadership of the American Counseling Association, she was in trouble when her state passed their new licensure law. The law required 60 graduate credits in counseling, and the regulations provided no means for grandparenting. Because her degree only had 30 graduate credits, she was going to have to close her practice if she was unable to get the regulations changed. Her first step would be to challenge the licensure board directly. If she was unsuccessful, she could then file a suit against the licensure board, and the courts would be called upon to decide the legality of the rule.

The APA says, in section 706, that courts can

decide all relevant questions of law, interpret constitutional and statutory provisions, and determine the meaning or applicability of the terms of an agency action. [It can]

1   compel agency action unlawfully withheld or unreasonably delayed; and
2   hold unlawful and set aside agency action, findings, and conclusions found to be
    A   arbitrary, capricious, an abuse of discretion, or otherwise not in accordance with law;
    B   contrary to constitutional right, power, privilege, or immunity;
    C   in excess of statutory jurisdiction, authority, or limitations, or short of statutory right;
    D   without observance of procedure required by law;
    E   unsupported by substantial evidence. . . .
    F   unwarranted by the facts to the extent that the facts are subject to trial de novo by the reviewing court. (5 U.S.C.§706)

The use of the courts in reviewing rulemaking is very frequent. However, the judiciary's impact on rulemaking varies because certain agencies' constituencies do not sue. This may be because they are in general agreement with the overall results, or they have worked with the agency to come up with the rules—as is the case for rules requiring technical expertise. It may also be because those damaged do not have the resources to sue. The "key variable that triggers the litigation that brings judicial oversight is the magnitude of the negative effects anticipated by parties that have the resources and willingness to sue" (Kerwin, 1994, p. 263). Litigation is confronted most often by major agencies of social regulation (such as the Environmental Protection Agency, the Occupational Safety and Health Administration, the Consumer Product Safety Commission, and the National Highway Transportation Safety Administration), because they have enormous effect on certain industries and sectors of the economy. Counselors and their consumers either have few resources or have an aversion to engaging in the courts' adversarial process. However, some participant advocates certainly felt that litigation might be useful when other means of advocacy had been exhausted. (Chapter 12 contains further information on use of the courts.)

Congress. Congress does not let go of the rulemaking process once a law is enacted. It maintains oversight to ensure that rules are true to statutory intent. It finds that "rulemaking is easier to track, observe, and intervene in than other forms of bureaucratic action" (Kerwin, 1994, p. 274). Congressional oversight can take many forms. Congress can write laws so precisely in terms of content, methods, and schedules that agencies have little discretion. Congress can specify various procedures very clearly, conveying explicit ideas of the substantive political result they want, even when these ideas are unstated in the content of the statute. They can institute hammers—provisions that will take effect on a certain date should the agency fail to issue an alternative regulation—and deadlines. Hammers and deadlines pressure agencies to expedite the rulemaking process, although many times deadlines are hopelessly unrealistic. Legislative oversight may involve fiscal oversight by appropriations committees, the review of programs and proposition of legislation to remedy deficiencies by authorizing committees, and investigation of fraud and abuse by the House Government Operations Committee and the Senate Government Affairs Committee.

Congressional appropriations have generally served a passively negative oversight function. Rulemaking is generally not adequately funded, regardless of the political standing of the rule. In fact, there is generally an inverse relationship between the rule-making responsibilities established in authorizing legislation and the funding provided in appropriations. Congress does, however, successfully send messages to agencies by increasing or decreasing appropriations, by cutting off, reducing, or earmarking funds.

Various tools are available to the overseeing committees. These include hearings and investigations; legislative veto; authorization, guidance, and direction; requiring reports; use of inspector generals; nonstatutory informal controls; audits by the General Accounting Office; ad hoc groups; the Senate confirmation process; program evaluation; casework (constituents seeking help in dealing with executive agencies); use of the Congressional Research Service, the Office of Technology Assessment, and the Congressional Budget Office's reports and studies; and oversight by individual members.

Due to limited resources, Congress usually does not oversee constantly, and its oversight is rarely coordinated or systematized. Some have thought that this means that congressional oversight is ineffective. However, the "fire alarm" method of oversight that Congress uses (that is, when a constituent or another politically significant actor complains, Congress acts [McCubbins & Schwartz, 1987]) actually can be very effective. The fire alarm approach is prevalent because it is the most efficient and effective means of oversight for individual members of Congress. Clearly, counselors and counseling professional associations can sound the alarm. For instance, counselors who were not receiving payment for services provided to CHAMPUS subscribers (health insurance for military dependents) contacted their member of Congress to try to get the problem rectified. In some cases they were successful.

The President. Presidential review via the OMB is an unparalleled opportunity for the president to affect the course of public policy, although OMB only reviews some rules. The president "seeks to ensure that the substantive policies and political agenda of the administration are reflected in the rules issued by federal agencies" (Kerwin, 1994, p. 157).

Presidential review and its impact on rulemaking is a relatively recent phenomenon, the rise of which coincides roughly with the rise of social regulation and the increasing body of rules that came with that expansion of the federal government. Different presidents have had different agendas in their oversight activities and executive orders. President Carter, who began the presidential review process, was very concerned with making rulemaking a better, more understandable, reasonable, and standardized process, clearing up inconsistencies, and involving the public. His approach was

> built on five principles: policy oversight of rulemaking by agency heads, increased participation by the public in the development of rules, regulatory analysis, 'sunset review' to eliminate rules no longer needed and to update or revise those that had become obsolete or ineffectual, and the use of 'plain English' in rules to make them more accessible to those who must comply with their provisions. (Kerwin, 1994, p. 123)

Although his plan was in effect for a mere three years, it has had enduring relevance and influence.

In Executive Order 12291, Reagan introduced the most significant changes since the basic process for rulemaking was established by the APA in 1946. His goal was to decrease the size of government and the number of rules. He halted further expansion of participation opportunities and installed counterweights to the influence exerted by advocates of big government. He felt that too much participation diminished the appropriate power of elected officials. He put a 60-day "moratorium on new rules, a mandatory cost-benefit analysis for all major regulations, a requirement that all such regulations meet a 'net benefit' criterion, and a review of all proposed and final rules by the Office of Management and Budget" (Kerwin, 1994, p. 125).

Under Reagan, OMB review became another point of decision making that groups and organizations could influence. It was more reasonable and cost-effective for groups to focus their influence at this higher level, because effective lobbying could delay or defeat the rule.

> If a given interest group was confident about securing a sympathetic ear, it could pursue a strategy of nominal involvement during the agency phase of rulemaking while putting heavy pressure on the OMB staff and officials responsible for the review of the rule. In this way the interest group could attain its goal at a comparatively low cost. (Kerwin, 1994, p. 183)

Bush kept virtually all of Reagan's program intact, and Clinton has continued to open OMB review to public scrutiny and to limit review to important rules.

Clearly, presidential influence through OMB review has been sophisticated, substantial, and influential. National counseling groups and coalitions of groups representing counselors and mental health consumers may be able to gain the attention of OMB on important rules, thus indirectly influencing the rulemaking process.

BEYOND RULEMAKING

The importance of rules cannot be overstated. However, while rules have a major impact on agency activities, politics and discretion also play significant roles. After agencies make rules, they implement their programs, plans, and services. During both rulemaking and implementation, agency personnel use a great deal of discretion; in other words, they make many decisions that are not clearly articulated in rules. Davis (1969) referred to this as "government by men," as contrasted with government by law. He claimed that discretionary decisions are usually intuitive and that discretion is much more influential than the broad policies of rulemaking.

Agency personnel use discretion when "initiating, investigating, prosecuting, negotiating, settling, contracting, dealing, advising, threatening, publicizing, concealing, planning, recommending, supervising" (Davis, 1969, p. 22). "Each of the [affected parties] endeavors to manipulate the [agency] structure and the assignment of program responsibilities so as to maximize its ability to obtain federal funds and to minimize federal interference in the allocation and use of funds" (Seidman, 1980, p. 35). In the counseling field, schools, community mental health centers, licensure boards, and departments of social services are agencies or agency programs. School principals must use their discretion to decide which school counselor to hire. School counselors must use their discretion to decide which students to focus most of their counseling attention on. Community mental health centers use discretion in deciding how much to charge those seeking services and which clients on the waiting list to treat first. Licensure boards use discretion in deciding whether applicants' qualifications meet the licensure standards and whether counselors have been negligent or committed ethical violations. Government contracted insurance plans use discretion in deciding which claims to pay. Departments of social services use discretion to decide which child abuse reports to act on and how.

Agencies use discretion in deciding which public counseling programs to fund and which to de-staff, and in deciding which agency will have jurisdiction over a program. "Each agency has its own culture and internal set of loyalties and values which are likely to guide its actions and influence its policies . . . and one way to kill a program is to house it in a hostile or unsympathetic environment (Seidman, 1980, pp. 19–20). Counselors may want to push for a program to be housed in an agency that is sympathetic to their needs. Further, different agencies have different organizational structures, and these structures are more or less useful depending on the type of program.

Agency personnel use their own discretion to try to "find the most satisfactory accommodation of the needs of effectiveness to the often conflicting needs of fairness, both substantive and procedural" (Davis, 1969, p. 9). In some cases, personnel have greater discretion than they should have in this process. In some cases, they must use their discretion because no one can figure out how to write meaningful rules for a particular situation. In other cases, rules have not been written because discretion is the only way to adapt law to individual cases, and to find creative solutions to problems. In fact, said Davis (1969), informal procedures are the lifeblood of the administrative process. So, the key is not to eliminate discretion, since "rigidity encourages corruption, which is the greatest danger to democracy" (Richard Nelson, program director for the Atlantic Council, personal communication, April 15, 1995). The key is to use rules effectively and eliminate unnecessary discretion.

The areas in which discretion is most needed for decision making are also the areas most susceptible to influence. This influence can be toward injustice or toward greater justice. Counselors can influence agency programs toward greater justice if they are aware of those areas in which greater discretion is used.

SUMMARY

Historically, many have complained about the rulemaking process in terms of volume, quality, timeliness, procedural requirements, inequities in participation, and levels of bureaucratic discretion. The volume and complexity of rules strains institutional capacity and results in delays and the impossibility of implementation or monitoring compliance. Rule complexity is often too great for the public to understand, resulting in feelings of vulnerability, exposure, and a seething resentment. The public increasingly feels they are losing private control of their own lives. The volume of changes in standards disrupts programs, requiring learning and adjustments of personnel in the field. "The greater the volume of rulemaking, the greater the likelihood that the resultant rules are being passed on to implementation and enforcement staffs with inadequate training and resources" (Kerwin, 1994, p. 94).

Whether rules are of high quality is questioned. Quality refers to the effectiveness of rules in producing program outputs with a level of cost that equals the benefits to society. Limitations of information, limitations of rulemakers, limitations in resources, complexity of problems, and controversy all hinder the production of quality rules in a reasonable amount of time.

Further, the growth in procedural requirements can be overwhelming. Shortages of resources affect agencies' abilities to follow more complex procedures. Management obstacles and deficiencies, shifts in priorities—by Congress or as a result of judicial rulings or internal decisions—all slow the rulemaking process. Sometimes inertia is experienced because the agency simply does not want to act.

In addition, although the principle of participation is a good one, it has been fraught with inequities. Participants need knowledge in order to participate fully, and this knowledge is not distributed equally. The volume of participation can also be overwhelming, especially when a controversial issue turns the process into an adversarial one.

Finally, some Constitutional questions have been raised about whether bureaucrats should have so much power. A similar Constitutional question arises about whether separation of powers really exists when Congress calls on the agencies for expertise in writing laws, and when agencies propose laws to Congress. Questions have been raised by the American Bar Association, which is worried that rulemaking threatens the supremacy of common law.

However, despite these concerns, rulemaking appears to be here to stay because the principal actors in our political system value the rulemaking process. Counselors need to become aware of and actively use the rulemaking process. Counselors can impact the content of rules through providing crucial information and analyses and through bringing

political pressure to bear on agencies. They can do the same with Congress, the president and the courts, thus influencing those actors' oversight of rulemaking. There are many stages in the rulemaking process in which counselors can have a say, and perhaps a greater say than that which is possible legislatively or judicially. "Involvement of the public in rulemaking may be the most complex and important form of political action in the contemporary American political system" (Kerwin, 1994, p. 116). It is critical to the maintenance of democracy.

Chapter 12

CHANGING PUBLIC POLICY THROUGH THE COURTS

"Litigation does not leap to mind as a major interest group strategy," particularly for counselors, who seem to have an aversion to the adversarial nature of the court system. However, "throughout the twentieth century . . . groups representing the disadvantaged (minorities) and the difficult-to-organize (consumers) have successfully, if unevenly, used the judicial system to win policy victories" (Epstein & Rowland, 1985, p. 275). One participant advocate said, "I feel the court can change things overnight because we have such a litigious society. I think we need to get litigious ourselves. Nice guy goes only so far. We need to stop abuse by whatever means necessary." In fact, Alexis De Tocqueville (1835/1969, p. 270) suggested that "there is hardly a political question in the United States which does not sooner or later turn into a judicial one." This gives judges a chance to influence the course of public policy, and judges have been more than willing to seize the opportunity. The courts have thus become "crucial policymaking institutions in the American system" (Schlozman & Tierney, 1986, p. 358).

Interest group litigation has reached an all-time high for several reasons. First, there is more interest group activity in general. Second, there is more litigation in general. Finally, justices seem to encourage group activity, because it informs them and thus assists them in their jobs. Judges frequently cite amicus briefs in their opinions, and seem to view interest groups as a routine part of the governmental process (Epstein, 1991).[1]

Litigation is not usually thought of as part of an interest group strategy because interest groups usu-ally seek to directly impact the political system—which they limit to the executive and legislative branches—and most believe that the judicial system needs to be free of political maneuvering in order to make just rulings. Certainly counselors' primary political strategies have aimed to impact the executive and legislative branches. Indeed, the judiciary is not linked to a constituency that votes them in or out of office, and it is removed from the temporary and partisan motives that drive other branches (Kerwin, 1994). "Judges may consider themselves above the ordinary pressure tactics used by groups to influence elected officials" because "the rules of the legal game simply prohibit direct encounters. [But] the environment within which the Court works has become increasingly populated by organized interests" (Epstein, 1991, pp. 335–336). Abortion cases clearly demonstrate the fierce involvement of organized interests. Further, judges read the paper, listen to people, and have their own views and opinions. Also, politics plays a big role in the process of judicial appointments (Kerwin, 1994). Academics took a long time to admit that politics influences the judiciary, but by 1951 Truman had declared, "The activities of the judicial officers of the United States are not exempt from the processes of group politics. . . . Though myth and legend may argue to the contrary . . . the judiciary reflects the play of interests, and few organized groups can afford to be indifferent to its activities" (Truman, 1951, 1971, p. 479). This includes counselors.

HISTORY

Classic interest group involvement in the courts was first described by Arthur F. Bentley (1967) in 1908. He claimed that groups lobby the courts in order to obtain desired policy proclamations. He felt

---

1. Amicus curiae briefs are documents submitted to the U.S. or State Supreme Courts by groups or individuals other than the litigants. They are intended to inform justices of legal precedents as well as technical "facts."

that groups were the engineers of government policy wherever the policy was created, including in the courts. Truman (1951, 1971) further pointed out that interest groups could use litigation to maintain the status quo on legislation they originated and now needed to defend. However, "because of the perceived apolitical nature of the courts, research on lobbying through litigation, at least through the 1950s, was almost nonexistent" (Epstein & Rowland, 1985, p. 276).

Why did academics fail to give the same attention to interest groups and the courts that they gave to interest group interactions with the other two branches of government? First, they felt it was impossible for the courts, which were clearly designed to be independent of political influence, to be so influenced. They asked why interest groups would even bother lobbying courts, since their efforts would fall on deaf ears. Second, it was hard to collect data about group involvement in the courts because justices were not available for interview and amicus briefs rarely identified group involvement. The only data available was from interest groups themselves, and using this source raised questions of reliability and validity. A third reason was that research efforts were complicated by the difficulty in defining success. Groups have different goals in approaching the courts. Sometimes they define success as the ability to see their policy goals etched into law (Vose, 1949, 1959). Other times they define it as gaining publicity for a cause and maintaining membership (Gates & McIntosh, 1989, as cited in Epstein & Rowland, 1985). As a result of their research, Caldeira and Wright (1988) defined success as influencing the court's formulation of its plenary docket; Orren (1976) defined success as the ability to gain access to judicial forums; Epstein (1985) defined it as providing a counterbalance to "cut their losses"; O'Connor (1980) defined it as garnering publicity for their causes and launching issues onto the national agenda; and Kobylka (1987) defined it as maintaining or attracting members.

A fourth reason that academics avoided this area of inquiry was that many researchers verified the belief that justices based decisions solely upon personal preferences, and that because they lacked electoral accountability, they did not have to cloak their views to satisfy any constituency (Rohde & Spaeth, 1976; Schubert, 1959, 1965; Spaeth, 1963). In fact, in the late 1960s, an article stating that group

litigation rarely occurred was published by Hakman (1969). He said that scholars should not "waste their time studying what was surely an arcane phenomenon" (Epstein & Rowland, 1985, p. 279). As a result, for more than a decade there were no studies on interest groups influencing public policy through the courts.

Now, however, this has changed. Academic attention to the courts and interest groups has increased partly because changes in rules for standing and for class action suits have opened the door for interest group litigation. A 1981 study replicating Hakman's research, found that although interest group participation in amicus curiae may have been sporadic at the time of Hakman's study, in half of all the noncommercial cases coming before the Supreme Court between 1970 and 1980, interest groups filed amicus curiae briefs (O'Connor & Epstein, 1981–1982). Other scholars have confirmed this increase in participation and have attempted to classify the types of participation (Schlozman & Tierney, 1986). Currently, conventional wisdom is that the environment in which justices operate is subject to the same political pressures as that in which legislative and executive branch policy makers exist (Epstein & Rowland, 1985), and that national organizations can achieve policy goals through concerted, long-term litigation strategies at the U.S. Supreme Court level (O'Connor & Epstein, 1981–1982).

The perception of interest group effectiveness in the courts has changed over the years. It was previously thought that cases were only decided on their merits, but now it is clear that interest group's amicus curiae briefs serve to set Supreme Court agendas (Caldeira & Wright, 1988). Also, scholars historically have believed that groups always won over nongroup adversaries, not so much by group influence as by having greater resources, expertise, information networks, persistence over the long term, forum shopping/case selection, and the ability to neutralize localism's disadvantages (Epstein & Rowland, 1985).

The belief that groups outperform their nongroup adversaries seems reasonable for a variety of reasons. First, private counsel is client oriented, and maintains the goal of immediate court victory. Group attorneys, however, are policy oriented, aiming to create national legal precedent consistent with their objectives. They thus select litigation that maximizes the possibilities of achieving this. Group tactics (explored later in greater depth) such as coalition building, requesting coalition members to file amicus briefs, becoming repeat players (Krislov, 1963; Puro, 1971, as cited in Epstein & Rowland, 1985), sustaining use of the courts over as long a period as possible (O'Connor, 1980), priming the courts through law reviews (Newland, 1959), and making use of social scientific evidence (Lempert & Sanders, 1986; Vose, 1958) are not always feasible or relevant to individual litigants (Epstein & Rowland, 1985).

Epstein and Rowland's 1985 study showed that groups and nongroups succeed about equally, but groups win two-thirds of their constitutional cases while nongroups win only one-third. In nonconstitutional litigation, nongroups beat groups. National organizations that are involved in constitutional cases account for more than one-half of all group victories over nongroups. All organizations perform poorly when pitted against the federal government, as did nongroups. However, national organizations were very successful when opposed to subnational governments, and definitely outperformed nongroups.

In short, the same groups lobby the courts as lobby the other branches of government (Epstein, 1991). Scholars no longer give preference only to research on interest groups' influence on the legislative and executive branches of government. In fact, their research indicates that groups are likely to outperform nongroups in constitutional cases and in cases between national organizations and subnational governments. Thus, professional associations of counselors that are looking to influence public policy through the courts should particularly consider cases that challenge a situation on constitutional grounds, or they should wait until the American Counseling Association or one of its national divisions is willing to challenge a state or local government on some needed issue.

WHY INTEREST GROUPS USE THE COURT

Why would counselors use the courts rather than the many other available methods to influence public policy? Cortner (1968, p. 287; see also O'Connor,

1980; Schlozman & Tierney, 1986) argued that politically disadvantaged groups

> are highly dependent upon the judicial process as a means of pursuing their policy interests usually because they are temporarily, or even permanently, disadvantaged in terms of their ability to attain successfully their goals in the electoral process, within the elected institution, or in the bureaucracy. If they are to succeed at all in the pursuit of their goals, they are almost compelled to resort to litigation.

Women and blacks, in particular, have had "to resort to litigation to secure the constitutional rights of their members," because these organizations "lack adequate levels of political, social, and economic resources" (O'Connor, 1980, p. 2; also, Vose, 1949, 1958, 1959). Usually these groups use the courts to bring an end to discriminatory practices, representing society's underdogs in cases of civil rights, defendants' and prisoners' rights, and other issues of individual freedom (Glick, 1990). Supreme Court Justice Brennan (*NAACP vs. Button*, 1962) even wrote that interest group litigation

> is thus a form of political expression. Groups which find themselves unable to achieve their objectives through the ballot frequently turn to the courts . . . and under the conditions of modern government, litigation may well be the sole practicable avenue open to a minority to petition for redress of grievances. (pp. 429–430)

Clearly cases to support the rights of the mentally ill or those who have been sexually or physically abused fall into this category.

However, although liberal interest groups have been highly visible since the early sixties, advantaged groups also use the courts (Epstein, 1991). Well-established and well-funded organizations have the advantages of going to court from a position of strength, availing themselves of the top attorneys and using many kinds of tactics to influence policy outcomes—because going to court produces the most leverage when used in combination with other efforts (Galanter, 1974). The courts are thus another point of access for politically powerful and advantaged groups (Schlozman & Tierney, 1986). Although counselors' "advantages" do not match those of large corporations, if counselors were to join together in a class action suit—for instance, regarding a restraint-of-trade issue—they certainly could be fairly "advantaged" in the courts.

Both advantaged and disadvantaged groups use the courts for a variety of reasons. For instance, although they may have won in the legislature, others may challenge their legislation in the courts, and they may need to protect their victories (Glick, 1990). Or they may have no choice but to participate in litigation because they find themselves being sued by other groups. Groups may feel that because the court is the final arbiter, the court decision will yield greater policy permanency than will legislation. Sometimes a group's financial interests are at stake, and the courts are the only way to protect these interests (Epstein, 1991). Groups may use the courts to create legitimacy or precedent for future change in policy,[2] or to focus the attention of decision-makers and the public on some "widely ignored problem or grievance" (Schlozman & Tierney, 1986, p. 358). They may institute litigation to build or maintain their membership. Rallying around an expensive cause may persuade potential membership of the group's viability (O'Connor & McFall, 1992; Schlozman & Tierney, 1986). Finally, "organizations support legal action because individuals lack the necessary time, money, and skill" (Vose, 1958, p. 20).

Of all the reasons cited, counselors have chosen only one. That is, counselors have participated in the courts when they have had no choice, because they have found themselves being sued for practicing psychology without a license (Sweeney, 1991) or because they (and their schools) were sued for mixing church and state by practicing the "religion" of "secular humanism" (Brigman & Moore, 1994). In both these situations, policy has been profoundly impacted. In a court ruling in Virginia in 1972, the judge indicated that counselors should have their own license under which to practice (*Weldon* vs. *Virginia State Board of Psychologist Examiners*, 1972), and this ruling generated the first counseling license in the country. By 1979, counselors had filed legal grievances against psychology boards in at least 20 states. With respect to the school censorship issue, courts are making rulings daily that impact school curricula and school counseling programs across the country.

Counselors also have *considered* filing suit over struggles with managed care and insurance companies. Class action suits on behalf of mental health

consumers who have been unable to get these companies to authorize or reimburse for necessary services have been suggested. Class action suits have also been suggested in situations where the insurance company policies, managed care company policies, or self-insured company policies will not recognize counselors as qualified mental health service providers, because these policies restrain the trade of counselors unnecessarily and unlawfully.

Counselors for the most part have not taken a proactive stance on these issues, however, because they prefer to use more conciliatory means to accomplish their goals. Counselors have involved themselves in the courts only reactively. Perhaps when conciliatory efforts fail or when counselors realize the benefits of lobbying in the courts they will also use the courts to advocate for themselves and their clients.

What other kinds of policy decisions could counselors feasibly use the courts to influence? One area might be the scope of a counselor's legal practice based on training and licensure. When counselors are sued for practicing psychology without a license, for doing psychological testing (because psychologists claim that only psychologists should do that), or for providing any mental health service for which they have been adequately trained, a court case might yield the opportunity to change the states' scopes of practice as stated in state licensure laws. Although counselors typically would pursue these changes legislatively, when sued one has little choice but to respond.

Counselors also have had criminal fraud suits brought against them by insurance companies for inappropriate filing of claims and for inability to justify these claims with documentation. Cases such as this have often involved seizure of client records from counselors' offices. These cases could give counselors the opportunity to address policy issues in areas such as confidentiality, insurance company rights to records, the documentation that counselors can be required to keep, risks to clients of insurance company investigations, and the validity of *Diagnostic and Statistical Manual of Mental Disorders* (American Psychiatric Association, 1994) diagnoses as justification for reimbursement of care.

Counselors could also initiate class action suits for themselves or for their clients. For clients these

---

2. Because legal decisions are based on previous legal decisions—or precedents—groups may involve themselves in a number of smaller cases designed to decide small parts of their long-range policy goals.

might involve inappropriate mental health care due to facility incapacity (for instance, funding limits that prevent adequate care to all who need it) or insurance/managed care company refusal to reimburse for necessary services. These cases would address the policy issues of how much mental health care the mentally ill should receive, who is eligible, and how it should be funded.

A class action suit might be filed by school counselors over the impossibility of fulfilling their counseling responsibilities when they have 500 students assigned to them. The issue would be argued on the basis of schools and counselors incurring unreasonable liability. The same issue might be raised if a school was sued for a counselor's failure to report child abuse or suicidal intentions in a child who the counselor had never been able to see because the counselor was responsible for so many students.

A class action suit against managed care companies might be filed by counselors because the company removed a provider from their panel or refused to credential the provider and thus add him or her to the panel. This type of case might question policies related to the restraint of the provider's trade, particularly when the provider is as qualified as or more highly qualified than the current panel members. It would certainly raise the private sector issues of the rights of private companies to make their own policies, the right to follow those same policies when the organization has government contracts, and the more general struggle over the economy's need for health care cost containment.

Counselors might also file a class action suit against managed care companies to address the illegal relationship the contracts with these companies require them to have with their clients. On the one hand, counselors are legally and ethically bound to provide adequate care for their clients. They are also not to engage in activities that would hinder their ability to provide adequate care, such as dual relationships. On the other hand, they are caught in a bind because managed care companies will drop them from their panels—a livelihood risk—if they see clients on average more than six to eight sessions. Because this average may not realistically meet the client's needs, this conflict of interest puts clients at risk. The counselor/client relationship is therefore illegal and unethical according to state licensure laws.

Employers whose job classification systems and hiring practices do not include counselors, despite counselors being adequately trained to meet position requirements, are inviting a class action suit by counselors, particularly when mental health providers with equal or lesser qualifications are included and hired. Potentially, these employers include schools, state hospitals, departments of social services, and public mental health centers. The public policy issues involved are discrimination and restraint of trade.

Finally, in almost any case involving criminal activity or social issues—such as abortion, sexual abuse, child abuse, racial discrimination, and sexual harassment—counselors can be involved as expert witnesses or amicus curiae (discussed further later). If these cases are appealed to higher courts, counselors' testimony or briefs can affect public policy quite broadly.

ABOUT THE COURTS

To more fully understand how counselors can impact public policy through the court system, it is necessary to understand the structure and process of the court system and how and where this system allows for interest group influence. The United States has a dual court system. Each of the fifty states operates its own judicial system: the state courts. The federal government also operates courts in the states. These systems are separate, but both can rule on the same case. Courts can only hear cases that fall under their jurisdiction. Federal courts resolve cases involving questions of federal law or the U.S. Constitution. State courts hear cases involving state law or the state constitution. In many situations, litigants can select to sue on the basis of state law or federal law, and thus can select which court system to use (Tarr, 1994).

Both state and federal courts are hierarchically arranged, so cases move from one court to another, proceeding step by step from the lowest court to the highest, if successfully appealed (see Figure 12.1). A case begins in a state trial court or federal district court, where a single judge hears witnesses testify about the facts of the case. The case then proceeds, upon appeal, to an appellate court. If that ruling is challenged, it can sometimes (although very seldom) be appealed to the Supreme Court (Tarr, 1994). In certain cases, litigants petition the Su-

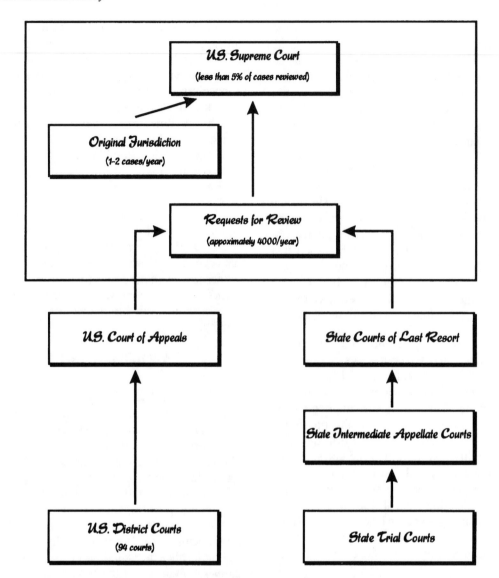

Figure 12.1. The Federal and State Court Systems. Adapted from K. Janda, J. M. Berry, and J. Goldman, *The Challenge of Democracy: Government in America, Fourth Edition.* Copyright © 1992 by Houghton Mifflin Company. Adapted with permission. (This material also appears in *The Challenge of Democracy: Government in America, Fifth Edition.*)

preme Court by writ of certiorari to review a case heard in a lower court. Only about 5 percent of those petitioned are heard.

Further, cases may be civil cases or criminal cases, and different statutes govern each. All cases that counseling professional associations are likely to be involved in are civil cases, although individual counselors might be involved in providing expert testimony in criminal cases, such as those related to child abuse, sexual abuse, or rape.

The Federal Courts

Article III of the Constitution established the Supreme Court and authorizes other courts to be established by Congress. These are known as the "constitutional" courts and include the district courts, the courts of appeals, and the Supreme Court. Most federal cases originate and terminate in the district court. Article I of the Constitution established legislative courts. These are specialized courts (such as Tax Court and Court of Military Appeals), and many times they have administrative and quasi-legislative responsibilities (Tarr, 1994).

If a litigant brings suit on an issue involving federal law, it generally must be heard first in a **district court.** There are 94 district courts, at least one in each state, with large states having as many as four. No district extends beyond the borders of a single state. Each district court has at least two judges, and the number of judges further assigned depends on the court's caseload. Congressional legislation and executive branch actions affect the number and types of cases brought before the district courts. District courts have no discretion over the cases they confront. "Any litigant who satisfies the jurisdictional requirements and follows proper legal procedures can initiate a case in federal district court" (Tarr, 1994, p. 40).

Litigants must have "standing," however, and an issue must be ripe for judicial remedy. Although standing used to be difficult to establish, it currently means that anyone who is aggrieved and articulating a complaint, who can demonstrate an "attenuated line of causation" between what the defendant does and the harm a complainant experiences, can be heard. The harm must be actual or potential, economic or otherwise, and must reflect a real dispute between the plaintiff and the defendant. No longer must a litigant prove that a specific constitutional or statutory boundary has been overstepped in causing injury. It must be clear that a court, by making a ruling, can provide the plaintiff with some relief. The plaintiff must have exhausted all other available remedies. This relaxation of the rules of standing has made courts much more accessible to interest groups (Kerwin, 1994; Schlozman & Tierney, 1986).

District courts are trial courts whose primary mission is the resolution of the disputes that created the cases in the first place. Rulings made are likely to affect only the disputants, since district court judges do not usually write opinions that could be used by other judges as precedent (Kerwin, 1994). District courts operate much as they have come to be seen on television or in the movies. Witnesses present testimony, lawyers direct questions to these witnesses, and a judge or jury decides the outcome. In many cases, guilty pleas are entered or settlements are reached before the case even comes before a judge (Tarr, 1994).

All litigants have the right to one appeal. The **appellate courts** are organized regionally, in "circuits" made up of three or more states. Courts of appeals primarily engage in error correction, overseeing the work of district courts. They review lower courts' briefs and trial transcripts, and sometimes hear oral arguments from attorneys (Tarr, 1994; see also Kerwin, 1994). In 99 percent of cases, the appeals decision stands, although some litigants appeal their case to the Supreme Court. The appeals courts hear more than 95 percent of cases in three-judge panels, deciding the cases by majority vote. Because decisions made depend on the composition of the panel, judges are rotated to avoid "stacking" the panels (Tarr, 1994). Appellate court opinions are written. They thus serve as precedent in other cases and impact public policy to a greater degree than do district court decisions. Before courts can impact policy, however, litigants must bring cases, because courts lack the authority to initiate cases by themselves (Kerwin, 1994; Schlozman & Tierney, 1986).

The **Supreme Court** is at the top of the apex. It has a limited original jurisdiction (one to two cases per year). It hears cases that are appealed from the U.S. Courts of Appeals, from state supreme courts, and sometimes from specialized courts. Very few cases come to the Supreme Court on direct appeal. Most cases are brought to the Supreme Court by a writ of certiorari. Even then, very few cases are heard by the Supreme Court. Of the 4000 cases petitioned to the Supreme Court each year, less than 5 percent are heard (Tarr, 1994).

Rule 17 (formerly Rule 19) of the Judiciary Act of 1925 sets forth criteria for acceptance of a case by the Supreme Court, but the court has a great deal of discretion in deciding to which cases to grant petition. The act's criteria are (a) the presence of important issues the Court has yet to decide, (b) conflict among the courts of appeals on an issue, (c) disagreement between the lower court and the Supreme Court's precedents, and (d) deviation from the accepted and usual course of judicial proceedings in a lower court. Although these criteria establish a starting point, empirical evidence suggests that Rule 17 does not explain how the court makes all of its gatekeeping decisions (Caldeira & Wright, 1988). Tanenhaus, Schick, Muraskin, and Rosen (1963) said that Rule 17 reasons appear in only two-thirds of cases carried over for a decision. Their research identifies

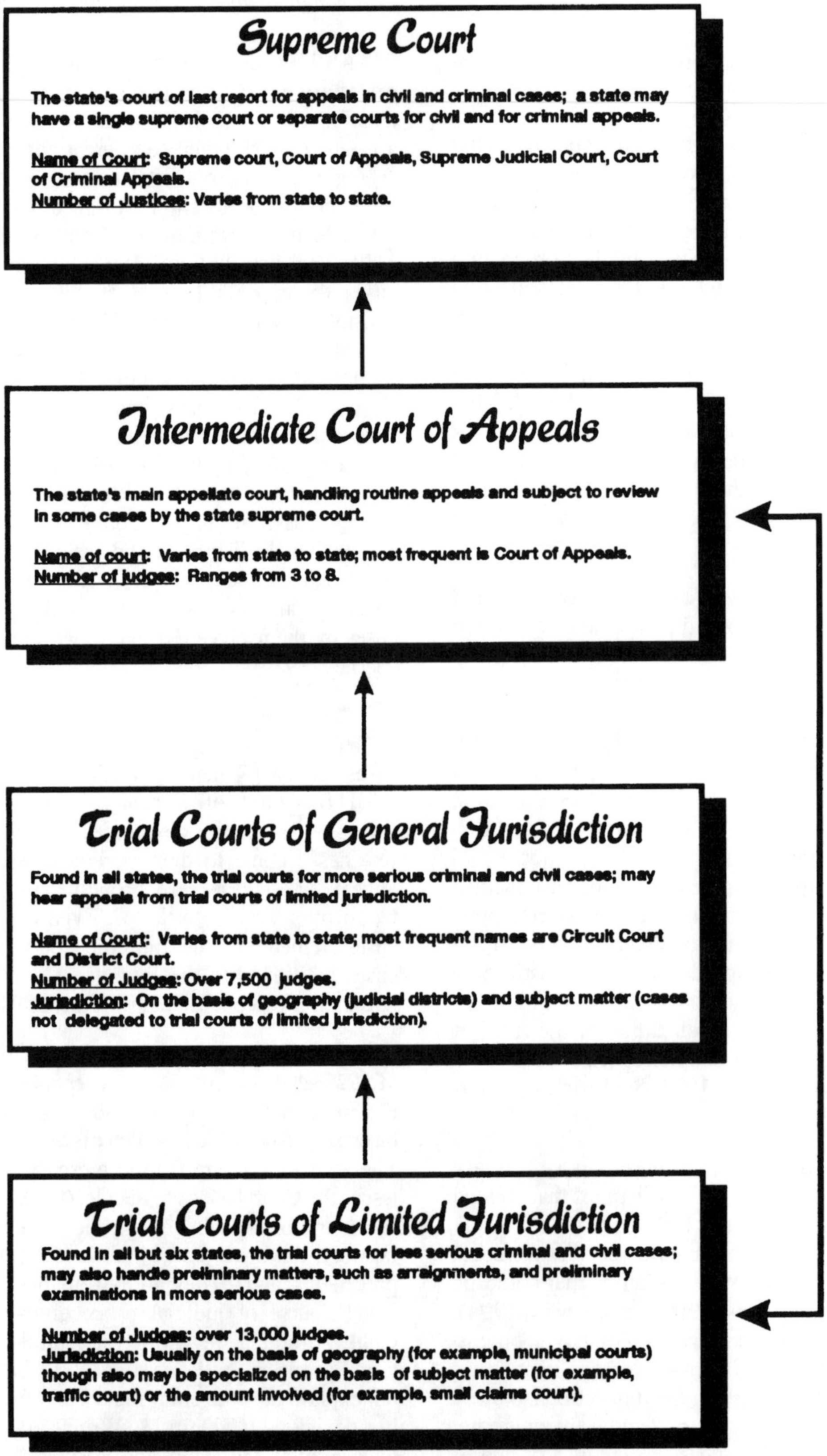

Supreme Court

The state's court of last resort for appeals in civil and criminal cases; a state may have a single supreme court or separate courts for civil and for criminal appeals.

<u>Name of Court</u>: Supreme court, Court of Appeals, Supreme Judicial Court, Court of Criminal Appeals.
<u>Number of Justices</u>: Varies from state to state.

Intermediate Court of Appeals

The state's main appellate court, handling routine appeals and subject to review in some cases by the state supreme court.

<u>Name of court</u>: Varies from state to state; most frequent is Court of Appeals.
<u>Number of judges</u>: Ranges from 3 to 8.

Trial Courts of General Jurisdiction

Found in all states, the trial courts for more serious criminal and civil cases; may hear appeals from trial courts of limited jurisdiction.

<u>Name of Court</u>: Varies from state to state; most frequent names are Circuit Court and District Court.
<u>Number of Judges</u>: Over 7,500 judges.
<u>Jurisdiction</u>: On the basis of geography (judicial districts) and subject matter (cases not delegated to trial courts of limited jurisdiction).

Trial Courts of Limited Jurisdiction

Found in all but six states, the trial courts for less serious criminal and civil cases; may also handle preliminary matters, such as arraignments, and preliminary examinations in more serious cases.

<u>Number of Judges</u>: over 13,000 judges.
<u>Jurisdiction</u>: Usually on the basis of geography (for example, municipal courts) though also may be specialized on the basis of subject matter (for example, traffic court) or the amount involved (for example, small claims court).

Figure 12.2. The Basic Structure of State Court Systems. Adapted by permission from page 48 of *Judicial Process and Judicial Policy Making* by G. A. Tarr; Copyright © 1994 by West Publishing Company. All rights reserved. Other information from *Book of the States, 1990–1991,* Lexington, KY: Council on State Governments.

four cues considered by justices, including the presence of the United States as a party (see also Ulmer, Hintze, & Kirklosky, 1972), the presence of a civil liberties issue, and dissension in the courts below. Ulmer (1983, 1984) persuasively showed that conflict among the courts of appeals on an issue and disagreement between the lower court and the Supreme Court's precedents dramatically raised the probability of justices placing a case on their agenda. Armstrong and Johnson (1982) and many others found that the Supreme Court took on a case when a lower court ruled contrary to their preferences, so that they could reverse the decision.

The State Courts

"What is most striking about state court systems is their bewildering organizational diversity" (Tarr, 1994, p. 49). Figure 12.2 outlines the basic structure of the state courts. Litigants in the state courts follow the same progression from lower to upper courts as they do in the federal courts. State courts "render final and determinative decisions in the vast majority of cases they consider, including most cases that announce major policy initiatives" (Tarr, 1994, p. 47).

Judicial Decision Making

In any case brought before them, "judges must determine what law is applicable, determine its meaning, and apply the law to the facts of the case" (Tarr, 1994, p. 269). Judges use the text of the applicable constitution, statute, or administrative regulation. They consult the "legislative history" of the enactment—that is, materials generated in the course of adopting a statute. They also explore precedent—that is, case law or decisions made in other courts. Courts follow the principle of *stare decisis,* which means that judges stand by precedents and do not disturb settled points. Judges also may apply principles of common practice and equity when laws and precedents are either inadequate or in conflict.

Judges are called upon to make a variety of types of decisions, and many of these decisions impact policy. Table 12.1 outlines the types of policy making and the jurisdictions under which they fall.

In more than two-thirds of cases decided by the Supreme Court there have been dissenting opinions.

These disagreements suggest that because more than one position is legally defensible, differing opinions may be subject to several influences, including politics. Researchers have tried to determine what factors—other than "legal" factors—impact judges' decisions. Researchers from the political perspective have found that the personal attitudes of judges determine what they want to do, feel is right to do, and find is feasible. Role orientations determine what they feel the role of a judge ought to be and what they think is appropriate judicial behavior. Institutional factors also play a role because appellate court decisions are group decisions and judges must be able to persuade other judges of their positions (Tarr, 1994). Figure 12.3 highlights the components of the political perspective.

As a result of their research, Carp and Rowland (1983) proposed the framework in Figure 12.4 to explain the impact of case content, law, and justices' backgrounds and environments on judicial decision making. Their research indicates that although case content exerts the major influence on the decisions— and therefore the traditional explanation that cases are decided on merits and on precedent is still correct in most situations—the traditional model has its limitations for cases in which precedents and evidence are about equally strong, for new areas of law where innovative decision making is required, and for issues about which the precedents and evidence are ambiguous or contradictory. For this small group of cases, "factors such as the judges' basic philosophy, the mores and traditions of their particular circuit or state, and the attitudes and values reflected in their own political backgrounds do indeed measurably affect their judicial decisionmaking" (Carp & Rowland, 1983, p. 165).

Whenever people disagree with the decisions of judges, they accuse them of operating inappropriately by acting on their own policy preferences rather than in accordance with the law. Although some people believe that judges interpret rather than make the law, others believe that interpreting the law inevitably involves judges in the policy-making process. "Their rulings may announce authoritative legal standards that define public policy within the jurisdiction they serve. In some cases, too, their rulings may influence political action and stimulate or retard societal change" (Tarr, 1994, pp. 303–304). The two perspectives can be complementary. "Whereas one view emphasizes that judicial rulings

Table 12.1. Types of Judicial Policy Making

Type of Policy Making	Definition	Major Policy Makers	Legal Basis
Constitutional	Judicial review of governmental action to determine its consistency with constitutional requirements	United States Supreme Court; state supreme courts	Federal Constitution, state constitution
Remedial	Establishment and implementation of requirements to eliminate constitutional violations or meet constitutional requirements	Federal district courts	Use of equity power to achieve constitutionally mandated situation
Statutory Interpretation	Interpretation and application of legislative enactments	Federal courts of appeals; state appellate courts	Federal legislation, state legislation
Oversight of administrative activity	Review of administrative activity to ensure that it is consistent with constitutional, statutory, and/or agency requirements	Federal courts of appeals; state appellate courts	Federal or state constitution; federal or state legislation; agency rules or other requirements
Common law	Judicial enunciation and application of legal standards in the absence of legislation or administrative action	State appellate courts	Judicial precedents, societal standards
Cumulative	Judicial development of policy through the exercise of discretion in resolving a large number of similar cases	State trial courts	Established practices within the court or jurisdiction

Source: Reprinted by permission from page 305 of *Judicial Process and Judicial Policy Making* by G. A. Tarr; Copyright ©1994 West Publishing Company. All rights reserved.

inevitably have policy consequences, the other view cautions that judicial rulings rooted solely in the policy views of the judges are inappropriate" (Tarr, 1994, p. 304).

Clearly, then, counselors desiring to influence public policy through the courts can do so by influencing these environmental and ideological factors, by choosing a venue with judges likely to be sympathetic to their concerns, and by being cognizant of the appropriate timing for advancing their case.

The Justices

No description of the courts would be complete without examining the positions and selection processes for the judges. The selection process is particularly important for counselors to understand because of its inherently political nature. "Basic to our understanding of a fair trial are the notions of judicial impartiality and neutrality, of rulings unaf-

fected by political considerations or by the identity of the litigants" (Tarr, 1994, p. 64).

Historically, many people have tried to influence judges. Threats of salary cuts or loss of position have been used to pressure judges in other political systems. To prevent similar pressures and to secure some degree of judicial independence, the U.S. Constitution guarantees that federal judges shall hold their offices for a life tenure and shall not have their salaries reduced. In order to provide some level of accountability, serious breaches of responsibility can result in impeachment (Kerwin, 1994; Tarr, 1994). However, this has only happened to two district court judges in recent years. So, once appointed, federal judges are the least constrained of public officials. They are invested with the power to declare the acts of other branches null and void. Justices are not immune from criticism or from politics, but they are better able to withstand attacks than those in the other branches of government (Kerwin, 1994).

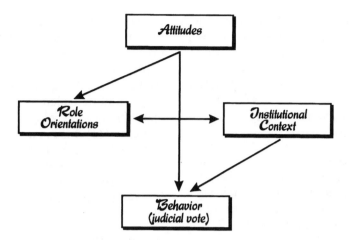

Figure 12.3. The Political Perspective on Judicial Decision Making. From "From Simplicity to Complexity: The Development of Theory in the Study of Judicial Behavior," by J. L. Gibson, 1983, *Political Behavior Journal, 5,* pp. 7–49. Copyright 1983 by Plenum Publishing. Reprinted with permission.

The states have gone further in attempts at accountability. Some require popular election, running for reelection, or some other manner of gaining public approval for their performance (Tarr, 1994). State court judge selections are good opportunities for counselors to influence future court decisions. The process of selecting state judges is more accessible to counselors than the process of selecting federal judges. There are more opportunities to impact the process because turnover is more frequent. Counselors can influence the selection process by building relationships with members of their state's Bar Association, as the Bar makes most of the recommendations for state judgeships.

Article II of the Constitution gives the president the power to appoint federal judges with the advice and consent of the Senate. The reality is complex. "The respective influence of the President and Senate on selection differs depending upon the level of court, upon the importance the President attaches to judicial appointments, and upon whether a single party controls both the presidency and the Senate" (Tarr, 1994, p. 79). Presidents nominate judges from their own party on the basis of their legal-political compatibility with the president's views. They sometimes try to be regionally and demographically representative (Tarr, 1994). However, as was evident in the Bork and Thomas nominations, the "Senate can assume an adversarial stance and conduct their own detailed investigation of the nominee's qualifications and constitutional views" (Tarr, 1994, p. 92). In the selection of district court or appeals

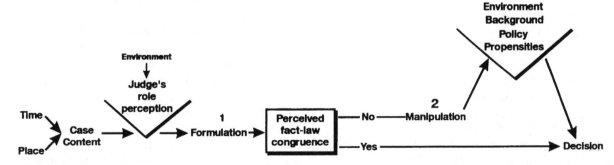

Figure 12.4. Framework for Analysis of Federal District Court Policy Decisions. From *Policymaking and Politics in the Federal District Courts* (p. 13), by R. A. Carp & C. K. Rowland, 1983, Knoxville: University of Tennessee. Copyright © 1983 by University of Tennessee. Reprinted with permission.

court judges, the senators usually have their own lists of potential judges, and the president merely confirms these recommendations. Appeals court judgeships are avidly sought with active campaigning (Tarr, 1994). "Anybody who thinks the judicial office seeks the man is mistaken. There's not a man on the court who didn't do what he thought needed to be done" (Howard, 1981, p. 101).

The American Bar Association is an unofficial participant in the process of selecting federal judges. Its Standing Committee on the Federal Judiciary does investigations and rates the nominees submitted to them by the president (Tarr, 1994).

Political conflict is never totally absent from the selection of judges. It was at its peak during the Bork nomination. "Judges in the United States may be appointed or elected, chosen by political officials, by 'merit selection,' or by popular vote. But no selection system altogether banishes political or ideological considerations. Different selection systems may affect who exercises political influence, but not whether it will be exercised" (Tarr, 1994, p. 63). In short, any process in which Senators, the Bar, or political parties are involved is open to influence by interest groups such as counselors. Clearly, influence requires staying aware of the backgrounds and ideological persuasions of potential judges. To do this and develop influence with those who make the recommendations and the decisions, counselors could use all of the advocacy strategies discussed in previous chapters. In addition, specialized methods are available when counselors try to influence the courts, and these are described in the next section.

INTEREST GROUP STRATEGIES

The strategies that interest groups use with the judiciary differ vastly from those used with legislatures and the administrative agencies. Most judges keep their distance from interest groups. The kinds of inducements that help create access to the legislative and administrative branches—PAC contributions, honoraria, lunches at posh restaurants, the implied promise of future employment—are off limits in the judicial setting (Tarr, 1994; Epstein & Rowland, 1985). Access is limited to formal courtroom settings governed by the strictest rules of procedure (Schlozman & Tierney, 1986). Although courts act only in cases between parties with con-

crete interests at stake, organizations concerned with the outcome may become quite active participants (Vose, 1958). They can participate when a suit is filed in (a) test cases, (b) class action suits, and (c) publicity litigation, (d) filing amicus curiae briefs, or (e) offering expert testimony. They can participate without a suit being filed in (a) judicial appointments and (b) shaping legal opinion. Organizations pursuing their goals through the courts "face a long slow process requiring patience and persistence" (Schlozman & Tierney, 1986, p. 360). The slowness is magnified by the fact that court decisions usually have quite narrow applications.

Affecting Policy When a Suit Is Filed

Litigation is not always pursued solely "to obtain policy objectives through favorable judicial determinations" (O'Connor, 1980, p. 2). But when an organization regularly brings **test cases** before the U.S. Supreme Court, it is called "outcome-oriented litigation." "Serious test cases argued by well-respected lawyers could bring favorable publicity to the organization, as well as spark a nonemotional discussion of the issue that previously had been clouded by other organizational stands on more controversial issues" (O'Connor, 1980, p. 142). Seventy two percent of organizations are involved in litigation at some point, making it 18th on a list of 27 techniques of exercising influence. Sponsoring litigation is a very direct way of influencing policy, but it is also very expensive and time-consuming to plan and execute (Schlozman & Tierney, 1986). With no delays, it takes an average of four years to pass a case through the lower courts to the Supreme Court. A series of cases on the same issue may extend over two decades or more (Vose, 1958). Therefore, while many organizations use this method, they use it rarely. Some organizations—such as public interest law firms—specialize in or were founded just to sponsor litigation on behalf of causes (Schlozman & Tierney, 1986). For instance, the NAACP has presented test cases to the Supreme Court and has won successive gains in protecting the rights of blacks to vote and to obtain housing, transportation, education, and the right to serve on juries. Charles Houston, special counsel for the NAACP in 1935, described the NAACP's use of the courts, saying that the legal campaign against inequality should be carefully planned "to secure decisions, rulings and public opinion on the broad principle instead of being devoted to merely miscellaneous cases" (Vose, 1958, p. 23). "Most organized interests, however, see litigation neither as their raison d'etre nor as something to be eschewed, but as an instrument to be used when it appears to be the best (or only) way of protecting or furthering organizational goals" (Schlozman & Tierney, 1986, p. 365; see also O'Connor, 1980).

Organizations sponsoring litigation want the courts to assess the constitutionality or application of a legislative or executive act. They institute the suit by choosing an unambiguous case. Careful planning is required so that the courts can be persuaded to rule on the intended issue. Sometimes this means violating the law intentionally so as to invite prosecution, or scouring the country to find an applicable situation or a desirable plaintiff. Organizations have greater ability than individuals to choose the cases, the forum, the attorneys and the strategies likely to help them gain a favorable ruling (Schlozman & Tierney, 1986).

Problems can arise in test cases, however, and must be anticipated. The defendant could move to another jurisdiction in which the issue is not an issue; he or she could get too old for it to be an issue; times could change, making the matter no longer an issue; the defendant could die or lose standing; or the defendant could get what he or she wants and not be willing to go forward due to the difficulties inherent in the case (Schlozman & Tierney, 1986). Sometimes defendants back out because of the unpopularity of the cause and the resulting threat to their employment or status (O'Connor, 1980).

Class actions are one way to minimize the problems arising from a one-defendant case. In class action suits a case is brought on behalf of a plaintiff and all other persons similarly situated (O'Connor, 1980; Schlozman & Tierney, 1986; Vose, 1958). The use of class actions has increased, and organizations regularly use them when a problem is not being addressed by Congress or an administrative agency (Schlozman & Tierney, 1986).

Many authors and researchers have attempted to determine what factors contribute to organizational success in litigation. As stated earlier, because organizations sponsor litigation for various reasons, sometimes just defining success is a problem. Cortner (1968) indicated, however, that critical to the success of aggressive litigants (those forced to re-

sort to the courts because of failures in other political forums) are creativity and innovation—mainly in the use of technical data—adequate financial resources, and public support for the idea. Defensive litigants-those who use the courts to urge the application of existing constitutional or legislative doctrines and who generally become defensive after some successes as aggressive litigants—use the same tactics that worked when they were aggressive. A defensive situation might exist when an organization successfully lobbies the legislature to pass laws, and then opponents challenge the laws in court.

Some of the other important factors necessary to successful litigation are (Belton, 1978; Cowan, 1977; Ginger, 1963; Greenberg, 1973; Krislov, 1963; Meltsner, 1973; Peltason, 1955; Sorauf, 1976; Vose, 1949, 1958, 1959, 1972):

1. Control of the information and the case, cohesion of the group, control of the group's litigation resources, and skill in managing its various resources. When several organizations are attempting to influence the same issue, a central organization might not have control of the litigation strategy. This hurts the overall chances of success.

2. Longevity, or the ability to stay in for the long haul. Actions often take years to get through the Supreme Court, and sometimes take as long as several decades.

3. Full-time skilled support staff and attorneys, or skilled and dedicated volunteers. This is critical because many law firms steer away from pro bono work and controversial issues brought by politically unpopular groups, claiming it scares away potential fee-generating clients. Volunteers work well if they are monitored closely by the staff.

4. Financial resources, including foundation support, because membership support may be unstable.

5. Technical data, such as scientific evidence or social science research data.

6. The ability to generate well-timed publicity to the public and to law reviews.

7. Close coordination between national headquarters and local affiliates, members, and the public.

8. Coordination and cooperation with other interest groups, in order to join resources, gain amicus assistance, and persuade the court to become involved—which they might not do if disagreement on the goals is present and widely reported. Disagreement may also diminish the organization's respectability.

9. The ability to persuade the Justice Department or the solicitor general to enter the dispute on the sponsoring organization's side. Filing of an amicus brief by a solicitor general almost guarantees a review of the case.

10. The organization's respectability and prestige.

11. A single issue focus, which allows for concentration of energies, development of competence on the issue, and Supreme Court familiarity with the group's expertise.

Sometimes organizations sponsor litigation knowing that a favorable ruling is unlikely. Organizations might sponsor this **publicity-oriented litigation** in order to enhance the organization's credibility with the public and its members, to attract new members, or to draw attention to "bad" laws that need changing. When the organization's issue attains the public eye, it may become part of a broader public agenda. Some groups never "win" a favorable ruling, but succeed anyway because their goals were to acquire publicity on their issue and/or gain remedy through the other branches of government (O'Connor, 1980).

A very important strategy and the one used most frequently by interest groups to influence public policy when a suit has been filed is **filing an amicus curiae brief** (Epstein, 1991; Vose, 1958). Because litigation is so expensive, an organization may choose not to sponsor a suit but to play a role in a U.S. Supreme Court or state supreme court case by participating as amicus curiae. An organization thus gains an opportunity to have input for only a fraction of the cost (Schlozman & Tierney, 1986); filing an amicus brief may cost as little as $6000 (Michael Anderson, McKenna & Cunio law firm, personal communication, July 1, 1995). "Organizations which [are understaffed, have] money problems, or [have] organizational difficulties, endeavor to supplement the positions of stronger associations that have the capacity to function as outcome-oriented litigants. They resort to amicus curiae activity on account of

their desire to get involved, coupled with the knowledge that they lack the resources to do more" (O'Connor, 1980, pp. 94-95).

Filing amicus curiae briefs is a relatively easy and informal mode of participation. It only requires preparation, printing, and filing of a brief, which is usually no longer than 25 pages (Schlozman & Tierney, 1986). Amicus curiae means "friend of the court," although those who submit the briefs are not so much friends of the court as they are friends of one of the litigating parties (O'Connor, 1980). To file an amicus curiae brief, an organization must either get permission from the litigating parties or from the court. Groups have 30 days to file the brief from the date on which the respondent receives the petition for writ of certiorari. To qualify as an amicus curiae, a nonparty must show that it has substantial interest in the legal question and must file the motion and brief in a timely fashion (Caldeira & Wright, 1988).

Caldeira and Wright (1989, as cited in Epstein, 1991) found in their research that groups file briefs with the Supreme Court for four reasons: the significance of the case to the group's members, the existence of conflict, the desire to keep group members satisfied, and the perceived efficacy of briefs. "Unsolicited amicus curiae briefs . . . may be filed by organizations that view a particular case as presenting issues of substantial concern or issues that could have an impact on their long range goals" (O'Connor, 1980, p. 4). An organization might want to inform the court of its stand on an issue, present new material, provide an additional perspective, show widespread support for a particular alternative in resolving the problem, or provide evidence to the public or the organizational membership that the organization is indeed active (O'Connor, 1980). Krislov (1963) indicated that the introduction of technical, nonlegal data by amicus curiae is really important to constitutional litigants, who may not otherwise have access to this data. Sometimes organizations file a brief because they are dissatisfied with the arguments presented to date. Other times they file them to indicate interest in the case. Still other times they file them at the request of one of the litigants who feels that filing it on his or her own might damage the case (O'Connor, 1980).

Overall, the use of amicus curiae briefs is strikingly similar to techniques used by lobbyists. Organizations furnish decisionmakers with evidence of why they should decide in a way that is favorable to the organization. Amicus curiae briefs make the courts aware that others are attentive to the issue at hand and care intensely about it. Amicus curiae briefs have become an advocacy document that allows an organization to publicize its position on an issue, to educate its own members on substantive points of an issue, or to impress its members with the organization's staff activity (Schlozman & Tierney, 1986).

The use of amicus curiae briefs has increased significantly, and a number of factors must be present if they are to be used effectively. First, lawyers must be willing to keep abreast of potential cases and the potential use of an amicus brief to strengthen the claims of the major parties. O'Connor (1980) claimed that amicus curiae briefs work best where a "loosely allied organizational network exists; that is, where associations are willing to work together to pursue common or similar aims" (p. 4).

Caldeira and Wright's (1988) research demonstrated that amicus curiae briefs not only inform the court but attract the attention of the court. In other words, when briefs are filed, they influence the chances that the Supreme Court will review the case, which is no small feat, since only approximately 170 of the 4000 requested are reviewed each year. Caldeira and Wright claim that this is because "the potential significance of a case is proportional to the demand for adjudication among affected parties and that the amount of amicus curiae participation reflects the demand for adjudication" (p. 1112). The *number* of amicus curiae briefs weighs more heavily than the substantive arguments presented in the case being reviewed. Even when the amicus curiae brief opposes the petition for certiorari, the chances of review are increased.

Perhaps the judicial area with which counselors are most familiar is serving as an **expert witness.** Forensics is a specialty area within the mental health field. By establishing this specialty and becoming known to the courts, counselors' testimony affects case outcomes. Counselors may be asked to evaluate parents and children in custody cases and make recommendations about which custody and visitation arrangements are in the child's best interests. They may be asked to testify to the psychological damage a client has sustained as the victim of a crime such as rape, burglary, or child physical or sexual abuse. They may be asked to make sentencing recommendations in cases where they have served as the probation or prison counselor. Each of these situations, though familiar, is only likely to affect the current disputants, unless the case is appealed to a higher court. In the higher courts, expert testimony affects precedent, and in the Supreme Court, it might affect decisions with wide social implications.

Affecting Policy without Filing Suit

Organizations can influence public policy through the courts without filing suit, by influencing judicial appointments, shaping opinion in the legal community, and using other, more creative strategies. As previously noted, all federal judges are appointed by the president with the consent of the Senate. Both the president and the Senate are subject to political pressure (Schlozman & Tierney, 1986). "From the onset of the Reagan administration in 1981, the politics of federal judicial appointments have become increasingly, although not universally, contentious" (DeGregorio & Rossotti, 1995, p. 215). Interest group politicking over the Bork and Thomas nominations was unprecedented and may have permanently changed the role of interest groups in Supreme Court nominations. Table 12.2 shows the strategies that interest groups used during these nominations. It is clear that because the Senate was involved, all of the lobbying strategies usually used to influence legislation were used to influence the judicial appointments. Organizations lobbied officials, held strategy sessions with key players, testified at public hearings, instituted letter-writing campaigns, inspired their members, coordinated their efforts with other groups, and used the media. Substantial resources—money, staff, active members, timely information, personal credibility, and personal rapport—were expended. Coalitions were formed to allow groups to share information, "brainstorm" about strategies, coordinate lobbying, target particular Senators, and capitalize on their strengths (DeGregorio & Rossotti, 1995).

It is also possible to influence the court by shaping opinion in the legal community. "Law review lobbying" involves publishing articles in law reviews and other legal journals or periodicals (Schlozman & Tierney, 1986; Newland, 1959).

Table 12.2. Priority Tactics as Employed by Advocates in the Bork and Thomas Confirmation Processes

Tactics	Total (N = 109)	Bork priority (N = 59)	Thomas priority (N = 50)
Internal Group Activities			
1. Lobbying Senate	65.0	59.3	72.0
2. Holding strategy sessions with member of Congress or staff	13.0	13.6	12.0
3. Preparing witnesses	13.0	10.2	16.0
4. Reaching out to group members	40.4	57.6	16.0
5. Coordinating internal group efforts	33.9	33.9	34.0
Intergroup Activities			
1. Coordinating activities with other groups	44.4	42.4	46.0
2. Participating in strategy sessions with other groups	30.0	37.3	22.0
External Group Activities			
1. Writing op-ed pieces, appearing on talk shows, etc.	20.0	20.3	20.0
2. Conducting polls or other research towards building mass appeal	4.6	6.8	2.0
3. Networking to keep presence in the media	18.3	22.0	14.0

Source: From "Campaigning for the Court: Interest Group Participation in the Bork and Thomas Confirmation Processes" (p. 223), by C. DeGregorio and J. E. Rossotti. In A. J. Cigler and B. A. Loomis (Eds.), *Interest Group Politics, Fourth Edition,* 1995, Washington, DC: Congressional Quarterly Press. Copyright ©1995 Congressional Quarterly Press. Reprinted with permission.

These articles advocate certain types of court decisions and legal reasoning or present scholarly analyses of constitutional issues or of legal remedies. Organized interests have encouraged sympathetic legal experts to write articles supporting particular viewpoints, particularly when the existing body of legal precedents runs counter to the organization's aims. In its litigation strategy, the NAACP has generated large numbers of favorable review articles before presenting an issue to the court (Schlozman & Tierney, 1986).

A related way to shape legal opinion is to speak at gatherings of law students, professors, and practitioners, or to write texts, as Ruth Bader Ginsberg did prior to initiating sexual discrimination cases. There is no way to tell how often this happens or how effective it is, but publishing in law journals is a legitimate and respectable way for organized interests to nurture a certain climate within the legal community (Schlozman & Tierney, 1986).

Finally, organizations have been very creative in developing other strategies to influence the court.

Close reading of the law often turns up loopholes that may benefit an interest group (O'Connor, 1980). Groups can give advice and service to litigants and can offer financial assistance (Caldeira & Wright, 1988). On the abortion issue in 1989, groups held vigils outside the court, marched and protested throughout the nation, and sought to influence public opinion through the media. They treated the Supreme Court as if it were Congress (Epstein, 1991).

SUMMARY

After reviewing the strategies interest groups use to influence public policy through the courts, several factors become clear. The counseling profession is unlikely to pursue aggressive litigation due its excessive costs. The only exception might be if counselors could persuade a public interest law firm to take on the case of an unjustly treated mental health consumer or student. Nevertheless, counselors might be forced into defensive litigation if other groups sue them, which is similar to what happens when counselors are sued for practicing psychology without a license or school districts are sued by groups who believe that the counseling curriculum is "religious." Counselors might also, in defensive litigation, support the government's case with information, evidence, and expert testimony when groups challenge legislation for which counselors have lobbied.

Particularly in cooperation with other mental health organizations, counselors can afford to file amicus curiae briefs in key cases. This would require, however, a change of focus for the counseling profession, since counselors rarely track the types of cases coming before the State and U.S. Supreme Courts.

Finally, if counselors do change their focus to include advocating through the courts and keeping abreast of cases related to mental health providers and consumers, they could effectively influence the courts in the same ways they influence legislatures and administrative agencies—by serving as a resource, writing articles, and generating publicity to influence public opinion.

Chapter 13

CONCLUSIONS

This book has looked at counselors as an interest group—not only as participants in the political process, but also as leaders helping to shape the counseling profession. It has presented a model of the stages of advocacy to organize advocacy efforts, and it has explained what is needed to achieve effective results.

Once again, these stages are

1. Development of a sense of professional identity

2. Problem identification

3. Resource assessment

4. Strategic planning

5. Training counselors for advocacy

6. Taking action

7. Victory celebration and regrouping

In its discussion of how counselors can best proceed through these stages, the book has brought together the public relations literature, public policy literature, and conflict resolution literature with the responses of a variety of people interviewed as part of the research for the book. *Making an Impact* also has explored extensively (a) the role of conflict in the advocacy process, (b) the process of coalition building, and (c) what's necessary to change public policy through rulemaking, the courts, and the legislature.

Certain essentials are required during each stage, and in fact should underlie all advocacy efforts. Counselors should have a strong sense of professional identity, strong leadership, organizational strength and unity, a "long view" in planning, good communication, adequate education and training, a consumer focus, a coordinated effort, perse-

verance—which research participants defined as "noodging people to death" and keeping advocacy "at the forefront of your brain all the time." Relationship building, communication, negotiation, conflict resolution, systems alteration, and consensus building—skills used daily by counselors—are also essential to advocacy.

Several facts that will surprise counselors but that could make it possible for them to be effective advocates have been clearly articulated by public policy scholars. First, neophytes can have significant influence. Second, the leadership of professional associations historically has advised counselors to do what professional lobbyists do. Third, most public policy and coalition initiatives come from organizational staff people, like those at the American Counseling Association (ACA), so the government relations staff working for counselors are not disadvantaged. Fourth, interest groups with "big bucks" are distrusted—to have influence they need more money because they often are viewed as "black sheep." Finally, times have changed; in the current political environment, expertise and substantive knowledge have more clout than the good ol' boys smoking cigars in the back room.

OBSTACLES TO EFFECTIVE ADVOCACY

Obstacles to counselor advocacy efforts remain, however. The book's discussion about advocacy activities, procedures, and attributes naturally implies that their absence would pose an obstacle to advocacy. But there are other obstacles. According to research participants, counselors' "wimpiness"—their seeming unwillingness to take a stand for themselves, for something they believe in, and to persevere at it—is an obstacle. "We are afraid of [advocacy]," said one counselor. Another knew that building relationships with advocacy targets is necessary but said, "I find that challenging and intimidating. I think many other people do as well." Complacence is the reason counselors sometimes do not choose to overcome this fear. "Apathetic people [are our greatest obstacle]. Ninety five percent of the work is done by less than 5 percent of the people." The problem, said another counselor, is "just not doing it. [Counselors want] results but [don't] want to do anything about it." In justifying his request that counselors write a letter or make a phone call once a year, one advocate said, "Excuse me, that is not too much to ask!" Perhaps too many people are willing to be satisfied with the status quo. Perhaps they lack self-esteem because they have been the underdog for so long. "I think we collectively have felt the need to defend so much that we often come off sounding like 'Oh, please let us in. We'll be good.'" Certainly, leaders of counselor advocacy consider one of their most difficult tasks to be motivating their membership.

Professional association leadership and organizational structure can also contribute to advocacy failures through poor management, poor communication, organizational bureaucracy, failure to celebrate successes, not knowing who the membership is, and lack of vision or focus. "The ACA governing council, rather than say professionalization was its highest priority, which the membership said it should be, didn't want to bite the bullet, because human concerns should be our highest priority. So, we prioritize them by alphabet. We alphabetized our strategic goals. That in itself speaks to a problem." Too much recycling of leadership and reinventing the wheel due to lack of continuity and archives are further cited as faults. It would seem difficult not to reinvent the wheel if leadership were not recycled, however. Another example of an obstacle was demonstrated when Dr. Clark from the National Institutes of Mental Health spoke with the leadership of the American Mental Health Counselors' Association (AMHCA) about the issue of subsidizing counseling training through grants. As the participant advocate remembered: "Someone from AMHCA was kind of pounding their fist and saying, 'You know, we've been trying for ten years.' He said, 'That should have told you something: that if you keep trying and it's not working, you're doing something wrong.'" Another felt that "the people that really have the skills to do all this stuff get caught up in political association issues. The association isn't here for the association, the association is here for the advancement of the profession."

Leadership that is burnt out and scattered also results in failure to use resources well. "There's a powerhouse of resource out there. We haven't tapped it." According to another advocate, "What we wind up doing when we don't ask people to participate in the advocacy process [is] . . . we waste an extraordinary amount of talent within our own professional ranks." Yet, "organizations cannot afford to be dysfunctional because when you have people who are stealing from themselves and their family, time, money, efforts, etcetera, on behalf of the organization, well then, the organization darn well better have its act together."

Other obstacles cited were lack of time, financial resources, and staff, and "turf wars." "Most counselors who are in jobs or in private practice don't have the time, or feel that they don't have the time. [They say:] 'My job takes up so much time and how do I have time left to do anything else?'" Turf wars, in which other mental health providers seek to exclude counseling from jobs, reimbursement, and pertinent legislation, are obstacles. These wars play on the public's lack of knowledge about who counselors are, and on their confusion about the different kinds of people who refer to themselves as counselors.

INCREASE IN ADVOCACY

Obstacles or not, advocacy activities nevertheless have increased exponentially since the mid-1950s (Loomis & Cigler, 1986; Schlozman & Tierney, 1986). Since 1960, 61 percent of all groups have opened an office in Washington (Schlozman & Tierney, 1986). Loomis and Cigler (1986, p. 9) called this a "participation revolution," and many authors have pointed to the causes of this explosion. A primary cause is that American culture and the constitutional arrangements of the U.S. government actively encourage the emergence of multiple political interests. The Constitution contributes to a favorable environment for group development because it guarantees free speech, the right of association, and the right to petition the government for redress of grievances, all of which are basic to group formation. Another cause is that "American political parties are less unified and disciplined than parties in many other nations. The resulting power vacuum in the decision-making process offers great potential for alternative political organizations such as interest groups to influence policy" (Loomis & Cigler, 1986, p. 5).

Another cause is that demystification of interest group politics has also made people aware of its great potential. This potential initially became apparent when Vietnam protest and civil rights groups succeeded in changing problem policies through protests. Although not all groups wanted a protest orientation, the general feeling was that government is overly biased toward business, and if other groups do not lobby, their interests will not be represented. Business groups, conversely, opened Washington offices because of the "plague of regulation" (Berry, 1989b, p. 35). If they did not act, their businesses would be encroached upon by federal regulatory bodies. Also, business increasingly felt the public's hostility, and so worried about their interests being represented (Berry, 1989b).

A final cause is that the government has directly sponsored citizen groups such as grassroots neighborhood associations, and has asked for citizen input on advisory councils (Loomis & Cigler, 1986). Thus, interest groups are clearly at the center of the American political process. "Through a troubled and turbulent time, the solution to the ills of our democracy was *more* democracy. More people needed to participate in politics so that policies would more closely approximate the true wishes of the citizenry. *More participation inevitably meant more interest groups*" (Berry, 1989b, p. 14). Overall, the citizenry has become more educated and aware, more empowered, and more certain that if they do not take action, they will lose. Counselors as an interest group are no exception.

Some, however, have criticized interest groups as preventing needed government action and as encouraging nonrepresentative government. "Expanding the role of interest groups has not . . . restored public confidence in the integrity of the political process. Rather, it has heightened unease about the role of interest groups in a democracy" (Berry, 1989b, p. 139). "Fear and fascination, trepidation and trust, despair and delight" (Petracca, 1992b, p. 10) characterize American feelings about interest groups. The concerns have been expressed since Alexander Hamilton, James Madison, and John Jay wrote the Federalist papers (Madison, 1787). Their dilemma about interest groups when composing the Federalist papers was that people would pursue self-interests even when those interests were in opposition to the best interests of the country at large, that "interest groups continually push government to enact policies that benefit small constituencies at the expense of the general public" (Berry, 1989b, p. 1; see also Petracca, 1992a).

Further, research demonstrates that interest groups are not representative of the general public, and that their composition has not changed much over time. Most groups (93 percent) represent business, the well-off, professionals, and managers against those representing the public interest or the disadvantaged. The "haves" are well-represented, while the "have nots" are not. Also, businesses have multiple representation by virtue of being members of numerous groups. "Members of the dominant age, gender and racial group . . . receive ample representation in the pressure community through their dominant role in the unions and business and professional associations that form the preponderance of organizations active in Washington" (Schlozman & Tierney, 1986, p. 74; see also Almond & Verba, 1963 and Wright & Hyman, 1958).

The nonrepresentative nature of interest groups is further accentuated because civic competence (the sense that one can affect the political system) is directly affected by education, occupation, and gender. Higher education, higher employment status, and being male correlate with higher civic competence (Almond & Verba, 1963).

Others are concerned that interest groups have caused politics to become shrill and unruly. They feel that interest groups have diverted policy makers from a long-run to a short-run focus, from the substantively meritorious to the politically exigent. Narrow interests seem to prevail over broad ones, and are often able to stymie policies designed to confront problems having society-wide implications (Petracca, 1992c; Tierney, 1992). Milbrath (1959) claimed that this source of private power, with no accountability, could usurp governmental power.

McFarland (1992) summarized these concerns in describing what he called interest group stasis. Interest group stasis means that those with the greatest economic stakes become the most organized and tend to control government policy in some area. Interest group stasis basically argues that

(1) many widely shared interests cannot be effectively organized within the political process; (2) politics tends to be fragmented into decisionmaking in various specific policy areas, which are normally controlled by special interest coalitions; (3) there are a variety of specific processes whereby plural elitist rule is maintained; and (4) a widespread ideology conceals this truth about American politics. (p. 63)

Stasis makes economic innovation very difficult because it is inherently unstable, and "quickly dissipates into the relatively simple organization of political-economic oligopoly" (p. 64). The government spends more and more, budget deficits increase as special interests acquire tax exemptions, and the economy deteriorates.

McFarland argues, however, that in the real world something stops this collapse: the "frequent appearance in the same decisionmaking situation of organized producer interests, countervailing power lobby, and autonomously acting government officials" (p. 66) are a countervailing power that provides some balance to the "skewed political world of plural elitism" (p. 70). The sources of this countervailing power may be issue networks, social movements, or interest group patrons—such as wealthy individuals, foundations, and government agencies.

In fact, "inequalities in representation are not necessarily translated into proportional inequalities in influence" (Schlozman & Tierney, 1986, p. 85). Those who are more poorly represented have won many victories. Sometimes other groups work in their behalf (such as teachers' groups working for students). Also, even though business is well-represented, it does not always speak with one voice. Further, interest group growth has increased the numbers of organizations represented in the political system; has offered "a direct link to government on the everyday issues that concern a particular constituency, but not the nation as a whole" (Berry, 1977, p. 231); and has replaced narrow subgovernments with a more open process in which more people can participate. As Madison said, if the government does not allow people to pursue their self-interest, then it takes away their freedom (cited in Berry, 1989b).

Counselor advocacy is critical to the continued existence and development of the counseling profession. The increasing number and activities of interest groups paradoxically means that individually groups have less impact. Thus, groups that organize stimulate other groups to organize, because if they do not they will lose (Petracca, 1992b). Lobbying firms, public relations companies, lawyers, trade association executives, company representatives, and public interest groups are all trying to win a precious time slot for their issues on the appointment schedule of one legislator or, through a hearing, of an entire committee. Counselors must either compete with these groups or work with them. In any case, each counselor must always remember that his or her voice is only one of many, and it is up to the individual to make that voice heard (Wittenberg & Wittenberg, 1989). Counselors must change their way of doing business to one that embraces advocacy as a way of life (Richards, 1990). They must accept a truth once heard at an Alanon meeting: "Crazy is doing the same thing over and over, and hoping for a different result." Continuing a course that does not include advocacy for the profession is crazy.

Appendix

ADVOCACY RESEARCH: PROCEDURES, PRECONCEPTIONS, AND LIMITATIONS

RESEARCH QUESTIONS

The research for this book explored the following questions

- What are the essential elements of counselor advocacy?

- What do counselor advocates believe works best in advancing the profession?

- What do counselor advocates do when advocating?

- What factors influence the choice of advocacy strategies?

- Who do counselor advocates consider the main targets of their advocacy?

- What are the obstacles to advocacy and how can they be overcome?

Particular attention was paid to the topics addressed in this book on advocacy, including establishing priorities and objectives, and assessing resources, including funding.

Defining what is outside the scope of research is as important as what is included. This research did not focus on anyone other than professional association leaders who might be involved in advocacy efforts; it did not focus on evaluating the actual success of advocacy, only on the advocates' beliefs about what works and on what advocacy methods are actually used; and it did not focus on advocacy efforts on a particular piece of policy (as public policy case studies do). Although many of these areas would be valuable research topics, and should be taken up later, they were beyond the scope of this research effort.

METHODS

Three approaches—participant-observation, key informant interviewing, and content analysis of advocacy documents—were used to understand counselor advocacy. Deciding what particular factors to attend to was based on the social engineering model of public policy research (Bobrow & Dryzek, 1987). In other words, attempts were made to access information from many different sources, and to develop a comprehensive model to inform advocacy efforts. Encouraging counselors to experiment with this model and developing a recursive dialogue about how to improve it should be responses to this portion of the research.

Respondents. Twenty-eight national and state counseling profession leaders who are and have been actively involved in advocacy were interviewed. Half were female and half were male. Two were from an ethnic minority. One quarter were aged 37 to 39; half were aged 40 to 49; and one quarter were 50 and older. Thirty two percent (9) had masters degrees, while 68 percent (19) had doctoral degrees. Three quarters (21) were licensed as counselors, while one quarter (7) were not. Sixty four percent (18) identified themselves as mental health counselors (to include clinical, marriage and family, and addictions), while 36 percent (10) identified themselves as school, college, rehab, or career counselors. Forty six percent (13) indicated that their primary work was counseling, 32 percent (9) indicated that they primarily worked in administration, 29 percent (8) primarily taught counseling, and 7 percent (2) were primarily researchers (the percentages add up to more than 100 percent because some respondents indicated several categories). Forty six percent (13) of the respondents indicated that they had been advocating for between 0 and 10 years, 36 percent (10) for between 11 and 20 years, and 18 percent (5) for 20 years or more. Fifty four percent (15) of the respondents had been active as advocates primarily at the national level, 36 percent (10) had been active at the state level, and 10 percent (3) indicated equal involvement at the state and national levels.

Sampling. Sampling consisted of purposive networking. Two key advocates, one from the American Counseling Association (ACA) and one from the American Mental Health Counseling Association (AMHCA), were selected to recommend others who were knowledgeable about and experienced in advocacy. Both of these key informants were women in their 40s who had been employed at their associations' national headquarters for about two years. Both had doctoral level degrees in counseling or a related field. They were selected because they each held critical advocacy positions, were centrally involved in their respective organizations, and were cognizant of the advocacy activities and participants in their respective organizations. Of the 32 advocates they recommended, 4 were not interviewed because they were not easily available and because "saturation" made further interviewing redundant.

Setting. Interviews with staff were conducted at the associations' headquarters and interviews with leadership were conducted at the annual ACA convention in April 1994 and by phone. An interview guide containing research questions was used, along with an informal, conversational interview style. Interviews were approximately one hour long, and face-to-face interviews were audiotaped. The tapes were transcribed. Five interviews were conducted by phone due to participant unavailability in person, and one participant wrote her answers to interview questions. During phone interviews, notes were taken, and typed up soon after. Researcher comments and observations were written during or immediately following the interview process, and were added to the interview transcripts.

Participant observation was done at the ACA headquarters one day per week between January and July 1994, and at the ACA national convention in April 1994. Approximately 150 hours of advocacy and organizational activities were observed. Participant-observation notes and comments were typed soon after the observations were made.

Advocacy documents were collected from the advocacy and government relations departments at ACA. Respondents were also invited to contribute documents they had used when advocating; however, only one respondent submitted documents. These documents were reviewed, and their content, use, style, format (how content was expressed), and essential elements were analyzed. These notes were also typed. Approximately 1,500 pages of typed data resulted from the three data collection methods.

Data analysis was done using *The Ethnograph* computer program (Seidel, Kjolseth, & Seymour, 1988). This required that data categories be established, data be coded according to these categories, and codes be entered into *The Ethnograph*. The data categories were:

1. targets for advocacy

2. advocacy activities (what is done)

3. advocacy process (how it is done)

4. advocacy issues

5. obstacles to advocacy

6. organizational conflicts and their impact on advocacy

7. overcoming obstacles and negative impacts of conflicts

A one-category search separated all of the data into categories. The separated data informed the research results.

RESEARCHER QUALIFICATIONS

Karen Eriksen is a member of both ACA and AMHCA. As such, she sees their advocacy role as critical to the counseling profession. From this belief comes her motivation to do research that might further that role.

Eriksen has been a mental health provider since 1980, and has only in the last few years identified herself specifically with the profession of counseling. Her master's degree was in psychology, and previous doctoral work and advanced training was in marriage and family therapy. In recent years, she has become conscious of sharing certain values with the counseling profession. These include inclusiveness, valuing diversity, building bridges, and a focus on health, growth, and competence. This consciousness led to her identification with the counseling profession, and further, gave birth to her desire to advocate for policy changes to include counselors as part of the community of recognized mental health providers at all levels of government, in public and private programs, in insurance reimbursement, and in legislation.

Eriksen has participated in advocacy efforts successfully for many years. Her specific experiences in advocacy have been:

1. working with professional organization leadership and members to write letters to insurance companies about including counselors as mental health providers.

2. working with professional organization leadership and members to write letters to legislators about including counselors in legislation or changing legislation to better provide for clients.

3. as a national professional organization leader (Advocacy Intern at ACA and District Consultant for AMHCA), meeting with, writing letters to, and phoning state leaders to assist them in their advocacy process. This has involved the sharing of information, networking, providing documents, being a resource, and connecting leaders to other appropriate resources.

4. as a private practitioner, establishing relationships with referral sources and clients, and dispersing materials about her own practice and about counselors.

5. planning and participating in lobbying efforts directed toward state and national legislatures.

6. teaching and supervising counselors in training.

7. educating hospital programs about counselors, providing them with documentation of which insurance companies reimburse counselors so that these hospitals would be able to access the services of counselors.

PRECONCEPTIONS

Eriksen assumed that her personal observations of counselors' avoidance of advocacy and the rea-

sons for this avoidance are widely held and valid. She also assumed that useful information presented in a manageable format would produce the desired goals of increased participation in advocacy. Further assumptions were:

1. The counseling profession should continue to exist and grow.

2. Advocacy is necessary to both existence and growth.

3. Observation, interviews, and artifact analysis will yield the most relevant data.

RESEARCH LIMITATIONS

The research has several limitations. First, it merely tries to ascertain the "what and how" of advocates' activities, without ascertaining their level of effectiveness (see chapter 6 for a discussion on effectiveness). Further, rather than trying to validate information by confirming it with multiple sources, all ideas were included as possibilities. The analysis attempted to classify or group these ideas into a useable model. As such, the data analysis was cursory, not attempting to develop analytic categories or go too far beyond the data.

Other concerns should also be noted. The phone interviews could not be audiotaped, and thus the notes lacked the depth and color of the word-for-word transcripts from the face-to-face interviews. These interviews therefore cannot be considered to have been weighted equally to the face-to-face interviews. Further, researchers are always concerned about those respondents who were recommended but not interviewed. Could their information have colored the research results differently? In this case, this is not likely. Interviews with the four remaining recommendees could have been pursued; however, the researcher had reached "saturation." In other words, interviewing and observation ended when the researcher had stopped discovering any new information. Finally, sampling was limited by the choice of the initial two key informants. Since one was from ACA and one from AMHCA, organizations in serious conflict at the time of the research, it was hoped that competing interests would lead to a balanced selection. However, when information on respondents was tallied, there was a significant imbalance in favor of mental health counselors.

Further research should expand the respondent base to include more counselors from other specialty groups.

Further research also needs to assess the effectiveness of the advocacy activities and methods. Perhaps use of this book will offer opportunities to ascertain which strategies and procedures work best. In addition, research should be done to determine whether the researcher's original assumption was true: that the book would increase counselor participation in advocacy and would increase the effectiveness of counselor advocacy.

REFERENCES

Administrative Procedure Act, 5 U.S.C. § 551 (4) (1946).

Administrative Procedure Act, 5 U.S.C. § 552 (1) (1946).

Administrative Procedure Act, 5 U.S.C. § 5 706 (1946).

Advocacy Institute (1990). *The elements of a successful public interest advocacy campaign.* Washington, DC: Author.

Almond, G. A., & Verba, S. (1963). The sense of civic competence. *The civic culture: Political attitudes and democracy in five nations.* Princeton, NJ: Princeton University Press.

American Counseling Association. (1992). *21 steps in a successful legislative process: A fact sheet.* Alexandria, VA: Author.

American Psychiatric Association. (1994). *Diagnostic and statistical manual of mental disorders* (4th ed.). Washington, DC: Author.

American School Counselor Association. (1981). *Organizing for action: Ideas for mobilizing resources on behalf of elementary guidance* (2nd ed.). Falls Church, VA: Author.

Armstrong, V. C., & Johnson, C. A. (1982). Certiorari decisions by the Warren and Burger courts: Is cue theory time bound? *Polity, 15*(1), 141-150.

Baker, S. B., Swisher, J. D., Nadenicheck, P. E., & Popowicz, C. L. (1984). Measured effects of primary prevention strategies. *The Personnel and Guidance Journal, 62*(8), 459-464.

Bauer, R. A., de Sola Pool, I., & Dexter, L. A. (1963). *American business and public policy: The politics of foreign trade.* New York: Atherton.

Belton, R. (1978). A comparative review of public and private enforcement of Title VII of the Civil Rights Act of 1964. *Vanderbilt Law Review, 31,* 905-961.

Bentley, A. F. (1967). *The process of government.* Cambridge, MA: Harvard University.

Berry, J. M. (1977). *Lobbying for the people.* Princeton, NJ: Princeton University Press.

Berry, J. M. (1989a). *The interest group society.* New York: HarperCollins.

Berry, J. M. (1989b). Subgovernments, issue networks, and political conflict. In R. A. Harris and S. M. Milkis (Eds.), *Remaking American politics.* Boulder, CO: Westview.

Birnbaum, J. H. (1992). *The lobbyists: How influence peddlers get their way in Washington.* New York: Time Books.

Blake, R. R., & Mouton, J. S. (1964). *The managerial grid.* Houston, TX: Gulf.

Blake, R. R., Shepard, H. A., & Mouton, J. S. (1964). *Managing intergroup conflict in industry.* Houston: Gulf Publishing.

Bobrow, D. B., & Dryzek, J. S. (1987). *Policy analysis by design.* Pittsburgh, PA: University of Pittsburgh Press.

Biklen, S. K. (1992). *Qualitative research for education: An introduction to theory and methods.* Needham Heights, MA: Allyn & Bacon.

Bone, H. A. (1958). Political parties and pressure group politics. *Annals of the American Academy of Political and Social Science, 319,* 73-83.

Borders, L. D., & Drury, S. M. (1992). Comprehensive school counseling programs: A review for policy makers and practitioners. *Journal of Counseling and Development, 70*(4), 487-498.

Braun, C. (1976). Teacher expectation: Sociopsychological dynamics. *Review of Educational Research, 46*(2), 185-213. 371 U.S. § 429-430 (1963).

Brigman, G., & Moore, P. (1994). *School counselors and censorship: Facing the challenge.* Alexandria, VA: American School Counselor Association.

Browne, W. P. (1986). Policy and interests: Instability and change in a classic issue subsystem. In A. J. Cigler & B. A. Loomis (Eds.), *Interest group politics* (pp. 183-201). Washington, DC: Congressional Quarterly Press.

Browne, W. P. (1988). *Private interests, public policy, and American agriculture.* Lawrence: University Press of Kansas.

Browne, W. P. (1995). Organized interests, grassroots confidants, and Congress. In A. J. Cigler & B. A. Loomis (Eds.), *Interest group politics* (4th ed.) (pp. 281-317). Washington, DC: Congressional Quarterly Press.

Burke, R. J. (1970). Methods of resolving superior-subordinate conflict: The constructive use of subordinate differences and disagreements. *Organizational Behavior and Human Performance, 5*(4), 393-411.

Caine, R., & Caine, G. (1991). Making connections: Teaching and the human brain. Alexandria, VA: Association for Supervision and Curriculum Development.

Caldeira, G. A., & Wright, J. R. (1988). Organized interests and agenda setting in the U.S. Supreme Court. *American Political Science Review, 82*(4), 1109-1127.

Carledge, G., & Milburn, J. F. (1978). The case for teaching social skills in the classroom: A review. *Review of Educational Research, 48*(1), 133-156.

Carp, R. A., & Rowland, C. K. (1983). *Policymaking and politics in the federal district courts.* Knoxville: University of Tennessee.

Cigler, A. J. (1986). From protest group to interest group: The making of the American agriculture movement. In A. J. Cigler & B. A. Loomis (Eds.), *Interest group politics* (pp. 46-69). Washington, DC: Congressional Quarterly.

Cigler, A. J., & Loomis, B. A. (1995). Contemporary interest-group politics: More than "more of the same." In A. J. Cigler & B. A. Loomis (Eds.), *Interest group politics* (4th ed.) (pp. 393-406). Washington, DC: Congressional Quarterly.

Clark, P. B., & Wilson, J. Q. (1961). Incentive systems: A theory of organizations. *Administrative Science Quarterly, 6*(2), 129-166.

Cobb, H. D., & Richards, H. C. (1983). Efficacy of counseling services in decreasing behavior problems of elementary school children. *Elementary School Guidance and Counseling, 17*(3), 180-187.

Conway, M. M. (1986). PACs and Congressional elections in the 1980s. In A. J. Cigler & B. A. Loomis (Eds.), *Interest group politics* (pp. 70-90). Washington, DC: Congressional Quarterly Press.

Conway, M. M., & Green, J. C. (1995). In A. J. Cigler & B. A. Loomis (Eds.), *Interest group politics* (4th ed.) (pp. 155-173). Washington, DC: Congressional Quarterly Press.

Cooper, J., & Fazio, R. H. (1979). The formation and persistence of attitudes that support intergroup conflict. In W. G. Austin & S. Worchel (Eds.), *The social psychology of intergroup relations* (pp. 149-159). Monterey, CA: Brooks/Cole.

Coopersmith, S. (1981). *The antecedents of self-esteem.* Palo Alto, CA: Consulting Psychologists Press.

Cortner, R. C. (1968). Strategies and tactics of litigants in constitutional cases. *Journal of Public Law, 17,* 287-307.

Coser, L. A. (1956). *The functions of social conflict.* New York: Free Press.

Coser, L. A. (1967). *Continuities in the study of social conflict.* New York: Free Press.

Costain, W. D., & Costain, A. N. (1981). Interest groups as policy aggregators in the legislative process. *Polity, 14*(2), 249-272.

Council of State Governments (1990). *The book of the States 1990–1991.* Lexington, KY: Author.

Cowan, R. B. (1977). Women's rights through litigation: An examination of the American Civil Liberties Union Women's Rights Project, 1971-1976. *Columbia Human Rights Law Review, 8,* 373-412.

Davis, K. C. (1969). *Discretionary justice: A preliminary inquiry.* Baton Rouge: Louisiana State University.

Deffenbacker, J. L., & Kemper, C. C. (1974). Counseling test-anxious sixth graders. *Elementary School Guidance and Counseling, 9*(1), 22-29.

DeGregorio, C., & Rossotti, J. E. (1995). Campaigning for the court: Interest group participation in the Bork and Thomas confirmation processes. In A. J. Cigler and B. A. Loomis (Eds.), *Interest Group Politics* (4th ed.) (pp. 215-238). Washington DC: Congressional Quarterly Press.

De Tocqueville, A. (1969). *Democracy in America* (J. P. Mayer, Ed.) Garden City, NY: Doubleday. (Original work published 1835)

Deutsch, M. (1973). *The resolution of conflict.* New Haven: Yale University.

Epstein, L. (1985). *Conservatives in court.* Knoxville: University of Tennessee.

Epstein, L. (1991). Courts and interest groups. In J. B. Gates and C. A. Johnson (Eds.), *The American Courts: A Critical Assessment* (pp. 335-371). Washington DC: Congressional Quarterly Press.

Epstein, L., & Rowland, C. K. (1985). Debunking the myth of interest group invincibility in the courts. *American Political Science Review, 85,* 205-217.

Evans, C. L., & Oleszek, W. J. (1995). Reform redux: Jurisdictional change and the new Republican house. A paper presented at the Annual Meeting of the Midwest Political Science Association, Chicago, IL, April 6-8, 1995.

Evans, D. M. (1986). PAC contributions and role-call voting: Conditional power. In A. J. Cigler & B. A. Loomis (Eds.), *Interest group politics* (pp. 114–132). Washington, DC: Congressional Quarterly Press.

Fiorina, M. (1982). Legislative choice of regulatory forms: Legal process or administrative process. *Public Choice, 39,* 33–66.

Folger, J. P., & Poole, M. S. (1984). *Working through conflict: A communication perspective.* Glenview, IL: Scott, Foresman.

Folger, J. P., Poole, M. S., & Stutman, R. K. (1993). *Working through conflict: Strategies for relationships, groups, and organizations.* New York: HarperCollins.

Follett, M. P. (1940). *Dynamic administration: The collected papers of Mary Parker Follett* (H. C. Metcalf and L. Urwick, Eds.). New York: HarperCollins.

Foreman, C. H. (1995). Grassroots victim organizations: Mobilizing for personal and public health. In A. J. Cigler & B. A. Loomis (Eds.), *Interest group politics* (4th ed.) (pp. 33–53). Washington, DC: Congressional Quarterly Press.

Galanter, M. (1974). Why the "haves" come out ahead: Speculations on the limits of legal change. *Law and Society Review, 9,* 95–151.

Garment, S. (1994). *The buck stopped with her.* Washington Post, March 20.

Gerler, E. R. (1980). A longitudinal study of multimodal approaches to small group psychological education. *The School Counselor, 27*(3), 184–190.

Gerler, E. R. (1985). Elementary school counseling research and the classroom learning environment. *Elementary School Guidance and Counseling, 20*(1), 39–48.

Gerler, E. R., & Anderson, R. F. (1986). The effects of classroom guidance on children's success in school. *Journal of Counseling and Development, 65*(2), 78–81.

Gibb, J. R. (1961). Defensive communication. *Journal of Communication, 11*(3), 141–148.

Gibson, J. L. (1983). From simplicity to complexity: The development of theory in the study of judicial behavior. *Political Behavior, 5*(1), 7–49.

Gilchrist, L. A., & Stringer, M. (1992). Marketing counseling: Guidelines for training and practice. *Counselor Education and Supervision, 31,* 154–162.

Ginger, A. F. (1963). Litigation as a form of political action. *Wayne Law Review, 9,* 458–483.

Glaser, W. (1969). *Schools without failure.* New York: Harper and Row.

Glick, H. R. (1990). *Courts in American politics.* New York: McGraw-Hill.

Glosoff, H. L., & Koprovicz, C. L. (1990). *Children achieving potential.* Alexandria, VA: American Association for Counseling and Development and the National Conference of State Legislatures.

Green, M. (1982, December 13). Political PAC-Man. *The New Republic,* pp. 18–25.

Green, R. L. (1988). Image-building activities for the elementary school counselor. *Elementary School Guidance & Counseling, 22*(3), 186–191.

Greenberg, J. (1973). Litigation for social change: Methods, limits and role in democracy. Thirtieth Annual Benjamin N. Cardozo Lecture delivered before the Association of the Bar of the City of New York.

Godwin, R. K. (1992). Money, technology, and political interests: The direct marketing of politics. In M. P. Petracca (Ed.), *The politics of interests* (pp. 308–325). Boulder, CO: Westview.

Gurney, P. (1987). Self-esteem enhancement in children: A review of research findings. *Educational Research, 29*(2), 130–136.

Hakman, N. (1969). The Supreme Court's political environment: The processing of noncommercial litigation. In J. B. Grossman & J. Tananhaus (Eds.), *Frontiers of judicial research.* New York: Wiley, 199–253.

Hall, J. (1986). *Conflict management survey: A survey on one's characteristic reaction to and handling of conflicts between himself and others.* Woodlands, TX: Teleometrics International.

Hawes, L. C., & Smith, D. H. (1973). A critique of assumptions underlying the study of communication in conflict. *Quarterly Journal of Speech, 59*(4), 423–435.

Hayes, M. T. (1986). The new group universe. In A. J. Cigler & B. A. Loomis (Eds.), *Interest group politics* (pp. 133–145). Washington, DC: Congressional Quarterly Press.

Heclo, H. (1978). Issue networks and the executive establishment. In A. King (Ed.), *The new American political system* (pp. 87–124). Washington, DC: American Enterprise Institute.

Heinz, J. P., Laumann, E. O., Nelson, R. L., & Salisbury, R. H. (1993). *The hollow core: Private interests in national policy making.* Cambridge, MA: Harvard University Press.

Hendrix, J. A. (1992). *Public relations cases* (2nd ed.). Belmont, CA: Wadsworth.

Hocker, J. L., & Wilmont, W. W. (1991). *Interpersonal conflict.* Dubuque, IA: Brown.

Hoge, R. D., & Luce, S. (1979). Predicting academic achievement from classroom behavior. *Review of Educational Research, 49*(3), 479–496.

Hook, J. (1989, December 16). New law leaves loopholes for benefits to members. *Congressional Quarterly Weekly Report,* pp. 3420–3424.

Howard, J. W. (1981). *Courts of appeals in the federal judicial system.* Princeton, NJ: Princeton University.

Hula, K. W. (1994, September). *Bedfellows and policy preferences: Interest group coalitions in national politics.* Paper presented at the 1994 annual meeting of the American Political Science Association, The New York Hilton.

Hula, K. W. (1995a). Rounding up the usual suspects: Forging interest group coalitions in Washington. In A. J. Cigler and B. A. Loomis (Eds.), *Interest group politics* (pp. 239–258). Washington, DC: Congressional Quarterly Press.

Hula, K. W. (1995b). Saddling up the posse: Rounding up coalitions in the Washington corral. A paper presented at the 1995 Annual Meeting of the Midwest Political Science Association, The Palmer House Hilton, Chicago, IL.

Huntington, S. P. (1975). The democratic distemper. *Public Interest, 41,* 9–38.

Janda, K., Berry, J. M., & Goldman, J. (1992). *The challenge of democracy.* Boston: Houghton Mifflin.

Jones, R. E., & White, C. S. (1985). Relationships among personality, conflict resolution styles, and task effectiveness. *Group and Organization Studies, 10*(2), 152–167.

Kerwin, C. M. (1994). *Rulemaking: How government agencies write law and make policy.* Washington DC: Congressional Quarterly Press.

Kingdon, J. W. (1984). *Agendas, alternatives, and public policies.* New York: HarperCollins.

Kobylka, J. F. (1987). A court-created context for group litigation: Libertarian groups and obscenity. *Journal of Politics, 49,* 1061–1078.

Kornhauser, W. (1959). *The politics of mass society.* New York: Free Press.

Krislov, S. (1963). The amicus curiae brief: From friendship to advocacy. *Yale Law Journal, 72,* 694–721.

Latham, E. (1952). The group basis of politics: Notes for a theory. *American Political Science Review, 46*(2), 376–397.

Lawrence, P. R., & Lorsch, J. W. (1967). *Organization and environment: Managing differentiation and integration.* Boston: Harvard Business School, Division of Research.

Lax, D., & Sebenius, J. (1986). *The manager as negotiator.* New York: Free Press.

Lempert, R., & Sanders, J. (1986). *An invitation to law and social science: Desert, disputes and distribution.* New York: Longman.

Levine, C. H., & Thurber, J. A. (1986). Reagan and the intergovernmental lobby: Iron triangles, cozy subsystems, and political conflict. In A. J. Cigler & B. A. Loomis (Eds.), *Interest group politics* (pp. 202–220). Washington, DC: Congressional Quarterly Press.

Lindblom, C. E. (1959). The science of "muddling through." In J. M. Shafritz and A. C. Hyde (Eds.), *Classics of Public Administration* (3rd ed.) (pp. 224–235). Pacific Grove, CA: Brooks/Cole.

Linzer, L. (1988). How to use research to get publicity. *Public Relations Journal, 44*(12), 29–31.

Lipsky, M. (1968). Protest as a political resource. *American Political Science Review, 62*(4), 1144–1158.

Loomis, B. A. (1986). Coalitions of interests: Building bridges in the balkanized state. In A. J. Cigler and B. A. Loomis (Ed.), *Interest group politics* (pp. 258–274). Washington DC: Congressional Quarterly Press.

Loomis, B. A., & Cigler, A. J. (1986). Introduction: The changing nature of interest group politics. In A. J. Cigler and B. A. Loomis (Eds.), *Interest group politics* (pp. 1–26). Washington DC: Congressional Quarterly Press.

Loomis, B. A., & Sexton, E. (1995). Choosing to advertise: How interests decide. In A. J. Cigler & B. A. Loomis (Eds.), *Interest group politics* (4th ed.) (pp. 193–214). Washington, DC: Congressional Quarterly Press.

Luttberg, N. R., & Zeigler, H. (1966). Attitude consensus and conflict in an interest group: An assessment of cohesion. *American Political Science Review, 60*(3), 655–666.

Madison, J. (1987). The Federalist, No. 10. In G. Wills (Ed.), *The federalist papers by Alexander Hamilton, James Madison and John Jay* (pp. 42–49). New York: Bantam. (Original work published 1787)

Mann, T. E. (1990). *A question of balance: The president, the Congress and foreign policy.* Washington, DC: Brookings.

Mansbridge, J. J. (1992). A deliberative theory of interest representation. In M. P. Petracca (Ed.), *The politics of interests* (pp. 32–57). Boulder, CO: Westview.

Maraniss, D. (1983, June 26). Competing interests snarl gas debate. *The Washington Post,* pp. A-1, A-14.

Marsh, H. W. (1984). Relations among dimensions of self-attribution, dimensions of self-concept, and academic achievements. *Journal of Educational Psychology, 76*(6), 1291-1308.

McCool, D. (1989). Subgovernments and the impact of policy fragmentation and accommodation. *Policy Studies Review, 8*(4), 264-287.

McCubbins, M., & Schwartz, T. (1987). Congressional oversight overlooked: Police patrols versus fire alarms. *American Journal of Political Science, 28,* 165-179.

McElreath, M. P., & Miller, P. W. (1991). *Introduction to public relations and advertising: A reader from the consumer's point of view.* Needham Heights, MA: Ginn Press.

McFarland, A. S. (1992). Interest groups and the policymaking process: Sources of countervailing power in America. In M. P. Petracca (Ed.), *The politics of interests* (pp. 58-79). Boulder, CO: Westview.

Meltsner, M. (1973). *Cruel and unusual punishment: The Supreme Court and capital punishment.* New York: Random House.

Mental Health Liaison Group. (1993). *The time is now: The case for a comprehensive mental health benefit in health care reform.* Washington, DC: Author.

Michels, R. (1958). *Political parties: A sociological study of the oligarchical tendencies of modern democracy.* New York: Free Press.

Milbrath, L. W. (1963). *The Washington Lobbyists.* Chicago: Rand McNally.

Miller, J. B. (1986). What do we mean by relationships? *Work in Progress: Stone Center Working Paper Series #22.* Wellesley, MA: Stone Center for Developmental Services and Studies.

Murray, J. S. (1986). Understanding competing theories of negotiation. *Negotiation Journal, 2*(2), 179-186.

Myers vs. *United States, 272* U.S. 52 (1926).

Myrick, R. D. (1993). *Developmental guidance and counseling: A practical approach* (2nd ed.). Minneapolis, MN: Educational Media Corporation.

NAACP vs. Button, 371 U.S. 429 (1962).

Newland, C. A. (1959). Legal periodicals and the United States Supreme Court. *Midwest Journal of Political Science, 3,* 58-74.

Newsom, D., Scott, A., & Turk, J. V. (1993). *This is PR: The realities of public relations.* Belmont, CA: Wadsworth.

North, R. C., Brody, R. A., & Holsti, O. R. (1963). Some empirical data on the conflict spiral. *Studies in International Conflict and Integration* (pp. 1-14). Stanford, CA: Stanford University.

O'Connor, K. (1980). *Women's organizations' use of the courts.* Lexington, MA: Lexington Books.

O'Connor, K., & Epstein, L. (1981-1982). Amicus curiae participation in U.S. Supreme Court litigation: An appraisal of Hakman's "folklore." *Law and Society Review, 16,* 311-320.

O'Connor, K., & McFall, B. S. (1992). Conservative interest group litigation in the Reagan era and beyond. In M. P. Petracca (Ed.), *The politics of interests* (pp. 263-281). Boulder, CO: Westview.

Oleszek, W. J. (1989). *Congressional procedures and the policy making process.* Washington, DC: Congressional Quarterly Press.

Olson, M. (1965). *The logic of collective action: Public goods and the theory of groups.* Cambridge, MA: Harvard University Press.

Orren, K. (1976). Standing to sue: Interest group conflict in the federal courts. *American Political Science Review, 70*(3), 723-741.

Peck, M. S. (1987). *The different drum: Community making and peace.* New York: Simon & Schuster.

Peltason, J. W. (1955). *Federal courts in the political process.* New York: Random House.

Peterson, M. A. (1992). Interest mobilization and the presidency. In M. P. Petracca (Ed.), *The politics of interests* (pp. 221-241). Boulder, CO: Westview.

Petracca, M. P. (1992a). The future of an interest group society. In M. P. Petracca (Ed.), *The politics of interests* (pp. 345-361. Boulder, CO: Westview.

Petracca, M. P. (1992b). Introduction. In M. P. Petracca (Ed.), *The politics of interests* (pp. xvii-xxv). Boulder, CO: Westview.

Petracca, M. P. (1992c). The rediscovery of interest group politics. In M. P. Petracca (Ed.), *The politics of interests* (pp. 3-31). Boulder, CO: Westview.

Phillips, E., & Cheston, R. (1979). Conflict resolution: What works? *California Management Review, 21*(4), 76-83.

Public Health Services Act, U.S. C. § 303.(d)(1).

Purkey, W. W. (1970). *Self-concept and school achievement.* Englewood Cliffs, NJ: Prentice Hall.

Putnam, L. L., & Folger, J. P. (1988). Communication, conflict and dispute resolution: The study of interaction and the development of conflict theory. *Communication Research, 15,* 349–359.

Richards, D. L. (1990). *Building and managing your private practice.* Alexandria, VA: American Counseling Association.

Rohde, D. W., & Spaeth, H. J. (1976). *Supreme Court decision making.* San Francisco: W. H. Freeman.

Sabatier, P. A. (1992). Interest group membership and organization: Multiple theories. In M. P. Petracca (Ed.), *The politics of interests* (pp. 99–129). Boulder, CO: Westview.

Sabato, L. J. (1984). *PAC power: Inside the world of political action committees.* New York: Norton.

Salisbury, R. H. (1969). An exchange theory of interest groups. *Midwest Journal of Political Science, 13*(1), 1–32.

Salisbury, R. H. (1990). The paradox of interest groups in Washington: More groups, less clout. In A. King (Ed.), *The new American political system* (pp. 203–230). Washington, DC: American Enterprise Institute.

Salmon, C. T. (1990). God understands when the cause is noble. *The Gannett Center Journal, 4*(2), 23–34.

Schattschneider, E. E. (1960). The semisovereign people. New York: Holt, Rinehart & Winston.

Schlozman, K. W., & Tierney, J. T. (1986). *Organized interests and American democracy.* New York: HarperCollins.

Schrader, M. K. (1989). The image of the school counselor: Whose responsibility? *The School Counselor, 36,* 229–233.

Schubert, G. A. (1959). *Quantitative analysis of judicial behavior.* Glencoe, IL: Free Press.

Schubert, G. A. (1965). *The judicial mind: Attitudes and ideologies of Supreme Court justices 1946–1963.* Evanston, IL: Northwestern University.

Seidel, J. V., Kjolseth, R., & Seymour, E. (1988). The ethnograph. [software manual]. Amherst, MA: Qualis Research Associates.

Seidman, H. (1980). *Politics, position, and power: The dynamics of federal organization.* New York: Oxford University Press.

Seitel, F. P. (1984). *The practice of public relations.* Columbus, OH: Charles E. Merrill.

Shapiro, M. (1986). APA: Past, present and future. *Virginia Law Review, 72,* 452.

Sherif, M., Harvey, O. J., White, B. J., Hood, W. R., & Sherif, C. W. (1961). *The robber's cave experiment: Intergroup conflict and cooperation.* Norman: University of Oklahoma, Institute of Group Relations.

Simmell, G. (1955). *Conflict* (K. H. Wolff, Trans.). New York: Free Press.

Smith, D. G. (1964). Pragmatism and the group theory of politics. *American Political Science Review, 58*(3), 600–610.

Sorauf, F. J. (1976). *The wall of separation: The constitutional politics of church and state.* Princeton, NJ: Princeton University.

Sorauf, F. J. (1995). Adaptation and innovation in political action committees. In A. J. Cigler & B. A. Loomis (Eds.), *Interest group politics* (4th ed.) (pp. 175–192). Washington, DC: Congressional Quarterly Press.

Spaeth, H. J. (1963). Warren Court attitudes toward business: The "B" scale. In G. A. Schubert (Ed.), *Judicial decision-making* (pp. 79–108). New York: Free Press.

Sweeney, T. J. (1992). Counselor credentialing: Purpose and origin. In F. O. Bradley (Ed.), *Credentialing in counseling* (pp. 1–12). Alexandria, VA: American Association for Counseling and Development.

Tanenhaus, J., Schick, M., Muraskin, M., & Rosen, D. (1963). The Supreme Court's certiorari jurisdiction: Cue theory. In G. A. Schubert (Ed.), *Judicial decision-making* (pp. 111–132). New York: Free Press.

Tarr, G. A. (1994). *Judicial process and judicial policymaking.* St. Paul, MN: West.

Thomas, C. S., & Hrebenar, R. J. (1992). Changing patterns of interest group activity: A regional perspective. In M. P. Petracca (Ed.), *The politics of interests* (pp. 150–174). Boulder, CO: Westview.

Tierney, J. T. (1992). Organized interests and the nation's capitol. In M. P. Petracca (Ed.), *The politics of interests,* (pp. 201–220). Boulder, CO: Westview.

Truman, D. B. (1951). *The governmental process.* New York: Knopf.

Truman, D. B. (1971). *The governmental process* (2nd ed.). New York: Knopf.

Ulmer, S. S. (1983). Conflict with Supreme Court precedent and the granting of plenary review. *Journal of Politics, 45,* 474–478.

Ulmer, S. S. (1984). The Supreme Court's certiorari decisions: Conflict as a predictive variable. *American Political Science Review, 78,* 901–911.

Ulmer, S. S., Hintze, W., & Kirklosky, L. (1972). The decision to grant or deny certiorari: Further consideration of cue theory. *Law and Society Review, 6,* 637–649.

Vose, C. E. (1949). Private attorneys-general: Group action in the fight for civil liberties. *Yale Law Journal, 58,* 574–598.

Vose, C. E. (1958). Litigation as a form of pressure group politics. *The Annals of the American Academy of Political and Social Sciences, 319,* 20–31.

Vose, C. E. (1959). *Caucasians only.* Berkeley: University of California Press.

Vose, C. E. (1972). *Constitutional change: Amendment politics and Supreme Court litigation since 1900.* Lexington, MA: Lexington Books.

Walker, J. L. (1983). The origins and maintenance of interest groups in America. *American Political Science Review, 77*(2), 390–406.

Wall, V. D., Galanes, G. J., & Love, S. B. (1987). Small, task-oriented groups, conflict, conflict management, satisfaction, and decision quality. *Small Group Behavior, 18*(1), 31–55.

Walton, R. (1969). *Interpersonal peacemaking: Confrontations and third party consultation.* Reading, MA: Addison-Wesley.

Wehlage, G. G., & Rutter, R. A. (1986). Dropping out: How much do schools contribute to the problem? *Teachers College Record, 87*(3), 374–392.

Weldon vs. *Virginia State Board of Psychologist Examiners, 1972.*

Whitmont, E. C. (1986). *Return of the goddess.* New York: Crossroads.

Wilmot, W. W. (1987). *Dyadic communication* (3rd ed.). New York: Random House.

Wilson, G. K. (1992). American interest groups in comparative perspective. In M. P. Petracca (Ed.), *The politics of interests* (pp. 80–95). Boulder, CO: Westview.

Wilson, G. K. (1986). American business and politics. In A. J. Cigler & B. A. Loomis (Eds.), *Interest group politics* (pp. 221–235). Washington, DC: Congressional Quarterly Press.

Wirth, S. (1977). Effects of a multifaceted reading program on self-concept. *Elementary School Guidance and Counseling, 12*(1), 33–40.

Wittenberg, E., & Wittenberg, E. (1989). *How to win in Washington.* Oxford: Basil Blackwell.

Wohlford, P., Myers, H. F., & Callan, J. E. (Eds.) (1993). *Serving the seriously mentally ill: Public-academic linkages in services, research, and training.* Washington, DC: American Psychological Association.

Wolpe, B. C. (1990). *Lobbying Congress: How the system works.* Washington, DC: Congressional Quarterly Press.

Wright, C. R., & Hyman, H. H. (1958). Voluntary association member ship in American adults: Evidence from national sample surveys. *American Sociological Review, 23,* cited in B. H. Zisk (1969). *American political interest groups: Readings in theory and research.* Belmont, CA: Wadsworth.

Zisk, B. H. (1969). *American political interest groups: Readings in theory and research.* Belmont, CA: Wadsworth.

INDEX

ABOUT THE AUTHOR

Karen Eriksen did doctoral work in counseling and in marriage and family therapy. She graduated from Mary Ann Walter's Extern Program with advanced training in Marriage and Family Therapy. She has been working actively as a psychotherapist since 1980, obtaining licenses in California, Michigan, and Virginia. She has worked in outpatient, hospital, and private practice settings with individuals, groups, marriages, and families of children and adolescents. Karen has extensive experience calling on a wide range of community resources to help clients. She has taught at George Mason University and Marymount University.

Karen is a leader spiritually, politically, and professionally. She has lobbied actively at the national and state levels for legislation protecting and benefiting clients. Serving as President of the Northern Virginia Chapter of Clinical Counselors and as Secretary and Board Member of the Virginia Association of Clinical Counselors, she has chaired political and professional conference committees. As founder and administrator for the Family Life Enrichment Center, she organized a network of churches to provide low cost preventive mental health care as a community outreach.

Please photocopy these next four pages, complete the survey, and mail to the address shown. If you so desire, you may remove these four pages and return them.

Advocacy Activities of Counselors

A Survey

The material in this book has been based on research into the advocacy activities of counselors. The research is continuing, and your willingness to participate would be greatly appreciated. The purpose of this survey is to determine counselors' levels of participation in advocacy activities. Completing the following survey should take approximately one-half hour. Please answer as forthrightly as possible. The survey's information will remain confidential. Your personal information will be detached from this survey and kept in a separate locked file, only accessed if a follow up is needed. NO ONE WILL BE ABLE TO ASSOCIATE YOUR INFORMATION WITH YOU. Only a code number is assigned to the survey.

Background Information

The following items collect background information on your age, gender, degree held, educational specialty, job responsibilities, ethnic group, and income.

1. Age: _____   2. Gender: _____   3. Highest Degree Earned: _____

4. Years full-time, post-master's, professional experience: _____
   If you have participated part-time, divide the numbers of years appropriately (for instance, 20 hours/week, divide years by 2)

5. Specialty area (choose **one** to indicate your primary area of specialization):
   mental health (clinical,   rehabilitation _____
   marriage & family,   employment/career _____
   addictions) _____   pastoral _____
   school _____   other _____

6. Choose the three of the following in which you professionally participate most. Rate them "1" through "3," in order of the degree of your participation, with "1" being greatest participation and "3" being least participation:
   teaching _____   counseling _____
   research _____   administration _____
   consulting/speaking/   other _____
   doing workshops _____   _____

7. Primary ethnic group:
   Black _____ Hispanic _____ Asian _____ Caucasian _____
   Native American _____ Other _____

8. Yearly personal income from counseling-related endeavors (this includes all of those listed under items 5 and 6): _____

– – – – – – – – – *This will be detached and your name and related personal data removed* – – – – – – – – – –

Name ....

Address ....

City .... State .... Zip ....

Work Phone .... Home Phone ....

Advocacy Participation

Counselor advocacy *is the promotion of counselors or the counseling profession to gain recognition, inclusion, reimbursement, or use of counselors as mental health professionals.* (This does not refer to advocacy solely for the benefit of clients.)

Advocacy targets *are legislators, government officials, courts, insurance companies and their representatives, schools, the public, members of counseling professional associations, other professionals, other organizations—any people or organizations toward which counselors direct their advocacy activities.*

Please indicate the number of hours you have spent in each of the following activities during the last **three (3) months** (indicate whole or partial hours). Your answers should pertain only to participation in counselor advocacy, not to advocacy solely for the benefit of clients.

	Number of Hours
9. Writing **letters and/or making phone calls** to advocacy targets:	_____
10. Making **face-to-face contact** with advocacy targets:	_____
11. Doing counseling-related **public speaking** to community organizations (<2 hours):	_____
12. **Planning** advocacy activities:	_____
13. **Testifying at hearings** related to mental health issues:	_____
14. Working on any **political campaign:**	_____
15. Writing for counseling-related **publications:**	_____
16. **Educating counselors** on how to participate in advocacy activities:	_____
17. Doing **background research** for policy documents, or to inform advocacy targets or position papers (on such things as the impact of proposed changes, legal precedent, causes of problems, arguments for and against changes, views of decision-makers and other publics):	_____
18. Participating in **coalitions** related to counseling's aims:	_____
19. **Filing suit/engaging in litigation** on behalf of counselors:	_____
20. Engaging in **protests/demonstrations:**	_____
21. **Developing publicity or media materials:**	_____
22. Giving **workshops** to non-counselors (>2 hours):	_____
23. Doing **pro-bono work** to increase counseling's visibility:	_____
24. **Preparing counselors-in-training** through teaching or supervision, on any counseling-related subject:	_____
25. **Presenting at** counseling-related state or national **conferences** on any counseling-related subject:	_____
26. **Preparing documentation** designed to persuade advocacy targets to take action:	_____
27. Working with **committees/advisory groups** designed to oversee mental health delivery systems, legislation, or programs:	_____
28. **Drafting** counseling or mental health **legislation:**	_____
29. Doing **research** to further the counseling profession or mental health treatment:	_____
30. Working toward or promoting counseling **accreditation or certification:**	_____
31. Performing **other** advocacy activities (specify:) _____	_____

Advocacy Experience

Please indicate the number of years you have spent in each of the following:

Number
of Years

32. As a member of a counseling professional association: _____

33. As an officer in a local counseling professional association: _____

34. As a board member (not as an officer) of a state counseling professional association: _____

35. As an officer of a state counseling professional association: _____

36. As a staff member for a counseling professional association: _____

37. As a committee member (not on board of directors or governing council) of a national counseling professional association: _____

38. As a board or governing council member for a national counseling professional association: _____

39. **Dollars contributed** within the past year to political campaigns/political action: _____

40. What persuades you to participate in the advocacy activities (see questions 9–31) in which you do participate?

_____

_____

_____

_____

41. What professional association most influences your participation in advocacy activities?

_____

42. For the advocacy activities you consider important, if you don't participate, please indicate your reason(s) for not participating:
    - _____ Lack of time
    - _____ Lack of money
    - _____ Personality unsuited to advocacy
    - _____ Dislike doing the activity
    - _____ Lack knowledge of how to do the activity
    - _____ Other

_____

_____

_____

Please return survey to: Karen Eriksen
6194 Old Franconia Road
Alexandria, VA 22310